The Green Thumb Directory

A WHERE-TO-BUY-IT GUIDE FOR GARDENERS

By Marion Schroeder

DOLPHIN BOOKS
DOUBLEDAY & COMPANY, INC.
GARDEN CITY, NEW YORK

Previously published as THE GREEN THUMBOOK

Illustrations from:
Garden Flowers, by Stefen Bernath,
Copyright © 1975 by Dover
Publications, Inc.: pages 1, 2, 3, 86, 90, 92, 102

House Plants, by Stefen Bernath,
Copyright © 1976 by Dover
Publications, Inc.: pages 82, 117, 118, 119, 120, 123, 124, 126, 129, 135, 136, 157

Library of Congress Cataloging in Publication Data

Schroeder, Marion.
  The green thumb directory.

  Published in 1975 under title: The green thumbook.
  Includes bibliographical references and index.
  1. Gardening—Directories. 2. Nurseries (Horticulture)—United States—Directories. 3. Gardening—Bibliography. I. Title.
SB44.S36 1977   338.1'7'5915202573
ISBN 0-385-12423-6
Library of Congress Catalog Card Number 77-2055

Contents

Introduction

The Green Thumb Directory—what it is and how to use it

In recent years millions of people have become gardeners, and every year more join their ranks. Gardening has become one of the most popular of all activities.

But a gardener, unlike a golfer or a bridge player, is hard to define. There are indoor gardeners and outdoor gardeners, city gardeners and homesteaders, orchid breeders and orchardists, specialists in begonias and devotees of bonasi. Some turn their backyards into arboretums, others create miniature landscapes in gallon jugs. But all of them are working with living plants—of which there are more than 350,000 known species.

Along with this increase in gardeners and their diverse interests has come an increasing demand for garden products of all types. Many are hard to find. No one company could supply all garden needs.

That is the reason we have compiled this book. It's a sort of "yellow pages" of gardening, a buyer's guide to sources—for seeds, plants, supplies, and information.

As gardening covers such a broad area, we could not possibly list all sources. But we have tried to include those that will be of most interest and help to all gardeners, from beginners to specialists.

The majority of the companies, nurseries, plantsmen, and suppliers listed in this book sell by mail throughout the United States and Canada. The few that limit sales to either country are indicated. Some are manufacturers who, while they do not make direct-mail sales, will send

you information about their products and refer you to retailers in your area.

The primary sources for many of your garden needs are the reputable nurseries and garden dealers in your own locality. We urge you to get acquainted with them and patronize them. These are people who will keep you in peat and pots and other basics, who stock many plant materials best suited to your area, who often will take the time to give you help and advice. The sources in this book are not intended to replace local dealers, but to supplement them.

To help you find information you are looking for and make this book easier to use, we have placed each source in a category that we think is most applicable. You'll find rose growers under "Roses," and specialists in orchids under "Orchids."

But many sources don't fit neatly under one heading. Jernigan's Gardens, of Dunn, North Carolina, for example, offer hundreds of varieties of iris and are listed under "Iris." But they also sell daylilies and a number of unusual hostas. Rather than repeating their listing in these two categories (and greatly increasing the size and cost of this book), we've cross-referenced them in the index.

If you check the index for hostas, you'll be referred to page 105. But the *next* listing in the

index after hostas is "Hostas; additional sources," and under this is a reference to Jernigan's Gardens. They're also in the index under "Daylilies; additional sources."

Whenever you're looking through a particular category—orchids, herbs, wildflowers, and so on—*always check the index for additional sources.* (One exception: the larger seed companies and nurseries are seldom included in a cross reference, because each offers such a wide variety of plant materials and supplies.)

You'll also find some plant categories in the index—such as holly, lilacs, and heaths and heathers—that do not appear as separate categories in the book. The index will refer you to sources that offer a fairly wide selection of these plants.

Many suppliers, in addition to mail-order sales, have retail nurseries, greenhouses, or shops open at regular hours. Others are "open to visitors." Hours are indicated, but if you're making a special trip, it's best to phone ahead, because these times may vary from season to season. In most cases these "open hours" do not apply to holidays. And please observe the request "visitors by appointment."

Catalogs, price lists, or brochures are sent without charge unless payment or postage is specified. When a supplier requests an "sase" this means a self-addressed, stamped envelope (always use a large, #10, envelope). When there is a charge for sales literature, send coins, a check, or a money order—*not* stamps. In many cases this money is credited toward a future order. A number of companies send several catalogs, price lists, or other material during the course of a year; we've just given an indication of their main sales literature.

If the minimum order handled is over $5.00, this is noted, and any charge cards accepted are listed. Abbreviations used are: AEX (American Express), BAC (BankAmericard), CB (Carte Blanche), CGX (Chargex), DC (Diners Club), and MC (Master Charge).

As in any business, garden suppliers move to new locations, change addresses, go out of business, and retire. Postal services for forwarding mail are becoming more limited. So, when writing to any source, it's advisable to use first-class mail, with your return address on it—especially if you're enclosing money. If your letter can't be delivered, it will be returned to you. Postcards, however, will *not* be returned, even if your address is on them.

When writing to suppliers, please mention *The Green Thumb Directory*. This will help them identify your inquiry and assure you of getting the material or information listed in this book.

Please remember—

This is *not* a guide to *free* information about gardening.

A few of the "sources" listed in this book are huge corporations whose advertising budgets run into hundreds of thousands of dollars.

But a far greater number are small growers or suppliers, and many are individuals who sell plants as a part-time activity or to share plants with other gardeners.

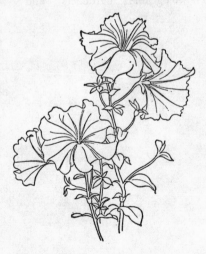

Their profit margins are not large —and printing and mailings are costly. So please do not ask for catalogs or price lists unless you have a definite interest—and when payment or postage is requested, be sure to include this.

Don't expect them to provide you with general information about gardening. Consult your state or provincial agricultural service instead; these agencies are supported by your tax dollars. If you do have a specific question about a supplier's plants or products, however, most will be glad to answer it. But do enclose a self-addressed, stamped envelope (SASE) or a postcard for their reply.

Our listing of a supplier, company, or plantsman does not imply our endorsement. While we are familiar with a great many, and others were recommended by knowledgeable gardeners and horticulturists, some we have accepted on their own word and description.

On the other hand, some plantsmen are not included because of their own request; they said they could not handle any more business. A few we chose to omit. Others are not listed because we did not have adequate information about them.

If you know of any sources you think should be included in any future listings, or if you receive poor services or materials from any source mentioned in this book, we'd appreciate hearing from you. Also, if a letter sent to any source is returned to you, we will try to find out if the address has changed or if the company is no longer in business. Just write to *The Green Thumb Directory*, Box 99, Cary, IL 60013.

Happy Gardening

Marion Schroeder

Seed and Plant Companies

Alberta Nurseries & Seeds, Ltd., Box 20, Bowden, Alta. ToM oKo. (403)-224-3362. Color illustrated catalog. Open Mon.–Fri., 9 A.M.–5 P.M.

Vegetable and flower seeds, including many houseplant seeds. Vegetable plants, perennials and bulbs, nursery stock, garden supplies and equipment. All plant materials are very hardy, suited to northern climates. In business over fifty years.

Allen, Sterling & Lothrop, 191 U.S. Rte. 1, Falmouth, ME 04105. (207)-781-4142. Price list. MC charge. Open Mon.–Sat., 8 A.M.–5 P.M.

Vegetable and flower seeds, lawn seeds, field grasses; packet and quantity sales. Also garden tools and equipment, bird food and bird feeders, peat pots, plastic and clay pots, insecticides, and fertilizers. Maine's largest vegetable-seed distributors.

Archias Seed Store Corp., 106–108 E. Main St., Sedalia, MO 65301. (816)-826-1330. Color illustrated catalog. BAC and MC charges. U.S. sales only. Open Mon.–Sat., 8 A.M.–5 P.M.

Plant materials especially adapted to the central states, including vegetable and flower seeds, field seeds, nursery stock, small fruits, perennials, and bulbs. Garden and greenhouse supplies and equipment. Company founded in 1884.

Bash's Seed Store, 130 N. Delaware St., Indianapolis, IN 46204. (317)-637-7333. Illustrated catalog, 50¢ (credited). AEX, BAC, and MC charges. Open Mon.–Sat., 8:30 A.M.–5:30 P.M.

Both bulk and packaged vegetable, flower, herb, and grass seeds. Also flowering bulbs, complete line of garden tools and accessories, chemicals and fertilizers, garden books, and various garden-related gift items.

Bash's, which opened in 1856, is the oldest seed store in Indiana and one of the oldest in the United States. The retail store in Indianapolis, across the street from the city market, still has antique seed bins, scales, and counters in use.

Burgess Seed & Plant Co., Box 221, Galesburg, MI 49053. (616)-665-7079. Color illustrated catalog. BAC and MC charges. Visitors by appointment.

Vegetable and flower seeds, nursery stock, perennials, bulbs, houseplants, wide range of garden supplies and equipment. Many exclusive introductions each year. The ten top-selling vegetables, "The Best of Burgess," carry a double-money-back guarantee.

"We are one of the few remaining consumer seed houses that still produce our own seed. On our Galesburg acreage we grow seeds of Burgess specialties, hard-to-grow varieties, and other items of which we have been unable to obtain products up to our quality standard."

Burnett Bros., Inc., 92 Chambers St., New York, NY 10007. (212)-227-6138. Color illustrated catalog, $1.50 (credited). Minimum order, $10. Open Mon.–Fri., 11 A.M.–3 P.M.

Vegetable and flower seeds, bulbs, perennials, greenhouse plants. Wide selection of garden tools, fertilizers, chemicals. Packet and quantity sales of seeds. Firm established in 1905.

W. Atlee Burpee Co. Headquarters: 300 Park Ave., Warminster, PA 18974. (215)-674-4900. Branches at: Box B-2001, Clinton, IA 52732; and 6350 Rutland Ave., Riverside, CA 92502. Color illustrated catalog. U.S. sales only.

Flower and vegetable seeds, bulbs, roots, nursery stock, and wide selection of garden aids. Over the years, the company has introduced many new varieties of vegetables and flowers. Several, dating back to the nineteenth century, are still popular today.

"W. Atlee Burpee Company, which was founded in 1876, dedicates its research to making good gardeners better."

D. V. Burrell Seed Growers Co., Box 150, Rocky Ford, CO 81067. (303)-254-3318. Color illustrated catalog. Open Mon.–Fri., 9 A.M.–5 P.M.

Vegetable and flower seeds; packet and quantity sales. Catalog has detailed cultural information for Colorado-area growers. Owned and operated by the Burrell family since 1900.

Comstock, Ferre & Co., 263 Main St., Wethersfield, CT 06109. (203)-529-3319. Illustrated catalog. MC charge. Open Mon.–Sat., 10 A.M.–4 P.M.

Vegetable, flower, and herb seeds; packet and quantity sales. Established in 1820; fifth generation of family now operates business.

The retail garden store in Wethersfield has a full line of seeds as well as perennials, houseplants, garden equipment, and a holiday decorating shop. All clerks are gardeners, known for their expertise.

William Dam Seeds, Hwy. 8, West Flamboro, Ont. LoR 2Ko. (416)-628-6641. Illustrated catalog. Open Mon.–Sat., 9 A.M.–5 P.M.

Untreated seeds. Flower and vegetable seeds; both packet and bulk quantities. Large selection of herb seeds. Specializes in European varieties with special strains of common and uncommon vegetables. Also houseplants, asparagus, rhubarb, artichokes, and horseradish. Organic plant foods and organic insect controls. Much information on organic culture in catalog.

"Our slogan is 'Untreated Seeds–Highest Quality.'"

DeGiorgi Company, Inc., 1411 Third St., Council Bluffs, IA 51501. (712)-323-2372. Illustrated catalog, 35¢.

Very large variety of seeds, including vegetables, flowers (annuals, perennials, and tropicals), and tree seeds. Many uncommon. Both packet and quantity sales. The catalog, described as "more than just a seed catalog," is packed with growing tips and advice. For example:

"Parsnip is very hard to germinate. Try sowing parsnip seeds with some radish seeds. Radish has vigorous sprouts that break up the hard top crust and if there is enough moisture in the ground you will get a perfect stand of parsnip that way, in the incredibly short time of from four to five days."

Early Seed & Feed, Ltd., 198 Idylwyld Dr. S., Saskatoon, Sask. S7K 3S9. (306)-652-4160. Illustrated catalog. Minimum order, $10.

Flower and vegetable seeds; grain, forage, and grass seeds. Packet and quantity sales. Varieties for western prairies area. Extensive selection of fertilizers, chemicals, garden tools, and supplies. Founded in 1907.

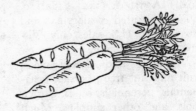

Don't Plant Too Much

Beginning vegetable gardeners tend to get carried away and plant too large a garden. About midseason they find out it's just too much work and lose their enthusiasm. USDA experts recommend a size no larger than 15 × 25 feet—an area that with a little daily effort will yield a surprisingly large harvest.

And if they want to garden organically, vegetables such as radishes, lettuce, beets, peas, spinach, sweet potatoes, turnips, onions, Swiss chard, leeks, and most herbs are good choices. They're easy to grow without using any chemicals.

Farmer Seed & Nursery Co., 818 N.W. Fourth St., Faribault,

6   THE GREEN THUMB DIRECTORY

MN 55021. (507)-334-6421. Color illustrated catalog. BAC and MC charges. U.S. sales only. Open Mon.–Fri., 9 A.M.–5 P.M.

Vegetable and flower seeds, large line of nursery stock, garden tools. Many hybrid introductions, including releases from the University of Minnesota and the University of New Hampshire, adapted to northern climates. Founded in 1888.

Henry Field Seed & Nursery Co., 407 Sycamore St., Shenandoah, IA 51602. (712)-246-2110. Color illustrated catalog. BAC and MC charges. U.S. sales only. Visitors by appointment.

Vegetable and flower seeds, fruit and nut trees, berries, ornamentals, perennials, bulbs, garden tools, and other supplies. Much planting and cultural information. First mail-order catalog sent out in 1899.

Germania Seed Co., 5952 N. Milwaukee Ave., Chicago, IL 60646. (312)-631-6631. Color illustrated catalog, $3.00 (credited).

Flower and vegetable seeds exclusively. Over 3,100 varieties— one of the most complete listings available. Both packet and quantity sales.

Gurney Seed & Nursery Co., Second & Capital, Yankton, SD 57078. (605)-665-4451. Color illustrated catalog.

Wide variety of vegetable and flower seeds, nursery stock, bulbs, perennials, garden supplies and equipment. Many novelty items. Catalog has much information about planting and, each year, has a folksy section in which gardeners tell about their experiences and show photos of their prize crops.

How Many Pounds in a Bushel?

If it's potatoes, a bushel will weigh a hefty 60 pounds. A bushel of tomatoes weighs almost as much, 56 pounds. Here's the poundage of some other vegetables, by the bushel: beets, 52; cucumbers, 48; green beans, 30; peas in pods, 30; lima beans in pods, 32; pepper, 25; and carrots without tops, 50.

Joseph Harris Co., Inc., Moreton Farm, Rochester, NY 14624. (716)-594-9411. Color illustrated catalog. Open Mon.–Sat., 8 A.M.–5 P.M.

Wide variety of vegetable and flower seeds, many developed by Harris plant breeders. Specialties include Moreton, Jet Star, and Supersonic tomato; Pioneer carrot; Elite zucchini; Harmony bicolor sweet corn; Black Magic eggplant; Frontier snapdragons; Sunnyside portulaca. Founded in 1879.

Visitors are welcome at the fifteen acres of flower trials any time from early summer into fall. Groups may make arrangements for a tour of the entire company.

The Chas. C. Hart Seed Co., 304 Main St., at Hart St., Wethersfield, CT 06109. (203)-529-2537. Illustrated catalog. MC charge. Open Mon.–Fri., 8 A.M.–5 P.M. Sat., 8 A.M.–noon.

Vegetable, herb, and flower seeds; lawn grasses. Packet and quantity sales. Both standard varieties and new introductions. In business since 1892.

H. G. Hastings Co., Box 44088, Atlanta, GA 30336. (404)-349-6600. Illustrated catalog. BAC and MC charges.

Flower and vegetable seeds, nursery stock, roses, perennials. One of the best selections of southern vegetable seeds available. Very extensive listing of garden tools, equipment, fertilizers and chemicals, bird houses and feeders, and garden books.

The company has retail stores in Atlanta and Birmingham, Alabama; Lawrenceville, Georgia; and Charlotte, North Carolina.

R. L. Holmes Seed Co., 2125 46th St., N.W., Canton, OH 44709. (216)-492-0123. Illustrated catalog.

Vegetable seeds, most in quantities of one ounce or more. Varieties listed are recommended for commercial growers or gardeners selling in roadside stands. Detailed information about yields in catalog.

Johnny's Selected Seeds (Rob Johnston), Albion, ME 04910. (207)-437-4303. Illustrated catalog, 50¢. Open weekdays, business hours.

Full line of organically produced vegetable and herb seeds, both common and unusual varieties. Heirloom dry and snap beans, non-hybrid (open-pollinated) corn, excellent strains of cabbage, tomatoes, peas, lettuce, cucumbers, and others. Also some oriental and other imported vegetables. Emphasis on short-season varieties.

Johnston says his is one of the few seed houses, shipping nationally and internationally, with an outright commitment to organic growing and organically produced seeds. His aim is to revive the small-farm style of seed growing, which has been largely replaced by commercial growers.

"Our concentration is on basic food plants—things that gardeners can really sink their teeth into. All in all, we are interested in providing folks with seeds for real food—not plants to impress neighbors, or varieties which will fit neatly into a packing crate."

J. W. Jung Seed Co., Randolph WI 53956. (414)-326-3121. Color illustrated catalog. Open Mon.–Fri., 8 A.M.–5 P.M.; Sat., 8 A.M.–noon.

Vegetable and flower seeds, berries, fruit and shade trees, shrubs, perennials, bulbs, and related items. Many Jung exclusives, such as Wayahead tomato, Spring Glory flowering crab, Honey Cream early dwarf sweet corn. Farm seeds sold through subsidiary, Jung Farms, Inc. Founded in 1907. Group tours of entire company offered; appointments must be made in advance.

Orol Ledden & Sons, Centre & Atlantic Aves., Sewell, NJ 08080. (609)-468-1000. Color illustrated catalog. BAC charge. Open

Mon.–Fri., 8 A.M.–9 P.M.; Sat. and Sun., 8 A.M.–5 P.M.

Complete selection of seeds, plants, farm and garden supplies, and tools. Established in 1864, the largest and oldest farm and garden center in the Delaware Valley area.

Dry Corn
(for Corn Meal and Feed)

It used to be that nearly every farmer had his own corn seed. A friend of ours remembers how, as a young boy, he rode with his father and bags of shelled corn to the mill, and watched the water wheel go around from the back of the wagon. Times have changed, but gardeners everywhere are once again discovering the simple pleasure of raising their own dry corn. Small, hand grinders are now widely advertised and easily available. Compare the flavor of your own corn meal with that of the store-bought kind. Use in cereals, breads, muffins, and pancakes.

—Rob Johnston
Johnny's Selected Seeds

Letherman's, Inc., 1203 E. Tuscarawas St., Canton, OH 44702. (216)-452-8866. Illustrated catalog. MC charge. Open daily.

Many varieties of vegetable and flower seeds. Also wide selection of chemicals, fertilizers, and garden supplies. In seed business over seventy years.

Lindenberg Seeds, Ltd., 803 Princess Ave., Brandon, Man. R7A 0P5. Illustrated catalog.

Vegetable and flower seeds, lawn seeds, roses, bulbs, fertilizers, and garden supplies. Plant varieties especially for Canadian prairie areas. Good cultural information. Fall bulb catalog sent on request.

Small-plot Spuds

Potatoes aren't usually considered a small-space crop. But Jim Simpson of Hendersonville, North Carolina, says he averages a bushel or more of prime spuds from his 8 × 10 patch.

In an article in *The Gardener*, publication of the Men's Garden Clubs of America, Simpson says secrets are fertile soil, a sunny location, and mulch—a six-inch layer of straw or hay plus another deep layer of oak leaves.

About four months after planting, tubers are waiting to be picked, and, boiled with a little butter, "they're a taste fit for a king."

Earl May Seed & Nursery Co., North Elm, Shenandoah, IA 51603. (712)-246-1020. Color illustrated catalog. BAC and MC charges. Open Mon.–Fri., 8 A.M.–5 P.M.

Vegetable and flower seeds and plants, nursery stock, garden supplies, and related equipment. The public is welcome at the seventy-six-acre test garden, which includes All-America flower and vegetable trials. Annual open house is held third or fourth Sunday in July.

"We try to help our catalog readers by describing in detail all the items we sell, including mature size and shape of trees and shrubs, details of flowers and fruit, length of time from planting to maturity, etc. In addition, we mark each shrub that attracts birds."

The Meyer Seed Co., 600 S. Caroline St., Baltimore, MD 21231. (301)-342-4224. Illustrated catalog. BAC and MC charges.

Vegetable, flower, lawn, and field seeds. Also vegetable plants and roots, flowering bulbs. Extensive line of garden supplies—almost one third of the catalog is devoted to tools, equipment, and other garden needs. Very good cultural information, including a planting calendar for flowers, a vegetable-planting guide, and a chart of yields.

The Natural Development Co., Box 215, Bainbridge, PA 17502. Illustrated catalog, 25¢.

Untreated seeds of vegetables, herbs, and flowers. Whole grains for sprouting. Garden tools and related supplies, including hand grist mills. A variety of organic foods and honey. Featured products are Fertrell and Nitrell, organic plant foods, and Tri-Excel, an organic plant protectant. These three products are also available at retail garden centers in a number of states.

Nicholson-Hardie, 5717 W. Lovers Ln., Dallas, TX 75209. Catalog.

Extensive listing of flower, vegetable, and herb seeds—all selected to give best results in southern regions of the United States.

"Today's inflation has hit hard. Every time we stand at the grocery store check-out counter we are reminded of this fact. Fight inflation with a back yard garden. Besides saving money you will be on your way to a fascinating and rewarding hobby."

L. L. Olds Seed Co., 2901 Packers Ave., Box 1069, Madison, WI 53701. (608)-249-9291. Color illustrated catalog, 25¢ (includes two packages of seeds). BAC and MC charges. Open Mon.–Sat., 8 A.M.–noon and 1 P.M.–5 P.M.

Vegetable and flower seeds, bulbs, nursery stock, garden supplies. Many introductions, including those of the University of Wisconsin, suitable for northern areas. Quantity price list available for market gardeners. Group tours, by appointment, of retail garden shop, mail-order department, seed-packeting plant, and seed-testing labs.

Geo. W. Park Seed Co., Inc., Box 31, Greenwood, SC 29647. (803)-374-3341. Color illustrated catalog. BAC and MC charges. Open Mon.–Fri., 8 A.M.–4:30 P.M.

About three thousand varieties of flower and vegetable seeds, many Park exclusives. Numerous hard-to-find flower seeds for both indoor and outdoor growing. Bulbs, plants, garden accessories, and growing supplies, including

Hobby House light-garden equipment. The catalog index includes a guide to germination time, best use, bloom time, and culture of hundreds of varieties of plants. Established in 1868; about 3 million catalogs mailed each year.

Pennington, Inc., Box 192, Madison, GA 30650. (404)-342-4100. Illustrated catalog. AEX, BAC, CB, and MC charges.

Vegetable and lawn-grass seeds, especially bred for southern growers. Packet and quantity sales. Also various home gardening supplies. A featured item is Pennington Green Coated grass seed. Seed plant in Madison, Georgia, is one of the largest in the United States.

All About Drying Food

Home gardeners are discovering that drying is an excellent way to preserve and store their harvests. A 122-page book, How to Dry Fruits and Vegetables at Home, by the food editors of Farm Journal (Dolphin Books, 1975), covers the subject thoroughly. There are instructions for making and using electric dryers, sun drying, packaging and storing, and, as a bonus, fifty-two recipes for cooking with dried fruits and vegetables. Available from booksellers, $2.95.

W. H. Perron & Co., Ltd., 515 Labelle, Chomedey, Laval, Que. H7S 2A6. (514)-332-3610. Color illustrated catalog, $1.00 (credited). CGX and MC charges. Canadian sales only. Open Mon.–Sat. (hours vary according to season).

Very extensive list of vegetable and flower seeds of all types. Also perennials, bulbs, nursery stock, and a wide selection of garden tools, supplies, chemicals, and fertilizers. Detailed cultural information and planting suggestions. (Plant shipments are limited to Montreal area.)

The company's Garden Center, situated on ten acres near Montreal, is one of the largest in Canada. A staff of eighty-six employees is maintained the year around, and at the height of the garden season the parking lot is often filled before the Garden Center opens. At times several people are kept busy just answering calls from gardeners asking for advice.

Reuter Seed Co., Inc., 320 N. Carrollton Ave., New Orleans, LA 70119. (504)-482-3141. Illustrated catalog. BAC charge. U.S. sales only. Open Mon.–Sat., 8 A.M.–5 P.M.

Complete line of vegetable and flower seeds, bulbs, and garden supplies. Vegetable varieties are adapted to and sold primarily in the southeastern states. Two of the most popular are Burpless hybrid cucumber and Green eggplant. In business for over ninety-five years.

Ritchie Feed & Seed, Ltd., 27 York St., Ottawa, Ont. K1N 5S7. (613)-236-0454. Illustrated catalog. Open Mon.–Fri., 8 A.M.–6 P.M.; Sat., 8 A.M.–5 P.M.

Flower and vegetable seeds for home gardeners. Garden supplies, tools, chemicals, and fertilizers. Detailed planting advice is in the catalog.

The Rocky Mountain Seed Co., 1325 15th St., Box 5204, Denver, CO 80217. (303)-623-6223. Illustrated catalog.

Vegetable, flower, grass, and field seeds. Packet and quantity sales. Also nursery stock, bulbs, seeds of native wildflowers. Variety of garden supplies. Plant stock especially suited to high-altitude gardens of the Rocky Mountain area.

Grow Your Own Peanuts

Peanuts are easy to grow in home gardens, says The Rocky Mountain Seed Co. A good variety is New Mexico Large Valencia. To roast peanuts in their shells, put in a 350-degree oven for 30–45 minutes. Shelled peanuts can be roasted with or without oil in a 350-degree oven, about 30 minutes. Stir occasionally and watch closely, as peanuts overcook very quickly. To salt before roasting, dip in water, salt, and drain well before putting in the oven.

Roswell Seed Co., 115–117 S. Main St., Box 725, Roswell, NM 88201. (505)-622-7701. Catalog. BAC charge. Open Mon.–Sat., 8 A.M.–5:30 P.M.

Vegetable, flower, and field seeds especially adapted to the Southwest. Packet and bulk sales. Also wide selection of insecticides, herbicides, fungicides, and fertilizers. Detailed planting information for the area. Company founded in 1900.

Seedway, Inc., Hall, NY 14463. (315)-596-6391. Color illustrated catalog. Open Mon.–Sat., 8 A.M.–5 P.M.

Vegetable and flower seeds, especially varieties for northeastern gardeners. Packet and quantity sales. Also lawn-grass seed, flowering bulbs, and garden supplies and equipment. World famous for hybrid sweet corn varieties.

R. H. Shumway Seedsman, 628 Cedar St., Rockford, IL 61101. (815)-964-7243. Color illustrated catalog.

Vegetable and flower seeds, plants, bulbs, nursery stock, and garden tools and supplies. Popular sellers are midget vegetables, such as Baby cabbage, four inches across; Tom Thumb head lettuce, about the size of a tennis ball; and Golden Midget sweet corn, with stalks about three feet high and four-inch ears. The company, founded in 1870, still retains a nineteenth-century look in its catalog.

Stokes Seeds, Inc., Box 548, Buffalo, NY 14240. (416)-685-4255. Color illustrated catalog.

Some 1,400 varieties of vegetable and flower seeds—many exclusive with Stokes. Seeds are especially selected for northern-U.S. and Canadian climates.

In July and August, visitors are welcome at trial gardens in St.

Catharines, Ontario. There are more than one half mile of annual flower beds plus All-America trial gardens.

Corn on the Cob—Everyone's Favorite

Corn ranks among the top three in favorite vegetables (along with tomatoes and potatoes). It's a native American plant. Indians taught early settlers how to cultivate it, and corn brought the Pilgrims through the winter in Plymouth when their wheat crops failed. In fact, it was such an important crop in colonial days that laws were passed requiring dogs to be tied by a leg so they couldn't dig up the fish planted for fertilizer in each corn hill.

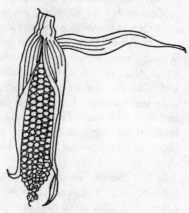

Thomas Seeds, R.F.D., Winthrop, ME 04364. (207)-377-6724. Illustrated catalog. Visitors welcome; phone ahead.

Vegetable and herb seeds; packet and quantity sales. Specializes in varieties best suited for northern climates. Most seeds offered are untreated; will send customers only untreated seeds if requested.

Thompson & Morgan, 401 Kennedy Blvd., Somerdale, NJ 08083. Color illustrated catalog.

The world-famous English seed company now has a U.S. branch. Seeds, however, come from parent company in England. Very wide selection of vegetable, flower, and tree seeds, many uncommon in this country. Included are seeds of numerous tropical and greenhouse plants.

The catalog has a great deal of information on nutrient content of vegetables; it claims one half cup of Thompson & Morgan's Soya or Vegetable bean is equivalent in usable protein to that in five ounces of prime steak.

"At a time when we waste literally millions of tons of protein for ourselves annually, in pursuit of producing highly expensive meat, we would like to show you how you can enjoy nutritionally sound and often superior protein from the richer and far more abundant sources that the earth provides. They are, too, many, many times less costly, healthier, and very enjoyable."

Otis S. Twilley Seed Co., Box 1817, Salisbury, MD 21801. (301)-749-3245. Illustrated catalog. Open Mon.–Fri.

Complete line of vegetable and flower seeds—emphasis on best of new varieties and disease-resistant strains. Packet and quantity sales.

"The seed business," says Twilley, "is my life and work. Sold first seeds of my own production at age seventeen. Took ten years out and worked for several of the largest seed companies in the country to learn their methods. Then started my own business again in 1936."

Vesey's Seeds, Ltd., York, P.E.I. C1A 7N8. (902)-894-8844. Illustrated catalog. Minimum order, $10. Open Mon.–Fri., 8 A.M.–5 P.M.

Vegetable and flower seeds; emphasis on the best of short-season varieties. Very good cultural information.

"In business since 1939. Started small. Have always market-gardened and still do. In this way acquire knowledge of new sorts suitable for short-season areas."

How to Grow More Vegetables than You Ever Thought Possible on Less Land than You Can Imagine is about the "biodynamic/French intensive method of organic horticulture." Sounds technical, but what it boils down to is workable ideas for getting the biggest yields from the smallest space with the least work, through organic methods. Highly recommended, especially for organic gardeners. Price is $4.00, from Ecology Action, 2225 El Camino, Palo Alto, CA 94306.

Ecology Action, a non-profit educational group, teaches classes on organic gardening and has an educational center, a library, and a store that sells seeds and organic-gardening supplies. Store hours are 10 A.M.–5 P.M., Tues. through Sat. Telephone: (415)-328-6752.

Wyatt-Quarles Seed Co., 331 S. Wilmington St., Box 2131, Raleigh, NC 27602. (919)-832-0551. Color illustrated catalog. Open Mon.–Fri., 8:30 A.M.–5:30 P.M.; Sat., 8:30 A.M.–1 P.M.

Wide selection of bulbs and plants in addition to vegetable, herb, flower, and grass seeds. Exclusive Carolina lawn-grass formula, especially adapted to the South. Also greenhouse supplies, planting mediums, containers, tools, chemicals, and other garden supplies.

"Our company was founded in 1881 by Job P. Wyatt. His grandsons and great-grandsons still operate the business. We offer the widest selection of flower and vegetable seeds in the area."

Where to Get Some Basic Advice on Vegetables

Most state cooperative extension services and provincial departments of agriculture publish a list of vegetable varieties best adapted to the area. Check with your state or provincial office.

Here are some USDA helps—order from **Supt. of Documents,** Washington, DC 20402.

Growing Vegetables in the Home Garden, NE-8, 95¢. A fifty-page, step-by-step guide, with

data on growing more than fifty specific vegetables.

Insects and Diseases of Vegetables in the Home Garden, G-46, $1.20. Tells how to recognize the most common insects and diseases that attack vegetables and how to prevent the damage they cause.

Minigardens for Vegetables, G-163, 35¢. How to be a gar-

dener without a garden; ideas for growing vegetables in pots, pails, and other containers.

A top-notch guide, *All About Vegetables,* has 112 pages of illustrations, information, and helpful tips. From your garden dealer or bookseller, or order from **Ortho Division, Chevron Chemical Co.,** 575 Market St., San Francisco, CA 94105. $3.98 plus 50¢ handling.

Especially for Canadian gardeners, the booklet *Planning Your Garden,* Nr. 1182, is $1.25 from **Information Canada,** Publishing Division, 171 Slater St., Ottawa, Ont. K1A 0S9.

The Food Garden

If you're looking for something different to grow in your garden, something that will add zest to your menus, something you can show off to your neighbors, or something you can't find elsewhere, browse through these pages.

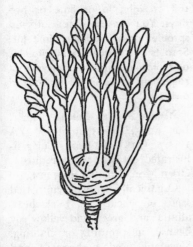

Abundant Life Seeds, Box 30018, Seattle, WA 98103. (206)-633-3057. Catalog, 50¢.

Seeds of vegetables and other food plants from the Pacific Northwest. Also regional varieties from Japan, Europe, and North America. All seeds are open-pollinated and untreated; many are home-grown and hand-collected and -cleaned. Wide variety of vegetables, herbs, seeds for sprouting, and also ornamentals.

Abundant Life Seed Foundation is a non-profit corporation dedicated to propagating and preserving native and naturalized plant species of the Pacific Northwest, particularly those not available commercially or that are rare and endangered. Workshops on seed raising and self-sowing gardens are offered to interested groups. And the foundation welcomes visitors, or correspondence from people who are propagating seeds and wish to exchange them and share their experiences.

Glecklers Seedmen, Metamora, OH 43540. Illustrated brochure, $1.00 (credited).

Glecklers conducts seed exchange and varietal research with over one hundred foreign countries. The result: many exclusive, rare, and unusual vegetable seeds. Among them are Imperial carrots (about a yard long), Peron Sprayless tomatoes, Aconcagua peppers (sweet as apples), Little

Gem squash (the size of an orange), and Evertender okra from India.

And also Gourmet, a greenhouse cucumber which, Glecklers says, proves women's lib has invaded the vegetable kingdom. Gourmet is a thenocarpic gynoecious hybrid. In simpler terms, it's a cuke with only female flowers, which produce fruit, in a closed greenhouse, without male pollen.

Can You Grow a Bigger Melon?

The world record for the biggest watermelon, according to Grace's Gardens (22 Autumn Ln., Hackettstown, NJ 07840), is a whopping 197 pounds. Some other record breakers: a 35-pound cabbage, a sunflower that topped 17 feet, and a 16¼-pound turnip. A lot of eating—if you like turnips!

If you can grow a bigger melon or break the record for some other fruits and vegetables, you may be eligible for a reward from Grace's Gardens. Details are in their illustrated catalog, which is 25¢ and includes a packet of gift seeds. The company specializes in seeds of unusual vegetables, with emphasis on the gigantic and the miniature, such as 4-foot-long squash, and carrots less than an inch long.

You're welcome to visit their trial gardens near Hackettstown, New Jersey, and Allentown, Pennsylvania. But phone first—(201)-637-4335.

Green Valley Seeds, 11565 E. Zayante Rd., Felton, CA 95018. Catalog; send SASE.

Seeds for sprouting, including alfalfa, mung bean, sunflower, fenugreek, lentil, red winter wheat, triticale, mustard, chick pea, and red clover. None treated with chemicals. Also sprouting screens, dried herbs, and books on sprouting and natural foods.

Green Valley is a non-profit cooperative organization whose aim is to promote collective health by making products available at lowest possible prices.

Almost-instant Vegetables

If you've never sprouted seeds, give it a try. Seeds sprout, without soil or light, in as little as two days. You can use a special seed sprouter or an ordinary fruit jar. Sprouts are loaded with vitamins and protein, and are delicious in salads or as additions to cooked dishes.

Metro Myster Farms, Rte. 1, Box 285, Northampton, PA 18067. (215)-262-6205. Color illustrated catalog, 50¢ (credited). Open Mon.–Fri., 8 A.M.–5 P.M.

Organically grown, untreated seeds of wheat, rye, buckwheat, alfalfa, and green and yellow soy beans, for sprouting or planting. Vegetable and herb seeds and plants, rhubarb, shallots, elephant garlic, sunchokes (improved knobless variety), comfrey, crownvetch crowns, and other seeds and bulbs. Complete planting instructions are sent with all bulb and root orders.

Nichols Garden Nursery, 1190 N. Pacific Hwy., Albany, OR 97321. (503)-928-9280. Illustrated catalog, 25¢. BAC and MC charges. Open Mon.–Sat., 9 A.M.–5:30 P.M.

Many rare and gourmet varieties of vegetable seeds, herb plants and seeds, organic-gardening aids, wine- and beer-making supplies, wheat grinders, and many books on gardening and related subjects. A very unique, interesting catalog with much advice on gardening and cooking.

One of Nichols' specialties is elephant garlic, a huge variety of garlic with a mild flavor. The nursery, the first to grow it commercially, introduced it to American gardeners and, because of its size, named it "elephant" garlic.

FOR PEOPLE PARTIAL TO PEPPERS

Along with some other unusual vegetables, **Paul F. Duke,** Fort George Star Rte., Box 280-A, Jacksonville, FL 32229, offers some forty varieties of peppers collected from around the world. Among them are Black Pods, from Guatemala; Peperoncini, a favorite sweet pepper from Italy; and long, slim, and hot Red Cayennes, from French Guiana. Pepper lovers can get a copy of Duke's seed list by sending 25¢.

Duke himself is very fond of peppers. He prepares an incendi-ary sauce by soaking peppers in vinegar and salt for six weeks, then boils it down and strains it, and pours it on everything from meat to scrambled eggs. He lays his stalwart taste buds to his Austro-Hungarian background.

Chili peppers are high in vitamins A and C—and the C content almost doubles when the chilies turn red. Christopher Columbus sent the first hot peppers back to Europe. Chilies can be dried, pickled, roasted, or frozen.

This chili lore comes from the brochure of Horticultural Enterprises, Box 34082, Dallas, TX 75234, specialists in chili peppers and imported Mexican seeds. Their illustrated brochure is 25¢. And if you'd like to learn Mexican cooking, the company says one of the most authentic guides is *The Complete Book of Mexican Cooking,* by Elisabeth Ortiz. It has 352 pages, and the price is only $1.60, postpaid.

GARDENING A LA FRANÇAISE

J. A. Demonchaux Co., Inc., 225 Jackson, Topeka, KS 66603. (913)-235-8502. Illustrated brochure.

"Gourmet Garden Seeds," imported from France. Some varieties: *Mâche à grosse graine,* corn salad that can be eaten alone or mixed with beets and potatoes; *Demi-nain choux de Bruxelles de la Halle,* semi-dwarf brussels sprouts; *Grosse blonde paresseuse,* a summer lettuce with "blond" leaves; and *Fraises des quatre saisons,* delicious little everbearing strawberries.

Demonchaux also has a number of books on gardening and cooking, all in French, but "easy to read and a good way to practice the language for those who want to improve their fluency in a useful and pleasant manner."

Le Jardin du Gourmet (Raymond Saufroy), Box 5, Rte. 15, West Danville, VT 05873. Illustrated catalog, 50¢. Open every day in season, 9 A.M.–6 P.M.

Seeds and plants, many imported and uncommon, of French vegetables and herbs. Included are shallots (the secret of French cooking), celeriac, onions, leeks, beans, cabbages, artichokes, and many more. Also, numerous books on herbs, cooking, and gardening, plus an assortment of gourmet foods. Saufroy, a Frenchman, former restaurant owner, and food consultant to a prominent publisher, includes many tantalizing recipes and cooking suggestions in his catalog.

These items are also for sale at Saufroy's shop in Vermont. Come and visit us, he says.

"And if I know my daughter, we'll also have flowers in pots, gadgets, perhaps some antiques. Dry flowers for winter bouquets. My neighbor is a potter, and some of his lawn creations will be on display also."

FOOD WITH AN ORIENTAL FLAVOR

Order some seeds from the following three companies, plant them, and while they're growing, read a good book on oriental cooking. You'll be all set for some unusual taste treats.

Kitazawa Seed Co., 356 W. Taylor St., San Jose, CA 95110. (408)-292-4420. Descriptive price list. Open Mon.–Sat., 8 A.M.–5 P.M.

An assortment of unique seeds. Gobo, an edible burdock with long, slender roots that are boiled until tender and tasty; Shingiku, an edible-leaved chrysanthemum; seven kinds of mustard, including Komatsuna, a mustard spinach;

Oshiro Uri, an oval melon good for pickling; and a lot more.

Taroko Company, Box 5, Warren, OH 44482. Descriptive price list.

Seeds of oriental vegetables such as Water Convolvulus (hollow stems, good for soup), Hong-Sing Tsai (sauté small leaves with slivered meat), and soy beans (grow your own protein).

Soy beans are easy to grow, says Taroko. But watch out for birds and rabbits. They *really* go for soy beans.

Tsang and Ma International, 1556 Laurel St., San Carlos, CA 94070. (415)-595-2270. Descriptive price list. Visitors by appointment.

Sixteen varieties of imported Chinese vegetable seeds. Owners, from Hong Kong, are experts in both planting and Chinese cooking. So to make sure everything goes right, each seed packet tells: what it looks like, how to plant it, how to grow it, when to harvest it, what it tastes like, how to prepare it, and how to cook it, and includes menu suggestions.

Kidney Beans . . . Pinto Beans . . . Soldier Beans . . . Adzuki Beans . . . Cow Pea Beans . . . Yankee Navy Beans . . . Pink Eye Purple Hull Beans . . . Dixie Speckled Butter Lima Beans

Name your bean. And most likely the **Vermont Bean Seed Company** will have it. They say they've got the largest selection of bean seeds in the country—over thirty-five different types. If beans

are your dish, write for a copy of their catalog. Their address: Way's Lane, Manchester Center, VT 05255. To make sure you prepare beans correctly, a country recipe is included with each variety you order.

If you're in the area, stop by and see their bean farm. But phone first, (802)-362-3900, to let them know you're coming.

Vegetable Plants

Here are some companies that will supply you with vegetable plants ready to set out in your home garden.

Brown's Omaha Plant Farms, Inc., Box 787, Omaha, TX 75571. Color illustrated brochure, 25¢.

Onion plants, including Crystal Wax Bermuda, White and Yellow Spanish, Red Hamburger, and others. Also cabbage, collards, brussels sprouts, broccoli, cauliflower, and sweet-potato plants. Minimum order for most varieties is one dozen.

"Our plants are not grown in hothouses, greenhouses, or cold frames. They are outdoor, open-field-grown, well-rooted, sturdy plants."

Evans Plant Co., Ty Ty, GA 31795. (912)-382-3106. Brochure.

Field-grown plants, including tomatoes, peppers, eggplants, cabbage, onions, collards, kale, leek, beets, cauliflower, head lettuce, broccoli, brussels sprouts. Plant growers for almost fifty years.

Fred's Plant Farm (Fred Stoker) Rte. 1, Dresden, TN 38225. (901)-364-3754. Descriptive price list. U.S. sales only. Visitors welcome anytime.

Fifteen varieties of sweet-potato plants, such as Running Puerto Ricos, Yellow Yams, Georgia Reds, Nuggets, Copperskins. Special collections available. Sold in quantities of twenty-five or more plants.

"We grow our own seed and plants, in open air and sunshine for toughness. Guaranteed safe delivery."

Should You Plant by the Moon?

Old-timers swore by planting at proper moon signs to make sure of bumper crops. If you'd like to learn how, read *Country Wisdom,* by Jerry Mack Johnson (a Doubleday paperback, $2.95 from booksellers). There's a wagonload of other rural facts and folklore thrown in for good measure.

Margrave Plant Co., 117 Church St., Gleason, TN 38229. (901)-648-5174. Illustrated price list. U.S. sales only. Visitors welcome anytime.

Sweet-potato plants—many varieties. Minimum order, twenty-five plants. Has been growing and shipping sweet-potato plants since 1933.

Mason's Plant Farms, Box 27, Reklaw, TX 75784. (713)-369-2283. Brochure and price list.

Onion, cabbage, broccoli, eggplant, tomato, brussels sprouts, cauliflower, pepper, and sweet-potato plants. Numerous varieties of each. Most plants available in quantities of one dozen or more. Air shipments are available.

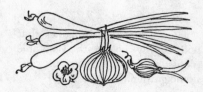

Piedmont Plant Co., Inc., 807 N. Washington St., Box 424, Albany, GA 31702. (912)-435-0766. Color illustrated catalog. Visitors welcome anytime.

Field-grown plants of hybrid and standard varieties of tomatoes, peppers, eggplant, cabbage, lettuce, broccoli, cauliflower, and onions.

"Our company is a family business started over seventy years ago. In a recent season we shipped 65 million plants."

Steele Plant Co., Box 191, Gleason, TN 38229. (901)-648-5476. Illustrated brochure. Open every day, April through June.

Many varieties of sweet-potato plants. Included with all orders is a booklet with 123 sweet-potato recipes (including cobblers, cakes, custards, pies, puddings, and biscuits).

Sweet potatoes, says Dudley Sanders of Steele Plant Co., are ideal for lazy gardeners. As they grow, their leaves shade the area, keeping weeds down and elimi-

nating the need for cultivation. After harvesting, the work is complete—no canning or freezing necessary. Just put the potatoes in a basket or crate, keep them from chilling, and the taste improves every day.

Texas Onion Plant Co., Box 871, Farmersville, TX 75031. (214)-782-7171. Price list. Open daily, January through May.

Several varieties of onion plants. Growing instructions are included with each order. The company has been growing and shipping plants for over forty years.

"Harvest onions as necks soften and tops begin to fall. Protect against freezing. Leave tops on. Tie in bunches with strings and hang on a wall in a ventilated enclosure. Or place onion in toe of discarded stocking, tie off with string, repeat process until stocking is full. Hang stocking by toe in ventilated area and remove onions as needed."

Plastic Gardens

For over ten years, Thomas E. Doyle has been growing plants in ground covered with a heavy, non-toxic plastic. Among the many benefits, he says, are larger plants, with no need for watering or cultivation. His methods must be good, because more than a thousand other gardeners in Daviess County, Indiana, where he lives, have plastic gardens, too. For a copy of his booklet Gardening Without Cultivation, which explains all about it, send $3.00 to Doyle, 10 Mill St., Washington, IN 47501. His garden at 1600 Bedford Rd. in Washington is on display from April to October. Phone: (812)-254-0947.

Herbs

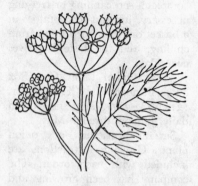

A.B.C. Herb Nursery (Viola Bennet), Rte. 1, Box 313, Lecoma, MO 65540. (314)-435-6389. Three price lists: Herbs; African Violets; and Terrarium and House Plants; send stamp for each. Open Mon.–Fri., 8 A.M.–noon; Sunday afternoon.

Herbs of all types. Over seven hundred varieties of African violets. Large listing of house and terrarium plants.

Saturday mornings, from May to October, the Bennets sell plants at the Ozark Farmers Market, near Rolla, MO—"well worth a planned visit."

"This is a fourth-generation family farm business. On Sunday afternoons we take time for visiting with anyone who comes to the farm."

Appalachian Root & Herb Co., 37 Center St., Rainelle, WV 25962. (304)-438-5211. Illustrated catalog. Open every day, 8 A.M.–4 P.M.

Some one hundred varieties of herb seeds and plants; primarily medicinal. Also terrarium plants, partridgeberries, rattlesnake plantain, sheet moss, and terrarium kits.

Casa Yerba, Star Rte. 2, Box 21, Days Creek, OR 97429. (503)-825-3534. Catalog, 50¢. Visitors by appointment.

About two hundred varieties of herb seeds—culinary, medicinal, dye, insect-repelling, and fragrant. A large selection of herb plants and roots. A very complete listing of herb books. The catalog has good descriptions of culture and uses.

"Casa Yerba is a family, homestead-type ranch. Streams and springs flow through our fifty-six acres plus. Everything we produce is 'naturally grown'—no chemical fertilizers or poison sprays are used. We love visitors, but do ask that they make an appointment. This is a working ranch, and it's difficult to be sociable during milking time or while cutting hay."

Cedarbrook Herb Farm, Rte. 1, Box 1047, Sequim, WA 98382. (206)-683-4541. Open Mon.–Sat., 10 A.M.–4 P.M., April through September.

Karmen and Don McReynolds, of Cedarbrook Herb Farm, have written a book, *Herbs, the Primer for Culture and Harvesting*, that has information about fifty of the most popular herbs, their uses, and propagation and drying methods. It's $2.00 postpaid.

The McReynoldses don't sell herbs by mail, but about one hundred varieties of potted herbs are for sale at their farm. And during August and September they have a supply of elephant garlic, a Cedarbrook specialty.

Fox Hill Farm, 434 W. Michigan Ave., Box 7, Parma, MI 49269. (517)-531-3179. Catalog, 50¢. U.S. sales only. Open Thurs. and Sun., noon–6 P.M.

About 130 varieties of herb plants and twenty varieties of scented geraniums. The catalog has good cultural information on herbs, and lists them under classifications such as culinary, fragrance, dye plants, insect-repelling.

A 30×75-foot Herb Sampler Garden and a solar-heated pit greenhouse are on display at the farm.

As for growing herbs indoors, Fox Hill Farm says:

"Yes, you can grow them indoors if you can grow a fibrous begonia, an ivy, or a geranium. And herbs are much more pleasant, because they smell good when you touch them and taste good when you eat them. Or, pluck a sprig to stick behind your ear or in your buttonhole."

Hemlock Hill Herb Farm (Mrs. Dorothy Childs Hogner), Litchfield, CT 06759. (203)-567-5031. Illustrated catalog, 50¢. Open Tues.–Sat., 10 A.M.–4 P.M.,

from May 1 to August 31. Other times by appointment.

Specializes in perennial culinary herb plants; many varieties. Also some scent and medicinal herbs. (No annuals.) Good descriptions and cultural information are in the catalog.

Besides growing herbs, Mrs. Hogner has written several books, including *Gardening and Cooking on Terrace and Patio,* and *Good Bugs and Bad Bugs in Your Garden—Backyard Ecology,* a fascinating book for children. She's also writing another book for children on endangered plants, such as cacti, lady's-slipper orchids, rare pitcher plants, Venus flytraps, and some species of milkweed that many people regard as common weeds.

Borage for Courage

One of her favorite annual herbs, says Dorothy Childs Hogner of Hemlock Hill Herb Farm, is borage (pronounce it to rhyme with courage).

"Plant it in a clump. Then, when you are bone-weary and ready to relax with a martini, drop one of the flowers in your drink. That is what the crusaders did when they had a stirrup cup before they took off on a crusade. They declared that borage gave them courage."

Herbs 'N Honey Nursery (Mrs. Chester C. Fisher, Jr.), Rte. 2, Box 205, Monmouth, OR 97361. (503)-623-4033. Catalog, 50¢ *or* self-addressed envelope with two

stamps. Open Mon.–Fri., 8 A.M.–
5 P.M. Other times by appointment.

More than 130 varieties of herb
plants; specializes in medicinal,
culinary, and tea plants. All
plants are organically grown; no
chemical sprays or fertilizers.

The nursery also publishes an
illustrated, 102-page *Herbal
Book*, $4.95 postpaid (catalog in-
cluded without charge). The
book contains a history of botanical remedies, how to prepare and
use herbal salves, ointments, etc.,
recipes for soaps and candles, plus
a complete description of each
herb, its culture, history, and lore.

Hickory Hollow, Rte. 1, Box
52, Peterstown, WV 24963. (304)-
753-9817. Illustrated brochure,
25¢.

Herb plants and various herbal
products. Jerusalem-artichoke tubers. Luffa (sponge-gourd) seeds.
Also plans for building a stove-
top unit for drying fruits, vegetables, and herbs.

Howe Hill Herbs, Howe Hill
Rd., Camden, ME 04843. (207)-
763-3506. Brochure and price list,
35¢. Minimum order, $8.00. Visi-
tors by appointment.

Herb plants, more than ninety
varieties. Scented geraniums, including rose, oak-leaf, pepper-
mint, pine, and lemon scent
groups; miniatures and dwarfs;
single- and double-bloom varieties.

The Christmas list (for a copy,
send a stamp in October) has
items such as terrarium kits, par-

tridgeberry bowls, wreaths of natural cones, mosses and berries,
and ivy and boxwood plants.

**North Central Comfrey Pro-
ducers**, Box 195, Glidden, WI
54527. (715)-264-2083. Illustrated brochure. Open every day,
daylight hours, May 15 to November 1.

Comfrey root cuttings, crown
cuttings, and plants. Dried comfrey leaves and leaf flour. Also
seedlings of native butternuts,
black walnuts, and hybrid pop-
lars.

Otto Richter & Sons, Ltd.,
Box 26, Goodwood, Ont. L0C
1A0. (416)-294-1457. Illustrated
catalog, 50¢. Open Mon.–Sat.,
8:30 A.M.–5 P.M.; Sun., 8:30
A.M.–4 P.M.

Over a hundred varieties of
herb seeds, many uncommon. Culinary, medicinal, dye, tea, and
others. Also books on herbs. Good
descriptions and cultural information are in the catalog.

Try Natural Plant Dyeing

Natural dyeing is growing in
popularity, according to Otto
Richter & Sons. In their catalog
they list more than twenty plants
that can be used to dye wool and
other materials. Many other herb
growers also offer dye plants.

The reason for the new interest
in natural dyes is the very reason
they were replaced by coal-tar
synthetic dyes in the late
1800s—the difficulty of stand-
ardizing colors. No two natural
dye lots are identical, producing

hues with subtle differences, appealing to those searching for the unique.

The how-to of natural dyeing is covered in two handbooks, $1.50 each, from Brooklyn Botanic Garden, 1000 Washington Ave., Brooklyn, NY 11225.

Dye Plants & Dyeing, Handbk. 46, illustrated with four color pages, explains plants and plant parts to use for coloring many fabrics.

Natural Plant Dyeing, Handbk. 72, has recipes and step-by-step procedures for creating vibrant colors through the use of plant materials.

Rocky Hollow Herb Farm, Box 354, Sussex, NJ 07461. (201)-875-5132. Illustrated catalog. Open every day, 10:30 A.M.–7 P.M., May through October.

Herb plants and seeds. Also dried herbs and herbal vinegars, oils, and other products. Many books on herbs.

Farm store and display gardens situated in a beautiful area, just outside Sussex.

"We have constructed herb gardens in various locations and would be happy to advise anyone interested in planting their own herb garden."

Sunnybrook Farms Nursery, 9448 Mayfield Rd., Chesterland, OH 44026. (216)-729-7232. Illustrated catalog, 50¢ (credited). Minimum order, $7.50. Open Tues.–Sat., 8:30 A.M.–5 P.M.; Sun., 1 P.M.–5 P.M.

Over 150 varieties of herb plants. A special Colonial Herb Garden with thirty-two plants, and planning and planting instructions. Also geraniums, cacti and succulents, and many exotic houseplants. In business since 1928; the second generation of the family is now operating the nursery.

Taylor's Garden, Inc., 1535 Lone Oak Rd., Vista, CA 92083. (714)-727-3485. Brochure, 25¢. U.S. sales only. Open daily, 8 A.M.–5 P.M.

Some two hundred varieties of herb plants, primarily cooking and medicinal. Garden has over two acres of cultivated and wild herbs. Conducted tours held every two months. Herbs are also available at Taylor's, 2649 Stingle Ave., Rosemead, CA 91770. (213)-280-4639.

Well-Sweep Herb Farm, 317 Mt. Bethel Rd., Port Murray, NJ 07865. (201)-852-5390. Brochure, 25¢. U.S. sales only. Open Mon–Sat., 9:30 A.M.–5 P.M.

Over three hundred types of herb plants and scented geraniums; also herb seeds. Many unusual varieties. Extensive listing of dried flowers.

"We have a large, educational display herb garden and fields where we grow our dried flowers, plus a barn filled with dried flowers for arrangements—all for visitors to enjoy."

The Yarb Patch, 3726 Thomasville Rd., Tallahassee, FL 32303. (904)-385-2647. Illustrated catalog, 25¢. BAC and MC charges. U.S. sales only. Open Mon.–Sat., 10 A.M.–5 P.M., September through May; noon–5 P.M., June through August.

Wide variety of herb seeds and plants. Also herbal products and vinegars; gourmet cookware. The catalog gives cultural tips for growing herbs in the South.

A retail shop and a semiformal herb garden are near a lake in a beautiful location near Tallahassee. Garden is at its best from April through October. Group tours arranged by appointment.

Yankee Peddler Herb Farm, Hwy. 36 N, Brenham, TX 77833. (713)-836-4442. Catalog, $1.00; price list, 25¢. BAC and MC charges. Open daily, 9 A.M.–5 P.M.

Wide variety of herb plants and seeds. Also scented geraniums, ornamental gourds, and ornamental grasses. Many uncommon. The catalog gives a thorough description of each herb, lists the common and the botanical names, and includes interesting notes about history and uses. Catnip, for example, was valued by old-timers for colicky babies, producing gentle sleep. And fresh juice from onions reputedly cures athlete's foot.

Seeds, plants, and books are available at the farm, which also has an antique shop and a display garden.

"Our goal is to include, along with the 'modern-day' herbs, as many of the hard-to-find varieties as possible—the rare, old-time botanicals that were used back in the days when botany and medicine were still coming along hand in hand. We are continuously adding new varieties as sources become available."

Helps for Herbalists

A basic guide is *A Primer for Herb Growing,* 50¢ plus 13¢ postage, from the **Herb Society of America,** 300 Massachusetts Ave., Boston, MA 02115.

Suggestions for growing and

cooking are included in the booklet *Herbs: Fun to Grow, Fun to Eat,* 25¢ from the **University of Vermont,** Publications Office, Morrill Hall, Burlington, VT 05401.

Herbs and Their Ornamental Uses, Handbk. 68, $1.50 from

Brooklyn Botanic Garden, 1000 Washington Ave., Brooklyn, NY 11225, describes the most attractive herbs for garden and kitchen use, and tells how to design knot, fragrance, and other herb gardens.

Fruits, Nuts, and Berries

The Adams County Nursery, Aspers, PA 17304. (717)-677-8338. Catalog. Minimum order, $15. Open Mon.–Sat., 7 A.M.–5 P.M. Other times by appointment.

Many types of fruit trees: apple, nectarine, pear, sweet and sour cherry, plum. Also Chinese chestnuts, grape vines.

Ahrens & Son Nursery, Rte. 1, Huntingburg, IN 47542. (812)-683-3055. Color illustrated catalog. Visitors welcome; phone ahead.

Specializes in strawberries; many varieties. The catalog has

much information on growing, several pages of berry recipes, and suggestions for operating a pick-it-yourself field. It also lists raspberries, blackberries, blueberries, grapes, gooseberries, currants, asparagus, and rhubarb.

"An interesting thing about strawberries is that they were once grown more for ornamental purposes than for eating. They still do make an attractive planting along a walk or as a ground cover."

Alexander's Blueberry Nurseries, 1224-A Wareham St., Middleboro, MA 02341. (617)-947-3397. Descriptive price list; send two stamps. Minimum order, $10. Open 10 A.M.–5 P.M. during fruiting season; other times by appointment.

Specializes in blueberries (several hundred varieties), lilacs, and raspberries. Also ground covers, small fruits, herbs, perennials, and ornamental shrubs. All plants are organically grown. Cultural directions are sent with orders.

When blueberries are ripe, you can pick your own at the nurseries. Call ahead to assure good picking, and bring containers. Plant customers may taste varieties to choose favorites for purchase.

"We are a small, family business, glad to offer personalized help to our customers. We offer a slide program on lilacs and a lecture on blueberry history, care, and culture at reasonable costs to organizations in the area."

W. F. Allen Co., Box 1577, Salisbury, MD 21801. (301)-742-7123. Color illustrated catalog. Visitors by appointment.

Strawberry plants, plus blackberries, raspberries, grapes, asparagus. Good cultural information. The oldest strawberry nursery in the United States; has been growing berries since 1885.

As American as Apple Pie

Apples, like the O'Tooles, Olsens, Schmidts, or Garcias, are American—but not like the Seminoles, Mohawks, Chippewas, or Apaches. The first apples were brought to North America by European settlers.

Baums Nursery, Rte. 2, New Fairfield, CT 06810. Descriptive price list. U.S. sales only.

More than 150 American and European varieties of apples, plums, and pears, both old and new types. A booklet, *Fruit Varieties of America and Europe,* $1.00 postpaid, provides detailed descriptions of all varieties.

Bountiful Ridge Nurseries, Inc., Box 249, Princess Anne, MD 21853. (301)-651-0400. Color illustrated catalog. BAC and MC charges. Minimum order, $10. Open Mon.–Fri., 8 A.M.–5 P.M.

Very extensive listing of peaches, apples, and grapes (including French hybrids and other wine grapes). Many patented and exclusive varieties. Also oriental persimmons, Chinese chestnuts, filberts, and pecans. A good selection of books on fruit culture. Founded before 1900, a fourth-generation business.

Brittingham Plant Farms, 2538 Ocean City Rd., Salisbury, MD 21801. (301)-749-5153. Color illustrated catalog. Open Mon.–Fri., 8 A.M.–5 P.M.

About thirty registered strawberry varieties. Also blueberries and raspberries. Growers for over thirty years.

Buntings' Nurseries, Inc., Dukes St., Selbyville, DE 19975. (302)-436-8231. Color illustrated catalog. Open Mon.–Fri., 9 A.M.–4 P.M.

Many strawberry varieties, including newest USDA introductions. Other small fruits as well as fruit, shade, and nut trees.

California Nursery Co., Box 2278, Fremont, CA 94536. (415)-797-3311. Descriptive price list. Minimum order, $15.

Large selection of fruit and nut trees, including almond, apricot, fig, nectarine, peach, plum, prune, cherry, pomegranate, lime, persimmon, and quince. Also grapes—both table and special wine varieties. Fruitgrowers since 1865.

C&O Nursery, 1700 N. Wenatchee Ave., Box 116, Wenatchee, WA 98801. (509)-662-7164. Color illustrated catalog. Open Mon.–Sat.

Fruit trees—apple, peach, quince, pear, nectarine, appricot, cherry, prune, plum—many patented. Also nut trees, berries. Good cultural information for orchardists.

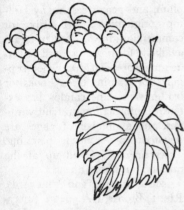

Common Fields Nursery, Town Farm Rd., Ipswich, MA 01938. (617)-356-5544. Illustrated price list. U.S. sales only. Open every day during season, 8 A.M.–6 P.M.

Cultivated blueberries—many new varieties. Also asparagus, raspberries, grapes, trees, and flowering shrubs. Emphasis on northern-grown stock.

The Conner Co., Box 534, Augusta, AR 72006. (501)-347-2561. Color illustrated catalog.

Arkansas state-certified strawberry plants; also other southern varieties from the USDA and North Carolina Experiment Station.

Cumberland Valley Nurseries, Inc., Box 430, McMinnville, TN 37110. (615)-473-2283. Price list. Minimum order, $25. U.S. sales only. Visitors by appointment.

Peach trees—more than sixty varieties. Also plum, nectarine, cherry, pear, apple, and pecan trees, and grapes.

Decorah Nursery, 504 Center Ave., Decorah, IA 52101. (319)-382-9311. Descriptive price list.

Black-walnut seedlings. World's largest black-walnut nursery, has several million one-year-old walnut seedlings. Founded by the late R. W. Daubendiek, known as "Johnny Walnutseed."

Florida's Vineyard Nursery, Box 300, Orange Lake, FL 32681. (904)-591-2525. Illustrated brochure. Minimum order, $10. Open Mon.–Sat., 9 A.M.–6 P.M.; Sun., 1 P.M.–6 P.M.

Fruits adapted to Florida and the lower Southeast. Golden and dark-skinned varieties of muscadine grapes; bunch grapes including Roucaneuf, a famous French wine grape. Also several varieties of blueberries and figs. Bare-root and containerized plants.

The nursery, which cooperates with the University of Florida in a wine-research program, is developing a premium wine estate. For visitors, there are tours of the vineyard and cellar, a preserve kitchen, a cheese *cave*, and gourmet dining. Also pick-your-own fruit in season.

Dean Foster Nurseries, Rte. 2, Hartford, MI 49057. (616)-621-4480. Color illustrated catalog. Open Mon.–Sat., 9 A.M.–6 P.M.

Asparagus plants, seed potatoes, strawberries, raspberries, blueberries, fruit trees, and evergreens. Nursery established in 1837.

Fruit Haven Nursery, Inc., Rte. 1, Kaleva, MI 49645. (616)-889-5594. Color illustrated catalog, 25¢.

Specializes in strawberries. Also raspberries, blackberries, rhubarb, and asparagus.

Galletta Brothers, Hammonton, NJ 08037. (609)-561-5033. Illustrated brochure.

Blueberry plants—both standards and new introductions. Available as rooted cuttings to bearing-age plants. The brochure includes a great deal of cultural information, even a recipe for old-fashioned blueberry pie.

Louis Geraldi Nursery, Rte. 1, O'Fallon, IL 62269. (618)-632-4456. Catalog. Open Mon.–Sat., 8 A.M.–6 P.M.; Sun., 10 A.M.–5:30 P.M.

Specialists, for over forty years, in all northern varieties of hardy, grafted nut trees.

Hilltop Orchards and Nurseries, Inc., Rte. 2, Hartford, MI 49057. (616)-621-3135. Western Regional Office: Box 2357, Wenatchee, WA 98801. (509)-663-1222. Color illustrated catalog.

Apple, cherry, peach, nectarine, plum, and pear trees; many Hilltop originations. Primarily for commercial growers, but trees are available for home orchards. Sturdee tree spreaders, hardwood supports for training trees. Books for fruitgrowers. The catalog has extensive information on fruit varieties, and a number of pages are devoted to orchard planning. Trees may be picked up at the nursery, but phone ahead.

Ison's Nursery and Vineyards, Rte. 1, Brooks, GA 30205. (404)-599-6970. Illustrated catalog. U.S. sales only. Open Mon.–Fri., 8 A.M.–6 P.M.; Sat., 8 A.M.–1 P.M.

Many varieties of muscadine grapes. Also blueberries and blackberries. Plants shipped bareroot. Over forty years of experience working with, cultivating, and propagating muscadines.

Potted plants for sale at nursery. Visitors at vineyard in the September-to-October ripening season will see grapes of all colors, large as half dollars.

America's Oldest Fruit Book

William Coxe was the first North American to write a definitive work on American fruits. His book, *A View of the Cultivation of Fruit Trees and the Management of Orchards and Cider,* published in 1831, did much to influence American tastes in fruit. The book has been republished in a limited facsimile edition by H. Frederick Janson of Pomona Book Exchange, Rockton, Ont. L0R 1X0.

Lawson's Nursery, Rte. 1, Box 61, Ball Ground, GA 30107. (404)-893-2141. Brochure. Open every day, 8 A.M.–5 P.M.

Devoted to growing old-fashioned types of apple trees— almost every turn-of-the-century variety from the southern Appalachians—such as Shockley, Old Fashioned Tender Rine, Yellow Sheepnose, and Limber Twig. Dwarf and semidwarf trees.

"This is a small family operation, started as a hobby to try to save the old varieties from extinction. You have to taste old-fashioned apples to know how good they really are. We're always happy to have friends come by to eat some apples and drink fresh cider with us."

Henry Leuthardt Nurseries, Inc., Montauk Hwy., East Moriches, NY 11940. (516)-878-1387. Illustrated catalog, 25¢. Minimum order, $10. U.S. sales only. Open Mon.–Sat., 9 A.M.–4 P.M., March 15 to May 15 and October 15 to December 15. Other times by appointment.

Specialists in espaliered fruit trees. Old-fashioned apple and pear types. Also grapes, raspberries, currants, gooseberries, blueberries. There is much information on the care of espalier-trained trees in the catalog.

Espaliered fruit trees, says Leuthardt, can be trained in many patterns and adapted to a variety of uses: below and between windows; along sides of buildings, fences, walls; edging for paths and driveways; as hedges or screens for borders; as a focal point of interest in gardens; arbors over a walk; to hide unsightly objects from view.

Edward Lowden, Box 10, Ancaster, Ont. L9G 3L3. Descriptive brochure, 50¢. Visitors by appointment.

Many varieties of red raspberries (early, main-crop, everbearing, and fall), black raspberries, blackberries (including the very hardy Lowden blackberry), strawberries, gooseberries, comfrey plants. Also many types of tomato seeds, especially Sub-Arctic early varieties.

An organic gardener, Lowden tests plants and seeds from all over the world on his experimental farm and does extensive plant breeding. In 1941 his Honey Gold melon won honorable mention in the All-America Selections.

Makielski Berry Farm, 7130 Platt Rd., Ypsilanti, MI 48197.

(313)-434-3673. Catalog. Open daily, 8 A.M.–8 P.M.

Small fruits, many uncommon varieties such as Lowden black raspberry, and Poorman, Captivator, and White Smith gooseberries. Numerous other types of raspberries, strawberries, currants.

The farm has more than thirty-six acres of U-pick raspberries in season. Check in advance for best picking times.

Test New Fruits

Dues of $4.00—which is credited if you buy fruits—will give you a membership in the New York State Fruit Testing Cooperative Association, Geneva, NY 14456, and a copy of their annual catalog. Members, throughout the world, can try new fruit varieties recommended by the New York State Agricultural Experiment Station. The catalog also has a great deal of cultural information for fruitgrowers. Visitors are welcome at the association offices, Mon.–Fri., 8 A.M.–5 P.M. Phone: (315)-787-2205.

May Nursery Co., 2215 W. Lincoln, Box 1312, Yakima, WA 98907. (509)-453-8219. Catalog. Minimum order, $10. Open Mon.–Fri., 8 A.M.–4:30 P.M.

Fruit trees, standard and dwarf. Patented apple varieties. Introducing a genetic dwarf peach, Canadian Wonder; height at ten years is only three to four feet. Also hop plants, shade and flowering trees, and flowering shrubs.

Mayo Nurseries, Lyons, NY 14489. Illustrated catalog. Minimum order, $10. Visitors welcome weekdays; phone ahead.

Apple trees; standard, dwarf, and semidwarf; many uncommon varieties. Also peach, apricot, prune, plum, pear, cherry trees. Flowering shrubs, shade and ornamental trees.

J. E. Miller Nurseries, Inc., 5060 W. Lake Rd., Canandaigua, NY 14424. (315)-394-0647. Color illustrated catalog. BAC and MC charges.

Dwarf and standard fruit trees, berries, table and wine grapes. Many varieties, both old and new, of apples and peaches.

Nourse Farms, Inc. (New Enland Strawberry Nursery), R.F.D., Box 485, South Deerfield, MA 01373. (413)-665-3078. Illustrated catalog. U.S. sales only. Open Mon.–Sat., 8 A.M.–4 P.M. at plant farms, River Rd., Whately, MA.

Strawberry plants, old and new varieties, adapted to the Northeast. Propagates virus-free stock with its own screen program. Also asparagus roots and McDonald strain of rhubarb, known for excellent quality and production. Largest strawberry nursery in New England; growers for forty-five years.

Rayner Bros., Inc., Box 1617, Salisbury, MD 21801. (301)-742-1594. Illustrated catalog. U.S. sales only. Open Mon.–Fri., 8 A.M.–5 P.M.; Sat., 7 A.M.–noon.

Strawberry plants; many new

introductions. Also blueberries, raspberries, blackberries, grapes, fruit and nut trees, asparagus roots. The catalog has excellent growing information, with special bulletins available on request.

Rider Nursery, Box 187, Farmington, IA 52626. Price list.

Dwarf and standard apples, sour and sweet cherries, peaches, dwarf and standard plums. Also raspberries, blackberries, boysenberries, grapes, blueberries, currants, strawberries, asparagus, rhubarb, and horseradish. Hardy, Iowa-grown stock.

St. Lawrence Nurseries, Rte. 2, Box 34, Heuvelton, NY 13654. (315)-344-6687. Price list, 25¢. Open every day; afternoons preferred.

Many uncommon fruit and nut trees; apples, including some very hardy, old varieties; very hardy pears and plums, mostly own introductions. Also American blight-resistant chestnuts, hardy black and Carpathian walnuts, butternuts, and hazelberts. Many varieties under test in experimental plots, including blight-resistant potatoes and very early peanuts.

Southmeadow Fruit Gardens, 2363 Tilbury Pl., Birmingham, MI 48009. (313)-644-1156. Descriptive price list. Minimum order, $7.50.

Rare and unusual varieties of fruit trees and plants: apple, peach, pear, nectarine, plum, apricot, cherry, quince, gooseberry, grape, and others. Many old American and foreign types, including plants for wildlife and conservation purposes.

A joint venture of Theo Grootendorst, a leading U.S. producer of fruit rootstocks, and Robert Nitschke, authority on fruit varieties and executive of the American Pomological Society.

For Fruit Connoisseurs

Southmeadow Fruit Gardens calls it a "catalog." But the 112-page illustrated book *Choice and Unusual Fruit Varieties for the Connoisseur and Home Gardener,* by Robert Nitschke (available for $5.00), is much more than that. The result of twenty-five years of study and observations of the best and most interesting fruit varieties, it includes history, descriptions, characteristics, and cultural information about hundreds of fruits.

Among the varieties included are Calville Blanc d'Hiver, a classic dessert apple grown in the 1600s for Louis XIII of France; Shinsei, a greenish-yellow apple from Japan; Merrill Delicious, one of the best-flavored of the early freestone peaches; Downer's Late Red sweet cherry, one of the oldest-known American varieties; and Lancashire Lad, a red, old English gooseberry.

A worthwhile addition to any fruitgrower's library.

Stark Bro's Nurseries, Louisiana, MO 63353. (314)-754-5511. Color illustrated catalog. BAC and MC charges. Open Mon–Fri., 8 A.M.–4 P.M.

Famous for its many fruit developments, particularly the Delicious apple. Catalog offers a wide selection of fruit trees and berries as well as general nursery stock, roses, shrubs, Stark orchard sprays, and other chemicals and fertilizers. Established in 1816, Stark Bro's is the oldest nursery in the United States—and the largest in the world.

Swedberg Nurseries, Inc., Battle Lake, MN 56515. (218)-864-5526. Color illustrated catalog. Open Mon.–Sat., 8 A.M.–7 P.M., April 10 to June 10. Other times by appointment.

Apples, pears, apricots, currants, plums, cherries, grapes, blueberries, strawberries, and other fruits. Emphasis on very hardy varieties, with many University of Minnesota introductions. Also nut trees, shade trees, evergreens, and other nursery stock.

Kiwi—the New Fruit Crop

A three-year-old kiwi vine (Actinidia chinensis, also known as Chinese gooseberry) produces fifty to sixty pounds of fruit a season, and when mature, up to three hundred pounds. The egg-shaped fruits taste something like gooseberries and are high in vitamin C and iron. Because of their big return on small plantings, kiwis are becoming a commercial fruit crop in California.

Home gardeners who would like to try kiwis can get a brochure and prices from Vallombrosa Gardens (Arthur & Vallie Wiebe), 1170 Vallombrosa Ave., Chico, CA 95926. (916)-342-7282. The gardens are open every day, 8 A.M.–5 P.M.

Fruitful Aids

The publications listed below, written by USDA and state horticulturists, offer expert advice for home fruitgrowers. Most are illustrated booklets, sold at cost. When ordering, be sure to list both *title and number,* and include payment with your order.

Order from the **Supt. of Documents,** Washington, DC 20402:

Dwarf Fruit Trees, L-407, 25¢.
Growing Blackberries, F-2160, 35¢.
Thornless Blackberries for the Home Garden, G-207, 30¢.
Growing Raspberries, F-2165, 25¢.
Growing Apricots for Home Use, G-204, 25¢.
Growing American Bunch Grapes, F-2123, 40¢.

Muscadine Grapes, F-2157, 30¢.

Insects on Deciduous Fruits and Tree Nuts, G-190, 40¢.

Order from **Michigan State University**, Bulletin Office, Box 231, East Lansing, MI 48824:
Fruit Pesticide Handbook, E-154, $1.00.

Peach Culture, E-509, 25¢.

Order from **The Ohio State University**, Extension Office, 2120 Fyffe Rd., Columbus, OH 43210:
Strawberries, RB-987, 50¢.

Bramble Fruit Culture, Nr. 411, 25¢.

Growing and Using Fruit at Home, Nr. 591, 40¢.

Order from **Cornell University**, Mailing Rm., Bldg. 7, Research Park, Ithaca, NY 14850:
Spraying the Home Orchard, IB-89, 15¢.

Blueberries in the Home Garden, E-900, 20¢.

Cultural Practices for Vineyards, E-805, 50¢.

Disease and Insect Control in the Home Orchard, E-1082, 25¢.

Order from **University of Massachusetts**, Cooperative Extension Service, 218 Stockbridge Hall, Amherst, MA 01002:
Currant and Gooseberry Growing, Nr. 121, 25¢.

Pruning Fruit Trees in the Home Orchard, Nr. 290, 25¢.

Order from **Purdue University**, Mailing Rm., Agricultural Administration Bldg., West Lafayette, IN 47907:
Strawberry Barrels, HO-68, 20¢.

Growing Pears, HO-108, 20¢.

Espaliered Fruit Trees, HO-110, 20¢.

Order from **University of Vermont**, Publications Office, Morrill Hall, Burlington, VT 05401:
Maple Sugaring in Your Backyard, BR-1220, 15¢.

Nuts You Can Grow

You can grow nuts in town or country, for profit or for pleasure, says the Northern Nut Growers Association. The following are good varieties for amateur nut growers: Carpathian or English walnuts; black walnuts; butternuts; heartnuts; chestnuts; filberts; pecans; hicans (hickory-pecan hybrids); hickory nuts; sweet acorn nuts; nut pines; persimmons; and pawpaws.

For information about joining the NNGA see its listing under "Plant Societies."

Information for Nut Growers

An illustrated booklet on nut culture, *Nut Growing*, IB-71, is 70¢ from **Cornell University**, Mailing Rm., Bldg. 7, Research Park, Ithaca, NY 14850.

Edible Nut Production, an eleven-lesson correspondence course, is $6.00; order from **Pennsylvania State University**, 307 Agricultural Administration Bldg., University Park, PA 16802.

Growing Black Walnuts for Home Use covers everything from selecting varieties to harvesting nuts. It's Nr. L-525, 25¢ from the **Supt. of Documents**, Washington, DC 20402.

Trees, Shrubs, and
Ground Covers

The following companies provide a broad range of plant materials, and many also handle garden seeds and supplies. Many of the larger seed companies also have nursery stock. But we have tried to put each source under the most appropriate and usable heading.

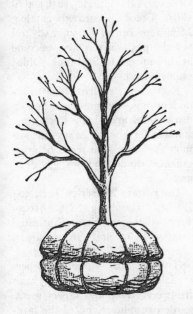

A rule of thumb—not *always* true—plants grown in a climate

similar to yours are your best choices.

Boatman Nursery & Seed Co., 212 S. Maple St., Dept. 101, Bainbridge, OH 45612. (614)-634-2741. Color illustrated catalog. BAC and MC charges. Open Mon.–Fri., 8 A.M.–5 P.M.

Some two hundred varieties of fruit and shade trees, berries and shrubs. Over five hundred varieties of vegetable and flower seeds. Garden equipment and supplies.

Southern orders are shipped from **Tennessee Nursery & Seed Co.,** Box 713, Dept. 101, Cleveland, TN 37311. (615)-476-4142. Open Mon.–Fri., 8 A.M.–5 P.M.

William Bradley Co., Nurseries, Box 345, Blairsville, GA 30512. (404)-379-3613. Illustrated price list. Open every day, 9 A.M.–9 P.M.

Nursery stock especially suitable for near southern areas. Shade trees, flowering shrubs, evergreens, fruit trees, berry plants, fertilizers, farm equipment, ground covers, bulbs, nut trees, lawn and garden supplies. Also decorative wrought-iron, bronze, and brass items.

"We're located in the north

Georgia mountains, an ideal growing area for stock that can be adapted to any climate."

Devon Nurseries, Ltd., 1408 Royal Bank Bldg., Edmonton, Alta. T5J 1W8. (403)-424-9696. Catalog. Nursery, in Devon, Alberta, open daily during planting season; hours vary; phone ahead (403)-447-3806.

Hardy northern stock. Evergreens, ornamental trees and shrubs, berries, alpine plants, fruit trees, wide selection of perennials, vines, and ground covers.

Buyer's Guide

The booklet *American Standard for Nursery Stock* will help you make sure you're getting quality plant materials. Prepared by the American Association of Nurserymen, it details recommended height, branching, caliper, root spread, and other relationships for nursery plants. Shrubs of certain sizes, for example, must have a certain number of canes; bareroot trees must have a minimum root spread depending on height. The booklet is $2.00 from the association, 230 Southern Bldg., Washington, DC 20005.

Emlong Nurseries, Inc., 2671 W. Marquette Woods Rd., Stevensville, MI 49127. (616)-429-3612. Color illustrated catalog. BAC and MC charges. Open every day, 9 A.M.–5 P.M.

General nursery stock. Wide variety of fruit trees (including dwarfs), berries, perennials, roses, ground covers, vines. Founded in 1900, a fourth-generation firm.

Earl Ferris Nursery, 811 Fourth St., N.E., Hampton, IA 50441. (515)-456-2563. Color illustrated catalog. BAC and MC charges. Open Mon.–Fri., 8 A.M.–5 P.M.; Sat., 8 A.M.–noon.

General line of nursery stock, with emphasis on evergreens and fruits. Many introductions, such as Maney and Ames juniper, Cyclone and Stoplight strawberry, Jonadel and Chieftain apple, Pink Princess weigela, and Black Hawk and Amethyst raspberry. Founded in 1869, the nursery is still in the same family.

Girard Nurseries, Box 428, Geneva, OH 44041. (216)-466-2881. Color illustrated catalog. Minimum order, $7.50. BAC and MC charges. Visitors are welcome at the nursery in Saybrook, Ohio; phone ahead.

Evergreens, azaleas, lilacs, rhododendrons, magnolias, hollies, ornamental and shade trees, trees suitable for bonsai. Many uncommon varieties. Also seeds of evergreens, rhododendrons, azaleas, and laurel.

Inter-State Nurseries, Inc., 504 E St., Hamburg, IA 51640. (712)-382-2411. Color illustrated catalog. BAC and MC charges. Open Mon.–Fri., 8 A.M.–5 P.M.

Trees, shrubs, vines, roses, perennials, bulbs, tree and bush fruits, vegetable and flower seeds, garden supplies. One of the largest mail-order nurseries in the United States.

Kelly Bros. Nurseries, Inc., Maple St., Dansville, NY 14437. (716)-335-2211. Color illustrated catalog. AEX, BAC, DC, and MC charges. U.S. sales only. Open Mon.–Fri., 8 A.M.–5 P.M.

Wide variety of shrubs, shade and ornamental trees, fruit trees, berries and grapes, perennials, roses, flowering bulbs, and other nursery stock.

"From a small beginning in 1880, we have grown to become one of the largest nurseries in the country, shipping millions of plants each year. The stock is grown on the finest land in New York State."

Custom-made Transplanting Tool

Cut a deep V notch in the end of a spade or a shovel if you're transplanting woody materials, recommends a South Dakota horticulturist. Sharpen the edges of the V and it will cut through roots easier and with minimum damage to them.

The Krider Nurseries, Inc., Box 29, Middlebury, IN 46540. (219)-825-5714. Color illustrated catalog. BAC and MC charges. Open Mon.–Sat., 7 A.M.–5 P.M.

General line of nursery stock, including some uncommon, imported trees. Vegetable and flower seeds. Over a hundred varieties of roses, including Festival Thornless rose. The nurseries were founded in 1896.

Kroh Nurseries, Inc., 5250 N. Garfield Ave., Box 536, Loveland, CO 80537. (303)-667-4223. Color illustrated catalog. BAC and MC charges. Open Mon.–Fri., 8 A.M.–4:30 P.M.

Fruit trees, ornamental shrubs, small fruits, hedging and windbreak plants, shade and ornamental trees, evergreens, roses, vines, perennials. Hardy stock especially for the Rocky Mountain and plains regions.

Mellinger's Inc., 2310 W. South Range Rd., North Lima, OH 44452. (216)-549-9861. Illustrated catalog; stamps appreciated. BAC and MC charges. Open Mon.–Sat., 9 A.M.–5 P.M.

Mellinger's advertises "1,000 horticultural items." Among them are many hard-to-find plant materials, nursery stock, fruits, nuts, berries, tree and shrub seedlings, bonsai stock, herbs, wildflowers, cacti, and tree and shrub seeds. More than fifty pages are devoted to tools, planting supplies, pots, chemicals, fertilizers, greenhouse and light-garden equipment, and organic gardening supplies. Very wide selection of books on both general and specialized horticultural subjects.

Ponzer Nursery, Lecoma Star Rte., Rolla, MO 65401. (314)-341-2593. Brochure and price list. U.S. sales only. Open Mon.–Sat., 9 A.M.–5 P.M.

General line of nursery stock, including evergreens, roses, fruit trees and small fruits, shade and ornamental trees, shrubs, and grasses. Some uncommon items, as pawpaw trees and old-fashioned winter onion sets.

Sheridan Nurseries, 700 Evans Ave., Etobicoke, Ont. M9C 1A1. (416)-621-9100. Color illustrated catalog, $1.00, Canada; $2.00, U.S. (credited). Minimum order outside Toronto-Hamilton and Montreal metropolitan areas, $40.

Very complete selection of nursery stock and related materials, including evergreens, rhododendrons, azaleas, deciduous trees and shrubs, roses, hedges, fruits, herbs, perennials, ornamental grasses, hardy ferns and wildflowers, grass seed, houseplants, fertilizers and other garden supplies, and garden books.

In addition, the catalog has much information on landscaping and site planning and on the use of native trees, shrubs, and wildflowers; lists of trees and shrubs for specific uses and locations; suggestions for planting in various soils; a Canadian plant-hardiness zone map; and recommended perennials. Much more than just a catalog—a reference book recommended for all gardeners in northern areas.

Sheridan has retail garden centers in Mississauga, Etobicoke, Unionville, and Toronto, in the Toronto metropolitan area, and in Beaconsfield and Montreal, in the Montreal area.

Skinner's Nursery, Ltd., Box 1030, Roblin, Man. R0L 1P0. (204)-564-2336. Catalog. Open Mon.–Fri., 9 A.M.–5 P.M.

Features trees, shrubs, fruits, and perennials that have proved to be hardy in the severe climate of northern Manitoba. Listings include apples, cherries, currants and other small fruits, hedge plants, roses, lilacs, ornamental crabs, evergreens, chrysanthemums, delphiniums, daylilies, iris, peonies, lilies, rockery plants, and ground covers. Many plants are developments of world-famous horticulturist Dr. F. L. Skinner.

The nursery has the most extensive private collection of trees, shrubs, and perennials on the Canadian Prairies.

Spring Hill Nurseries Co., Inc., 110 Elm St., Tipp City, OH 45371. (513)-667-2491. Color illustrated catalog. AEX, BAC, DC, and MC charges. Open every day, 8 A.M.–6 P.M.

Complete line of nursery stock, ornamental plants, vegetable seeds and plants, bush and tree fruits, houseplants, garden supplies. Many miniature roses. One of the country's oldest mail-order nurseries, founded in 1849. Most plants are grown in the fertile valley of Ohio's Miami River.

Stanek's Garden Center, 2929 27th Ave. East, Spokane, WA 99203. (509)-535-2939. Color illustrated catalog. BAC and MC charges. Open weekdays, 8 A.M.–6 P.M.

General nursery stock, especially suited to the Pacific Northwest. Roses, shade trees, perennials, evergreens, flowering shrubs, vines, bulbs, fruits, and garden supplies.

The retail garden center includes a garden store, a flower and gift shop, and one of the largest Christmas decorating shops in the West.

The Fight to Save the Elm

The American elm has been described by some botanists as the most beautiful thing that grows in the Western Hemisphere. But in past years Dutch elm disease has wiped out countless numbers of these magnificent trees.

However, the non-profit Elm Research Institute, founded in the late 1960s, is making encouraging progress against the disease. Tests show that a new, non-toxic fungicide used to inoculate healthy trees gives them a 99 per cent chance of survival.

For information about saving priceless elms in your community, send 10¢ to the Elm Research Institute, Harrisville, NH 03450, for the brochure Specialized Elm Care.

A word of warning: Before using any product claimed to be a cure for Dutch elm disease, write or call the institute. ERI has comprehensive files on almost all elm "cures," and their unbiased opinion and evaluation is yours for the asking. Telephone number is (603)-827-3048.

Stern's Nurseries, Inc., 404 William St., Geneva, NY 14456. (315)-555-7371. Color illustrated catalog, 50¢. AEX, CB, BAC, DC, and MC charges. Open Mon.–Fri., 8 A.M.–4 P.M.

Roses, fruits and berries, hedge plants, ground covers, perennials, and other nursery stock. Developers of many varieties of subzero roses. Also Miracle-Gro plant foods (available from many garden suppliers as well as from Stern's). Plants especially useful in attracting and keeping birds, "the best insecticide ever devised," are marked with a picture of a cardinal.

Valley Nursery, Box 845, Helena, MT 59601. (406)-442-8460. Price list. Minimum order, $10. Open daily, 9 A.M.–5 P.M.

Diverse list of nursery stock—ornamental trees and shrubs, conifers, fruit trees—many unusual or rare. All plants are in containers—raised from seeds collected in very cold areas and propagated at the nursery.

Clayton Berg, of Valley Nursery, says it has the widest variety of hardy woody ornamental, fruit, and shelter plants for cold areas ever assembled in the United States, and is dedicated to promoting research of woody plant materials.

Watch Your Eyes!

With the increase in home gardeners, there's also an increase in eye injuries, says the American Optometric Association. It recommends wearing sunglasses or safety goggles, especially when you're doing the following:

Digging. Dust and grit can blow into your eyes.

Cutting grass or weeds, particularly with power equipment. Mowers and sickles can toss rocks in the air.

Spraying chemicals or applying dry fertilizers.

Pruning bushes or trees. It's easy for a branch to snap back and hit your eye.

Working with cultivators.

Chipping stone for walls or gardens.

Working with wire to tie up vines or plants.

Harvesting crops from thorny bushes or from trees.

Waynesboro Nurseries, Inc., Box 987, Waynesboro, VA 22980. (703)-942-4141. Color illustrated catalog. BAC charge. Open Mon.–Fri., 8 A.M.–4:30 P.M.

Shade and flowering trees, fruit and nut trees, berries, bulbs, flowering shrubs, evergreens, roses, vines, ground covers. Many uncommon plant materials. Founded in 1922, the nursery operates more than two thousand acres, with approximately one thousand acres planted in nursery stock.

The Wayside Gardens Co., Hodges, SC 29695. Color illustrated catalog, $1.00 (credited). BAC and MC charges.

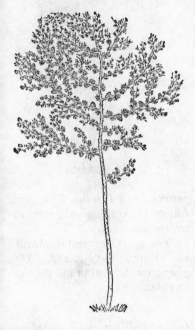

Many rare, uncommon, or hard-to-find plant materials. Very wide variety of perennials; ornamental shrubs, trees, and vines; ground covers; fruit trees; roses; and gardening supplies. The catalog has top-quality color illustrations and extensive descrip-

tions. For many years in Mentor, Ohio, the company relocated to South Carolina in 1975.

White Flower Farm, Esther Ln., Litchfield, CT 06759. (203)-567-9415. Two catalogs and three "Notes" each year, $4.00 (credited). Minimum order, $10. U.S. sales only. Open every day, 9 A.M.–5 P.M., April to November; remainder of year, Mon.–Fri., 9 A.M.–5 P.M.

Specialized nursery stock. Many unusual plant materials, including bulbs, perennials, dwarf evergreens, English Blackmore & Langdon begonias and delphiniums, ericas, azaleas, and numerous uncommon ornamentals. In addition to very complete descriptions of plant materials, along with drawings, the catalogs offer cultural information and advice on numerous garden subjects ranging from making a compost heap to proper care of a lawn. A worthwhile reference for every gardener's library.

Zilke Brothers Nursery, Baroda, MI 49101. (616)-422-1651. Illustrated catalog. Open daily, 8 A.M.–5:30 P.M., during planting season.

General nursery stock, fruit and nut trees, berries, roses, bulbs, perennials. Recent introductions in dwarf fruit trees. Catalog has very complete descriptions of plants.

Plant-Hardiness Zone Map

Just 25¢ from the **Supt. of Documents**, Washington, DC

20402, this huge map shows temperature zones of the United States and also lists typical plants that will survive in each zone. Ordering number is 0100-0434.

Expert Advice on Trees, Shrubs, and Vines

The following booklets, written by government horticulturists, may be ordered from the **Supt. of Documents**, Washington, DC 20402.

Shade Trees for the Home, AH-425, 75¢. Describes more than two hundred shade trees; covers selecting, planting, and care.

Growing Ornamentals in Urban Gardens, G-188, 30¢. Recommends plants most resistant to polluted air; tells how to plant and best ways to protect from damage.

Selecting Shrubs for Shady Areas, G-142, 30¢. Easy-to-grow shrubs that thrive in shady areas —their selection and care.

Shrubs, Vines, and Trees for Summer Color, G-181, 30¢. A guide to plants that add color to gardens after spring blossoms have faded; lists varieties suited to all areas.

Pruning Shade Trees and Repairing Their Injuries, G-83, 25¢. Advice on keeping your trees attractive and healthy.

Pruning Ornamental Shrubs and Vines, G-165, 25¢. Why, when, and how to prune your ornamentals.

Woody Seedlings and Transplants

A small investment in money and time—but considerable patience—can result in landscape-size trees, idle land producing Christmas trees, or reforestation of stripped woodlands.

Bakers' Tree Nursery (Gary L. Baker), 13895 Garfield Rd., Salem, OH 44460. (216)-537-3903. Catalog. Visitors welcome; phone ahead.

Seedlings and transplants of

numerous varieties of pines, firs, and spruces. Good descriptions in catalog. A booklet, *How to Retail Christmas Trees,* sent on request.

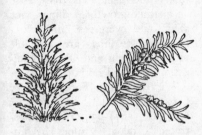

Carino Nurseries, Box 538, Indiana, PA 15701. (412)-463-3350. Illustrated catalog. Open Mon.–Sat., 8 A.M.–4:30 P.M.

Evergreen and deciduous seedlings and transplants for Christmas-tree growers, nurserymen, farmers, and homeowners. Situated in Indiana County, Pennsylvania—the Christmas-tree capital of the world.

"We specialize in superior seed sources for planting stock and take particular care in shipping top-quality stock which will grow."

Eccles Nurseries, Inc., Drawer Y, Rte. 1, Rimersburg, PA 16248. (814)-473-6265. Illustrated catalog. Open Mon.–Sat., 8 A.M.–5 P.M.

Seedlings and transplants of evergreens, hardwoods, shade and forest trees, and ornamental shrubs. Introduced "Norwest," a new strain of Scotch pine. Special collections of seedlings available. Also stock-planting bars and shearing knives.

Flickingers' Nursery, Sagamore, PA 16250. (412)-783-6528. Illustrated price list. Minimum order, $10. U.S. sales only. Open Mon.–Fri., 8 A.M.–5 P.M.

Seedlings and transplants of evergreens, deciduous trees, and shrubs, including European white birch, paper birch, dogwood, autumn olive, Russian olive, and Chinese chestnut. Also a variety of ground covers.

Musser Forests, Inc., Rte. 119 North, Indiana, PA 15701. (412)-465-5686. Illustrated catalog. Open every day, 9 A.M.–5 P.M., March 30 to November 15.

Evergreen and hardwood seedlings; evergreen transplants; rhododendron, yew, azalea, juniper, arborvitae, and barberry rooted cuttings. Also ground covers, landscape-size ornamentals, and container-grown plants.

Pikes Peak Nurseries, Box 75, Rte. 1, Penn Run, PA 15765. (412)-463-7747. Illustrated Catalog. U.S. sales only. Open Mon.–Sat., 8 A.M.–4 P.M.

Seedlings and transplants of deciduous and evergreen trees, rhododendrons, flowering trees, and shrubs. Also container and ball-and-burlap stock.

The nursery's Tree Shopping Center, in Penn Run, has a variety of nursery stock ready to go.

Silver Falls Nursery, 19542 Jack Ln. S.E., Box 84, Silverton, OR 97381. Catalog, 25¢. U.S. sales only.

Wide variety of woody plants (approximately 150 North American and foreign species). Sizes up to twenty-four inches. Many suitable for bonsai. Included are varieties of fir, maple, azalea, cedar, flowering quince, dogwood, cotoneaster, crab, juniper, larch, spruce, pine, flowering cherry, oak, arborvitae, and hemlock.

Vans Pines., Inc., Rte. 1, West Olive, MI 49460. (616)-392-

How to Plant Evergreen Seedlings, F-55, 20¢ from **Purdue University,** Mailing Rm., Agricultural Administration Bldg., West Lafayette, IN 47907.
Growing Trees in Small Nurseries, IB-68, 30¢ from **Cornell**

Seeds of woody plants, tropicals, ornamentals, perennials, and others—many uncommon, rare, or unusual
John Brudy's Rare Plant House, Box 1348-GT, Cocoa Beach, FL 32931. (305)-783-4225. Color illustrated catalog, $1.00 (credited).

1446. Illustrated catalog. BAC and MC charges. Visitors by appointment.

Seedlings and transplants of conifers and deciduous trees. Also accelerated-growth seedlings, tree seeds, and evergreen cones. Prepackaged seedlings are available to garden clubs and other organizations for fund raising.

Western Maine Forest Nursery Co., 36 Elm St., Fryeburg, ME 04037. (207)-935-2161. Illustrated catalog. Visitors by appointment.

Evergreen seedlings, especially for Christmas-tree plantings and reforestation. Also rhododendron and mountain-laurel seedlings; evergreen cones. Booklet, *Christmas Tree Grower's Guide,* sent on request.

Booklets to Aid Tree Growers

University, Mailing Rm., Bldg. 7, Research Park, Ithaca, NY 14850.
Tree Planting, Nr. 771, 20¢, **Michigan State University,** Bulletin Office, Box 231, East Lansing, MI 48824.

Seed Specialists

Uncommon, hard-to-find, and special-purpose seeds collected from around the world, mostly of tropical and semitropical plants. Among the listings are seeds of the Brazilian fern tree, Hawaiian ti plant, passionflower, hedge acacia, sensitive plant, flowering cabbage, asparagus fern, Egyptian

paper plant, eucalyptus, philodendron, and many more. Also
some plants, palm seedlings, and
rooted cuttings. All seeds are
identified by genus and species.
Two pages of the catalog are devoted to germination and care of
seeds and seedlings.

Brudy's background as an engi-
neer in the space program led to
travel in many tropical areas and
a resulting interest in propagating
tropical plants. "Since I was a
farm kid in the first place," he
says, "this was easy and rewarding work."

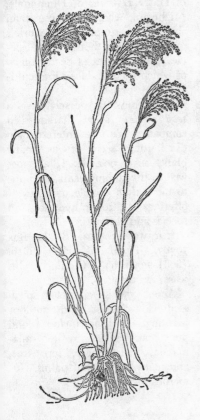

The Butchart Gardens, Box
4010, Station A, Victoria, B.C.
V8X 3X4. (604)-652-2222. Illustrated catalog.

Seeds of annuals, perennials,
and rock plants—similar to plants
growing in the world-famous
Butchart Gardens.

The thirty-acre gardens, thir-
teen miles from Victoria, are part
of an estate of the late Mr. and
Mrs. Robert Butchart and are
open to the public the year
around. Of special interest are
the English rose garden, a Japanese garden, and a formal Italian
garden. A gift shop and a restaurant are open during the summer
months.

Ornamentals for Canadian Gardens

An excellent guide to the best
varieties of woody ornamentals
and their culture is the 198-page
book *Ornamental Shrubs for Canada.* $3.50 from **Information
Canada,** Publishing Division, 171
Slater St., Ottawa, Ont. K1A 0S9.

De Sylva Seeds, 32192 Paseo
de Manuel, San Juan Capistrano,
CA 92675. Descriptive price list,
25¢.

Seeds for tropical and subtropical plants; many suitable for
bonsai. Numerous varieties of
palms, guavas, passion fruits, mac-
adamia nuts, kiwis, bananas. Also
seeds of pines, maples, and other
trees, which can be used for bonsai or grown outdoors to full-size
trees.

Exotica Seed Co. (Steven
Spangler), 820 S. Lorraine Blvd.,

Los Angeles, CA 90005. (213)-935-8181. Illustrated catalog, 50¢. Visitors by appointment.

Seeds of unusual and rare tropical and subtropical fruit trees and vines, palms, flowering trees, ornamentals, flowers, and wild plants. Among the many varieties are mountain papaya, chewinggum tree, edible dessert bananas, twelve types of grapes, and many kinds of edible passion fruit. Spangler makes frequent seed-gathering trips to add to his list.

A limited supply of plants, such as figs, mulberries, passion fruits, papayas, bananas, and guavas are available at the nursery.

"A venture to spread unusual plant varieties. More important is the purpose of healing the earth."

Ference's Nursery, Rare Plants, Point Pleasant, PA 18950. (215)-297-5296. Brochure and price list. Visitors welcome, afternoons.

Seeds of rare hybrid rhododendrons, Exbury azaleas, Japanese umbrella pines, and similar plants suitable for home growers. Included with seed orders is literature on special, exclusive method of raising seeds. Literature is $1.00 without seed order.

Harrold's, Box 29, Grants Pass, OR 97526. Catalog, 25¢.

Specialized flower seeds; many own originations and others from seed specialists throughout the world. Included are violas, pansies, begonias, coleus, gesneriads and primulas. Offerings in pansies, violas, and primulas are among the most extensive available. Seed specialists for seventy-five years.

J. L. Hudson, Seedsman (World Seed Service), Box 1058, Redwood City, CA 94064. Catalog, 50¢.

Very extensive list of seeds, many rare, of flowers, trees, shrubs, vines, vegetables, ornamental grasses, herbs, unusual plants of all types. Plants are indexed by their respective edible, medicinal, dye, bee, scent, fiber, and other useful properties.

Hudson is continuing the work of Harry E. Saier of Dimondale, Michigan, who, for more than sixty years, supplied the world's gardeners with thousands of species and varieties of seeds, many of which he introduced into cultivation.

"We think of ourselves as a *seed service* rather than a seed company. We are interested in distributing seed of as many plants as is possible. If all goes well in the coming years, we hope to more than double our present offerings of three to five thousand species and varieties."

Hurov's Tropical Seeds, Box 10387, Honolulu, HI 96816. (808)-735-1909. Catalog plus seasonal listings.

About 750 species of tropical seeds for indoor and outdoor plantings—such as Norfolk island pine, candlenut, Brazilian allamanda, shell ginger, fern tree, and many varieties of palms. Numerous rarities.

Clyde Robin Seed Co., Inc., Box 2855, Castro Valley, CA 94546. (415)-581-3467. Color illustrated catalog, $1.00.

More than 1,400 varieties of native seeds: wildflowers, trees, shrubs, vegetables, herbs; many very rare. Also about seven hundred varieties of plants. Listings range from *Abelia hirta*, a colorful flowering plant, to *Zizyphus jujuba*, a small tree with edible date-like fruits.

Special items are a collection of twenty-five vacuum-sealed, untreated vegetable seeds, enough to plant one third acre, and a "Survival Garden," which has vacuum-packed, untreated seeds with a seed life of twenty-five years or more, enough to plant a garden the size of a basketball court and feed ten to fifteen people for up to six months.

F. W. Schumacher Co. (Spring Hill Farm), Spring Hill Rd., Sandwich, MA 02563. (617)-888-0659. Catalog and price list. Open Mon.–Fri., 9 A.M.–5 P.M.

Seeds for a wide variety of trees and shrubs, including azaleas and rhododendrons, many imported items. Also many books on seed propagation. A fourteen-page pamphlet, *How to Grow Seedlings of Trees and Shrubs,* by F. W. Schumacher, is 25¢ (sent without charge with orders totaling $15 or more). Also a selection of vegetable seeds for home gardeners.

Woodlot Seed Co., Box 36, Norway, MI 49870. Price list; send stamp.

Seeds of evergreen and deciduous trees, deciduous shrubs, vines, rhododendrons. Detailed planting instructions are included.

"Hunters and fishermen are taking packets of seeds suitable for wildlife use to the woods when they fish or hunt. They scrape off a foot or two of surface soil with a boot or stick, drop in a seed, cover lightly with soil or leaves, step on it—and each has left his mark for the future."

Camellias

know, for they emulate and surpass in beauty nearly all the different flowers that we value. Each new variety is an adventure, bringing pleasure and excitement."

Redwood Empire Camellias, Inc., 7949 Lynch Rd., Sebastopol, CA 95472. (707)-823-6993. Catalog; send stamp. Open every day except Wed., 8 A.M.–5 P.M.

Container-grown camellias; japonicas, sasanquas, reticulatas, hybrids. Well described in catalog with good cultural information.

G. C. Robinson Nursery, 56 N. Georgia Ave., Mobile, AL 36604. (205)-433-7712. Price list.

Rare varieties of *Camellia japonica.* Also other camellias, and azaleas and gardenias. Available as rooted cuttings or small plants.

Tammia Nursery, Box 157, Slidell, LA 70459. (504)-643-3636. Price list. U.S. sales only. Open every day, 7 A.M.–4 P.M.

Camellias—japonicas, reticulatas, and hybrids; over 150 listings. Numerous Tammia introductions. Available as one- to six-year grafts.

Many other unusual plants on display at forty-acre nursery.

Nuccio's Nurseries, 3555 Chaney Trail, Altadena, CA 91001. (213)-794-3383. Catalog. Open Mon., Tues., Fri., and Sat., 8 A.M.–5 P.M., May to October.

Many varieties of japonica, sasanqua, reticulata camellias; Nuccio originations and others. Also an extensive listing of azaleas. Many rarities. Plants available in sizes from twelve to thirty-six inches.

Orinda Nursery, R.D., Box 135B, Bridgeville, DE 19933. (302)-337-7580. Illustrated catalog, 50¢ (credited). Open Wed.–Sat., 10 A.M.–4:30 P.M.

Camellias—standard and rare japonicas. Also many uncommon hybrid rhododendrons. Most plants three to five years old. Complete cultural information sent with each order.

"Camellias are the most elegant and variable flowers that we

To Read:

The Camellia: Its Culture for Beginners, $1.25 from the American Camellia Society, Box 212, Massee Ln., Fort Valley, GA 31030.

Check List of the Cultivated Magnolias, a seventy-two-page book compiled by members of the American Magnolia Society. Available for $5.00 from Plant Sciences Data Center, American Horticultural Society, Mount Vernon, VA 22121.

F&R Farrell Co., 6810 Biggert Rd., London, OH 43140. (614)-877-3134. Illustrated brochure. U.S. sales only.

Gossler Farms Nursery, 1200 Weaver Rd., Springfield, OR 97477. (503)-746-3922. Illustrated brochure, 50¢. Visitors by appointment.

Clematis

Some fifty varieties of rare and unusual clematis vines; most extremely hardy. Specializes in small-flowered species and hybrids. The company also offers a fiberglass "Rosebush Winterizer" with a three-year guarantee.

"A world of beauty awaits gardeners who will interest themselves in these beautiful clematis which bear flowers that are less than four inches in diameter. What they lack in size they make up in numbers. Flowers appear in great clusters, and they vary in form and shape from dainty bell-shaped clematis to lantern-shaped clematis."

The D. S. George Nurseries, 2491 Penfield Rd., Fairport, NY 14450. (716)-377-0731. Price list; send stamp. Visitors welcome; phone ahead.

Specialists, since 1894, in large-flowering, hardy clematis vines. Over thirty different varieties.

Magnolias

More than fifty varieties of evergreen and deciduous magnolias, with many rarities and new introductions. Also companion plants, such as *Cornus capitata* (Him-

Infer Landscape Co., 3995
12th St. S.E., Salem, OR 97302.
Price list; send stamp. Minimum
order, $10. Visitors welcome.

Some twenty-five varieties of
magnolias, ranging from seedlings
to specimen plants (five feet and
larger).

Little Lake Nursery (Mr. and
Mrs. Edward Hetzer), 4700 Muir
Mill Rd., Box 782, Willits, CA
95490. (707)-459-2669. Catalog,
35¢. Visitors by appointment.

Magnolia specialists, with over
one hundred species and cultivars; many very rare and not
listed elsewhere. Also some extremely rare members of the magnolia family, as michelia, illicium,
manglietia, and drimys. Other
listings include twenty-four
named varieties of flowering
quince, some twenty-five daphne
species and cultivars, and more
than fifty varieties of lilacs.

alayan dogwood), *Davidia invo-
lucrata* (dove tree), *Franklinia
alatamaha,* and *Styrax japonica*
(snowbell tree).

"We are a family operation
and a relatively small specialty
nursery. But we are growing
larger and have many new hybrids coming in from arboretums
and plantsmen."

Rhododendrons, Azaleas, and Companion Plants

Baldsiefen Nursery, Box 88,
Bellvale, NY 10912. (914)-986-
4222. Color illustrated catalog,
$2.00 (credited). Visitors by ap-
pointment.

Hardy rhododendrons, best of
old and new varieties. Own introductions as well as those of other
hybridizers; many rare hybrids
unobtainable elsewhere. Plants
are field-grown in a northern climate, exposed to temperatures as
low as —20° F.

"Our catalog is an indis-
pensable guide to better rhododendron growing. Less than half
of the 57 pages are devoted to
plant description—balance is valuable information on culture, diseases, growing, pruning, and alka-
line areas, plus a U.S. hardiness
zone map, and 37 natural-color
pictures."

Beaver Dam Creek Nursery
(R. P. Clark), 43 Davos Rd.,
Bricktown, NJ 08723. (201)-295-

1684. Descriptive price list. Open every day, 9 A.M.–5 P.M.; phone ahead.

Dexter hybrid rhododendrons and evergreen azaleas; new hybrid introductions not generally available.

The Bovees Nursery, 1737 S.W. Coronado, Portland, OR 97219. (503)-244-9341. Illustrated catalog, 25¢. BAC and MC charges. Open every day except Mon., 10 A.M.–6 P.M. (Open by appointment only, mid-July to mid-September and mid-December to February.)

Specializes in low- and/or slow-growing rhododendrons and azaleas. Many Bovees hybrids. Both new and old hybrids and species, particularly ones not commonly available. Also uncommon or rare trees and shrubs, native plants and bulbs, alpines, dwarf conifers, and many plants suitable for bonsai.

"Increasingly, we try to provide more choices for the extremes in climate, as we find that there is a growing interest in rhododendrons and azaleas all over the country."

Carlson's Gardens, Box 305, South Salem, NY 10590. (914)-763-5948. Color illustrated catalog, $1.00 (credited).

Largest mail-order selection of hardy azaleas and rhododendrons grown in the Northeast. Specializes in hardy deciduous azaleas; grows and propagates over 170 named varieties. Also a selection of evergreen azaleas including North Tisbury, Gable, a limited number of the hardier Glenn Dales, and Great Lakes azaleas from northern Ohio. Many uncommon and hard to find.

Azalea and rhododendron fanciers can enjoy the beauty of these flowering plants all year with a selection of color photos available from Carlson's. On the back of each print, the bloom is identified, along with the bloom time.

Rhododendrons and Their Relatives is the title of a beautifully illustrated guide to these plants. It has growing, propagating, and buying tips for rhododendrons, azaleas, heather, mountain laurel, and others. Handbk. 66, $1.50 from **Brooklyn Botanic Garden,** 1000 Washington Ave., Brooklyn, NY 11225.

Clarke Nursery (J. Harold Clarke), Rte. 1, Box 168, Long Beach, WA 98631. (206)-642-2241. Price list. Open daily, 8 A.M.–4:30 P.M.; phone ahead.

Many unusual species and varieties of rhododendrons; all

with American Rhododendron Society merit and hardiness ratings.

Greer Gardens, 1280 Goodpasture Island Rd., Eugene, OR 97401. (503)-686-8266. Color illustrated catalog, 50¢. BAC and MC charges. Open every day in peak season, 9 A.M.–6 P.M.

Some six hundred varieties of rhododendrons. Also 125 varieties of maples, many dwarf conifers, kalmias, lewisias, and other rockgarden materials. Many plants suitable for bonsai. Plant sizes from liners to specimen plants. One of the most complete listings of rhododendrons and maples available.

"We import large quantities of our own and those of other hybridizers so there is always something new. Growing and introducing the new, the rare, and the unusual is our specialty. We try to offer plants that are not available elsewhere."

Hall Nursery, 135 Norlen Park, Bridgewater, MA 02324. (617)-697-2695. Descriptive price list.

Hybrid and species rhododendrons; plant sizes from six to ten inches. The plants are raised from cuttings in greenhouse, then set out in beds for one year.

Thomas Henny Nursery, 7811 Stratford Dr. N.E., Brooks, OR 97305. (503)-792-3376. Catalog. Open every day, 8 A.M.–4 P.M.

About two hundred varieties of rhododendrons; dwarf and regular, both hybrid and species. Also Glenn Dale, Gable, and Exbury azaleas.

Island Gardens, 701 Goodpasture Island Rd., Eugene, OR 97401. (503)-343-4711. Illustrated catalog, $2.00 (credited). BAC and MC charges. Garden shop open daily, 10 A.M.–5 P.M.

Specialist in Exbury azaleas. Also rhododendrons, dwarf conifers, and maples. The catalog has excellent cultural information.

Houseplants and gift items are available at the garden shop.

H. L. Larson, Rhododendrons, 3656 Bridgeport Way, Tacoma, WA 98466. (206)-564-1488. Price list. Open daily, 9 A.M.–noon and 1 P.M.–4 P.M.

Hand-pollinated rhododendron seeds; extensive list. Many extremely rare, including second-generation yakusimanum hybrids. Instructions for germinating the seeds are included with the list.

Larson has introduced over thirty new rhododendrons, including a true blue and a compact maroon-colored rhododendron. The nursery has one of the largest collections of hybrid and species rhododendrons in the world. The flowering season extends from mid-January to mid-September, with peak bloom from April through June.

E. B. Nauman, 11 Casale Dr., Warren, NJ 07060. Catalog.

Hybrid and species rhododendrons, azaleas, hollies, and other broadleaf evergreens in small sizes for the collector. Specializes in newer and more unusual varieties, many not available elseswhere in the eastern United States. The

catalog has detailed descriptions of plants plus cultural information.

"We sell broadleaf evergreens for the gardener who wants something different, something he can't always find at the local nursery. We also serve the hobbyist who is intent on developing a collection of plants or who is starting a large landscaping project. Finally, we serve the patient gardener, who enjoys starting with small plants, who is willing to trade a little extra time for a considerable saving in money."

Rhododendron Ratings

The American Rhododendron Society rates flowers and plants on this scale: 5, superior; 4, above average; 3, average; 2, below average; and 1, inferior. A rating of 4/3 means an above average flower on an average plant.

Hardiness ratings, which indicate the minimum temperature a mature plant will usually withstand are H1, −25° F; H2, −15° F; H3, −5° F; H4, 5° F; H5, 15° F.

You'll find these ratings used in many catalogs and books on rhododendrons.

Orchard Nursery (James G. Thompson), Box 7224, Mobile, AL 36607. (205)-344-0732. Illustrated catalog. Minimum order, $10. U.S. sales only. Open Mon.–Sat., 8 A.M.–5 P.M.

Azaleas, including Kurume, Pericat, Glenn Dale, Gable, and Satsuki hybrids; rooted cuttings and 2½-inch pot sizes and larger. Also numerous varieties of camellias and magnolias. Good cultural information is in the catalog.

Orlando S. Pride Nurseries, Box 1865, Butler, PA 16001. (412)-283-0962. Catalog. U.S. sales only. Open Mon.–Sat., 9 A.M.–4 P.M.

Specialist in hybrid azaleas, rhododendrons, and hollies. Many own originations. Good selection of hardy hollies.

More than ten thousand hybrid rhododendrons may be seen at the nursery.

Rainier Mt. Alpine Gardens (Jim Caperci), 2007 S. 126th St., Seattle, WA 98168. (206)-242-4090. Price list. Open every day, 10 A.M.–5 P.M.

Extensive list of species rhododendrons. Also hybrid rhododrons and dwarf conifers; many plants suitable for bonsai.

Caperci, an expert on species rhododendrons, is a judge and gold-medal recipient from the American Rhododendron Society.

A. Shammarello & Son Nursery, 4508 Monticello Blvd., South Euclid, OH 44143. (216)-381-2510. Color illustrated catalog. Open Mon.–Sat., 8 A.M.–4:30 P.M.; Sun., by appointment.

Azaleas and rhododendrons; all introductions of Shammarello, an internationally known hybridizer since 1940. Good descriptions and cultural information are in the catalog. The plants are balled and burlapped, and range in size

The Garden Spot (W. O. Freeland), 4032 Rosewood Dr., Columbia, SC 29205. (803)-787-7463. Price list; send SASE. Visitors welcome, daylight hours.

Plants and cuttings of some one hundred ivies—species, varieties,

from nine to eighteen inches.

Sweet Gum Farms, Inc. (Wanda S. Mandel), Rte. 2, Alma, GA 31510. (912)-449-4359. Catalog, 50¢. Visitors welcome; phone ahead.

Azaleas, in 2½-to-3-inch pots. Many varieties of Kurume, Kaempferi, Pericat, Gable hybrids; also evergreen azalea species and a variety of ground covers. The catalog lists the order of bloom of the plants.

Ivy and Ground Covers

and a host of cultivars. Freeland has the largest collection of ivies grown in an open garden, ships to customers around the world, writes a newspaper column, "About Gardens" (a sample copy is included with each price list), and does a horticultural program for South Carolina Educational TV. All this has taken place since 1948, when he retired from a management job and settled down in South Carolina.

"If there is an ivy on your 'wish list' that is not on our sales list, please ask about it, for we grow a total of 200 cultivars and just might have enough to share. If we hear of any ivy we don't have, we soon will—by hook or by crook!"

Peekskill Nurseries, Box 25, Shrub Oak, NY 10588. (914)-245-5595. Illustrated brochure, plus color postcards.

Permanent evergreen ground-cover plants. Specializes in *Pachysandra terminalis*—grows over six hundred thousand plants yearly.

Also Baltic ivy, euonymus, myrtle, and junipers.

Rock and Alpine Plants, Dwarf Conifers, Uncommon and Rare Hardy Plants

Alpenglow Gardens, 13328 King George Hwy., Surrey, B.C. V3T 2T6. (604)-581-8733. Catalog, $1.00 (credited). Minimum order, $15. Open Mon.–Sat., 1 P.M.–5 P.M.

Many uncommon dwarf conifers, suitable for bonsai or landscape plantings. Also unusual hardy alpine plants, hardy orchids, saxifrages, heaths and heathers, dwarf rhododendrons, hardy geraniums, and many other rare plants and shrubs not generally available.

"We especially wish to draw attention to the dwarf conifers which can be used in so many ways, in the garden, the rockery, or for bonsai. The popularity of these little gems is rapidly increasing. It is no surprise to us to learn that garden enthusiasts have fallen under the spell of these charming little shrubs."

Alpines West Nursery, Rte. 2, Box 259, Spokane, WA 99207. (509)-926-3108. Descriptive price list, 50¢. Minimum order, $25. Visitors by appointment.

Rare alpine and rock-garden plants, western wildflowers, dwarf rock ferns, many dwarf conifers. Will collect specimen trees for bonsai enthusiasts on request.

Brimfield Gardens Nursery, Inc., 3109 Main St., Rocky Hill, CT 06067. (203)-529-0795. Catalog, $1.00. Visitors welcome; phone ahead.

Large collection of rare trees, shrubs, and dwarf evergreens. Listings include ornamental dwarf maples, dogwoods, hawthorns, magnolias, crab apples, azaleas, witch hazels, hollies, brooms, mountain laurels, ferns, rhododendrons, heaths and heathers, ivies, bamboos.

Carroll Gardens (Pat Donofrio), 444 E. Main St., Box 310, Westminster, MD 21157. (301)-848-5422. Catalog. MC charge. U.S. sales only. Open daily; phone ahead.

Rock plants, wildflowers, perennials, bulbs, roses, flowering shrubs and trees, vines, ground covers, wide selection of dwarf and rare evergreens, many herbs. Numerous uncommon varieties. Owner Pat Donofrio has had forty-four years of gardening experience.

Country Garden Nursery, 555 Irwin Ln., Santa Rosa, CA 95401. (707)-544-0882. Price list. Open Mon.–Sat., 8 A.M.–5 P.M.

Dwarf olives, dwarf geraniums, miniature roses, crab apples, walnuts, grapes, and other nursery stock. Also various houseplants.

The Cummins Garden, Box 125, Colts Neck, NJ 07722. (201)-946-4225. Catalog, 50¢ (credited). Minimum order for plants, $10. U.S. sales only.

Dwarf conifers, deciduous azaleas, dwarf rhododendrons, heaths and heathers, and companion plants for rock gardens. Many unusual varieties in all categories. Also extensive list of books on these plants and related subjects. Will do custom propagating.

Lamb Nurseries, East 101 Sharp Ave., Spokane, WA 99202. (509)-328-7956. Catalog. Open Mon.–Sat., 8 A.M.–5 P.M.; Sun., by appointment.

Very complete listing of alpines, rock plants, and hardy perennials, many uncommon. There are good descriptions in the catalog, along with cultural information and suggestions for use. The catalog also "pronounces" botanical names.

Laura's Collectors' Garden,

5136 S. Raymond St., Seattle, WA 98118. Descriptive price list, 50¢. Minimum order, $15. Visitors by appointment only.

Very rare and extremely rare alpines and rock plants. Good collection of cassiopes and lewisias plus miniature plants for containers and trough gardens. Primarily a botanist/plant collector—especially interested in dwarf conifers and miniature plants.

Minature Gardens, Box 757, Stony Plain, Alta. ToE 2Go. (403)-963-3447. Catalog, $1.00. Minimum order, $10. Open Tues.–Sat., 9 A.M.–5 P.M.; Fri., to 9 P.M.; May to September.

Unusual alpines, rockery plants, dwarf perennials, ornamental shrubs, dwarf conifers. Plants suitable for containers, miniature gardens, and bonsai. Largest collection of unusual dwarf perennials in North America.

"We are a family operated nursery, specializing in dwarf plants. These plants are grown naturally, not forced in any way, and seldom, if ever, found in ordinary nurseries."

Palette Gardens, 26 W. Zion Hill Rd., Quakertown, PA 18951. (215)-536-4027. Color illustrated catalog, 50¢. MC charge. Minimum order, $10. U.S. sales only. Open every day, daylight hours.

Dwarf conifers, bamboos, exotic maples, ferns, hostas, sedums, sempervivums, ornamental grasses, hardy cacti, alpine plants,

and various other perennials. Many plants rare or uncommon.

The gardens have ten acres of formal rock-garden display, with seven thousand different plants growing and over six hundred unusual and dwarf conifers.

Rakestraw's Gardens, G-3094 S. Term, Burton, MI 48529. (313)-742-2685. Illustrated catalog, 50¢. U.S. sales only. Open every day, 9 A.M.–7 P.M.

Rock-garden plants, including extensive collection of sedums and sempervivums, hard-to-find perennials, alpines, and dwarf conifers. Many rare and uncommon plants.

"Serious rock gardeners for 20 years, we strive to supply quality plants and each order is given our personal attention. We welcome visitors to our gardens."

Raraflora (Fred W. Bergman), 1195 Stump Rd., Feasterville, PA 19047. (215)-357-3791. List, by botanical name, of all plants propagated from Raraflora Arboretum, 25¢. U.S. sales only. Visitors by appointment.

Very rare, slow-growing dwarf conifers collected from around the world; largest collection in existence. Many aged specimens; choice bonsai material. Raraflora is a private arboretum, developed by Bergman over the past thirty years and devoted to rare plants. While plants can be ordered by mail, Bergman prefers personal inspection, as, he says, "It is usually unsatisfactory to describe rare plant material in print."

The Rock Garden, Rte. 2, Litchfield, ME 04350. Catalog, 40¢. Visitors by appointment.

Plants especially suitable for rock gardens: sedums and sempervivums, saxifrages, phlox, primulas, heaths and heathers, dwarf conifers and other dwarf shrubs. Many hard-to-find varieties.

"A fine rock garden is an enjoyable hobby but it is a high-maintenance garden. The pleasure is often in the challenge of growing difficult plants."

Siskiyou Rare Plant Nursery, 522 Franquette St., Medford, OR 97501. (503)-772-6050. Catalog, 50¢ (credited). Minimum order, $10. U.S. sales only. Open daily, 9 A.M. to dark; phone ahead.

Hundreds of varieties of ferns; rock-garden, alpine, and native plants; dwarf conifers; trees and shrubs—almost all are rare or uncommon. Each year, several hundred new plants are introduced; many are received in exchange from England, Switzerland, and New Zealand.

"This is a hobby business but has grown out of proportion to our space and facilities. We do the best we can for what we feel is a need—introducing new plants and propagating native plants for future enjoyment. We welcome visitors who are interested in exchanging rare plants."

Joel W. Spingarn, 1535 Forest Ave., Baldwin, NY 11510. (516)-623-7810. Catalog, 50¢. Minimum order, $10. U.S. sales only. Visitors by appointment.

Very rare dwarf and pygmy conifers and other dwarf plants. Spingarn propagates the better forms of plants of this type and has a private arboretum and an alpine garden. Catalog does not include prices, as they depend on availability. In his catalog introduction, Spingarn writes:

"The plants listed herein have been searched for and gathered together from many countries of Europe, Asia, and the North American continent. Many forms

Mountain Plants of Utah, EC-319, $1.50, and *A Beginner's Guide to Mountain Flowers,* EC-355, 75¢, are illustrated guides to these plants. Order from **Utah State University,** Extension Publications Office, Logan, UT 84322.

have been made available through the cooperation of various botanical gardens and arboreta, and many through exchanges with private collectors. They represent a collection of the rarest conifers in existence today."

Tingle Nursery, Drawer D., Pittsville, MD 21850. (301)-835-2101. Price list. Open Mon.–Fri. 7:30 A.M.–4 P.M.; Sat., 8 A.M.–noon.

Very broad listing of woody ornamental plants, winter-hardy in Maryland. Many uncommon, as *Franklinia alatamaha* and *Acer griseum.* Also azalea and rhododendron seedlings, heaths and heathers, and others. Plants available as "lining out" or specimen stock.

Wildwood Gardens, 14488 Rock Creek Rd., Chardon, OH 44024. (216)-286-3714. Price list; send stamp. Open daily, noon–8 P.M.; phone ahead.

Many rare and dwarf plants, suitable for rock gardens or bonsai, tray, or terrarium plantings. Numerous varieties of conifers, deciduous trees, grasses and ground covers, rhododendrons, and carnivorous plants.

Related Reading

Ornamental Grasses, IB-64, 30¢, has information on uses in home gardens. Available from **Cornell University,** Mailing Rm., Bldg. 7, Research Park, Ithaca, NY 14850.

Rock Gardens, Handbk. 10, has ideas on design, construction, care, appropriate plants, plus 125 photos.

Dwarf Conifers, Handbk. 47, culture and uses of dwarf evergreen, with description of varieties.

These two handbooks are $1.50 each from **Brooklyn Botanic Garden,** 1000 Washington Ave., Brooklyn, NY 11225.

Wildflowers and Native Plants

plants unobtainable elsewhere in the country, and to diffuse a love and knowledge of them."

Terry Barnes Nursery, Rte. 2, Box 239, McMinnville, TN 37110. (615)-668-9091. Illustrated price list.

Native wildflowers, ferns, and ground covers. List includes botanical names, descriptions, and cultural information. Also rhubarb, asparagus, small fruits, bulbs, and perennials.

Appalachian Wildflower Nursery (Donald Hackenberry), Honey Creek Rd., Rte. 1, Box 275A, Reedsville, PA 17084. (717)-667-3140. Catalog, 25¢. Visitors welcome; phone ahead.

Native wildflowers and plants, especially bulbous plants and hardy orchids (European and Asiatic species of the latter). Many uncommon, as *Cypripedium cordigerum* and *C. montanum, Crocus goulimyi, Fritillaria persica,* and others. Participates in seed exchange with botanical gardens in temperate regions of the world, resulting in much choice material.

"I hope to make available

Conley's Garden Center, 145 Townsend Ave., Boothbay Harbor, ME 04538. (207)-633-5020. Brochure and price list, 35¢. BAC and MC charges. Open every day, 8 A.M.–6 P.M.

Extensive list of native wildflowers, ferns, vines, and other native plants. The brochure includes both botanical and common names and good descriptions. A two-hundred-page book with more than a hundred photos, *Conley's Guide to Landscaping and Gardening Handbook,* a compendium of useful information, is $3.30 postpaid.

The retail garden center is one of the most complete in New England and has a selection of rare and dwarf evergreens—not available by mail.

Dutch Mountain Nursery (Cliff Walters), 7984 N. 48th St., Rte. 1, Augusta, MI 49012. (616)-731-5232. Illustrated catalog, 25¢. Visitors by appointment, 9 A.M.–5 P.M.

About 150 varieties of plants that attract birds and other wildlife. Trees, shrubs, and vines, such as paperbark maple, red Japanese maple, cutleaf elderberry, dwarf birch, buttonbush, and silverthorn. Also available from the nursery is a card file of five hundred ornamental plants, describing native habitat, form, color, soil preference, culture, growth rate, flower, and fruiting season; the price for the set is $8.75. Walters publishes an interesting newsletter, *F.B.I.—Fruit for the*

Birds International; a copy is included with the catalog.

Fern Hill Farm, Rte. 3, Box 191, Greenville, AL 36037. Descriptive brochure. U.S. sales only.

Native ferns and wildflowers; bare-root plants. Also tree seedlings suitable for bonsai. Very informative brochure.

"I am an elderly, retired teacher and have always collected plants. The name of my farm is from one of my favorite poems, 'Fern Hill,' by Dylan Thomas."

About Wildflowers

The New England Wild Flower Society has a number of publications on wildflowers. See its listing, under "Plant Societies," in this book.

Gardening with Wildflowers, Handbk. 38, has informative articles about wildflowers in all parts of the United States, tells how to know them and grow them. $1.50 from **Brooklyn Botanic Garden,** 1000 Washington Ave., Brooklyn, NY 11225.

Ferndale Nursery & Greenhouse, Box 218, Askov, MN 55704. (612)-838-4262. Illustrated price list; send SASE. U.S. sales only. Open Mon.–Fri., 9 A.M.–5 P.M.

Hardly wildflowers and ferns, including Showy Ladyslipper, the Minnesota state flower. In business since 1906—one of the oldest wildflower nurseries in the United States.

Visitors can see a display garlen of wildflowers; Showy Lady-slippers usually in bloom by June 20.

"Our stock comes from a natural habitat that demands ruggedness and hardiness."

Game Food Nurseries, 4488 Hwy. 116 East, Box V, Omro, WI 54963. (414)-685-2929. Illustrated catalog, $1.00. Minimum order, $8.00.

Seeds, roots, tubers, and plants of pondweed, wild celery, wild rice, duckwheat, water cress, wild roses, wild berries, "ecology grasses," blue water iris—and many other wild, aquatic, and bog plants. Especially for wildlife and conservation plantings. Much information on conservation and culture in catalog. For over seventy-five years the nursery has specialized in development of feeding and breeding grounds for migratory birds, fish, upland game birds, and other wildlife. It offers a professional planning and planting service for marshes, ponds, and streams.

"The planting of natural foods is conservation in the highest degree. It provides both food and cover essential to the existence of waterfowl, fish, and other wildlife at all seasons of the year."

Gardens of the Blue Ridge, Box 10, Pineola, NC 28662. (704)-756-4339. Illustrated catalog. Visitors welcome; phone ahead.

Many hardy native plants—wildflowers, orchids, ferns, aquatic and bog plants, vines, and shrubs. Plants suitable for rock gardens and naturalizing. Informative, well-illustrated catalog.

Green Horizons—Texas Wildflower Specialists (Carroll Abbott), 500 Thompson Ave., Kerrville, TX 78028. (512)-257-5141. Illustrated catalog; send SASE. Visitors welcome, daylight hours.

Some 150–200 species of native Texas plants and seed. Many quite rare, such as Indian Paintbrush, Mountain Pink, and Texas Bluebells. Also cactus seeds and fern plants. Is developing a "pink" bluebonnet and a "yellow" bluebell.

Abbott, who has driven over 300,000 miles of Texas highways in recent years as a political consultant, now devotes full time to collecting and campaigning for wildflowers.

"Wildflowers need to be preserved, because they're a feast for the eyes and food for the soul. There's just no tangible measurement of what wildflowers do to you. They give you a feeling you can't hold on to, a good feeling."

Griffey's Nursery, Rte. 3, Box 27, Marshall, NC 28753. (704)-656-2334. Price list. Open Mon.–Sat., 8 A.M.–6 P.M.; phone ahead.

Wild native plants, including orchids, violas, and other perennials, wild azaleas and rhododendrons, vines, creepers, ferns, aquatic plants, berries, holly, and evergreens.

Wild Plants of the Canadian Prairies is a 536-page reference invaluable for anyone with a serious interest in wild and native plants. Price is $4.50 from **Information Canada**, Publishing Division, 171 Slater St., Ottawa, Ont. K1A 0S9.

Henderson's Botanical Gardens, Greensburg, IN 47240. (812)-663-6587. Price list. Open Sun., by appointment.

Hardy wildflowers, native ferns, bog and aquatic plants, native lilies and bulbous plants, medicinal plants—many uncommon.

"The bog or that permanently moist location may be made an area of unrivaled beauty. Bog plants are acclaimed again and again because of their contrasting colors and regal stateliness."

Island Gardens, 28542 Chatham, Grosse Ile, MI 48138. (313)-676-2763. Illustrated catalog; send stamp. Visitors by appointment.

Native wildflowers, ferns, and

bulbs. The catalog includes several varieties of ladyslippers and six of trilliums (snow, purple, painted, rose, red toad, and yellow.) Also hybrid lilies and ground covers.

Jamieson Valley Gardens, Rte. 3, Box 646-W, Spokane, WA 99203. Illustrated catalog, $1.00. U.S. sales only.

Many rare and unusual wildflowers, both eastern and western natives. Native bulbous plants, ferns, trees and shrubs, perennials, berries. Numerous rare alpines.

"All our plants are nursery grown. We are conservationists by nature and believe that our wildlands should be preserved. You will find many nature-lore stories in our catalog."

Several plants, says Jamieson Valley Gardens, lend themselves to almost a wall-to-wall effect. "The creeping thyme makes a lovely wooly carpet as it follows the contour of the ground, covering humps or rocks. *Veronica pectinata* has the appearance of a wooly carpet with a deep pile. Then for a mossy green carpet the cotula is a choice subject in sun or shade. All these are easy doers and stay neat the year around, and their spreading propensities are easily controlled with a trowel."

Edgar L. Kline, 17495 S.W. Bryant Rd., Lake Grove, OR 97034. (503)-636-3923. Price list-brochure. Minimum order, $6.00. Open Mon.–Sat., 9 A.M.–5 P.M.

Extensive list of native American bulbs and allied species. Largest American collection of hardy cyclamen, brodiaea, calochortus, erythronium, American species of iris, lily species, trillium, and many other species of bulbs and roots not generally available. Growers, exporters, and importers since 1930.

Visitors are welcome at five acres of display gardens.

Lounsberry Gardens, Box 135, Oakford, IL 62673. (217)-635-5645. Color illustrated catalog, 25¢. U.S. sales only. Open Sun., by appointment.

Hardy wildflowers and ferns, perennials, rock plants. Well-illustrated catalog with detailed plant descriptions.

"Drifts of wildflowers under protecting trees and shrubs serve a double purpose. Besides making a beautiful carpet of bloom, they help to keep dead and decaying leaves nestled where they can act as a mulch and food supply for the larger plants."

Midwest Wildflowers, Box 64, Rockton, IL 61072. (815)-624-7040. Illustrated catalog, 25¢.

Seeds of wildflowers native to the Midwest, such as cardinal flower, shooting star, jack-in-the-pulpit, and wild columbine, along with about seventy other species. Many types difficult to acquire. Catalog describes and illustrates plants, and also includes facts and folklore associated with them.

"We hand-strip seeds from local meadows and woodlots as a part-time activity and as a service to wild gardeners."

Mincemoyer Nursery, County Line Rd., Jackson, NJ 08527. (201)-363-3215. Descriptive price list. Open every day except Mon., 9 A.M.–5 P.M., mid-March to mid-November.

Plants of many varieties of wildflowers and woodland ferns.

Other wildflowers, as well as a complete selection of nursery stock, tropical plants, and garden supplies, are available at the nursery.

How About an International Wildflower Preservation Society

Donald Hackenberry, of Appalachian Wildflower Nursery, feels there's a need for such an organization, and he'd like to get it started. The title may be different, he says, but that suggests its goals: using all beneficial means to preserve the world's wildflowers, maintain records, disseminate information, and preserve habitat through botanical and private gardens.

"At this point," says Hackenberry, "I know absolutely nothing about starting a non-profit corporation of this type." But he'll welcome letters from anyone who is interested. "Please advise readers who respond," he says, "to be patient, and that it will start small. But I feel it will grow."

[Note: As this is a "non-profit" venture, we urge anyone who writes to Hackenberry to include an SASE for his reply.]

70

THE GREEN THUMB DIRECTORY

Northplan Seed Producers, Box 9107, Moscow, ID 83843. (208)-882-8040. Price list. Visitors by appointment.

Seeds of native wildflowers, shrubs, and trees, gathered in the western states—such as wild hyacinth, dog's-tooth violet, flax, Oregon grape, red mountain heath, black locust, and Engelmann spruce. Quotations for large quantities on request.

Orchid Gardens (The Clair Phillips), Splithand Lake Rte., Grand Rapids, MN 55744. (218)-326-6975. Illustrated catalog, 35¢. Open Tues.–Sun., daylight hours.

Native, hardy wildflowers, ferns, orchids, mosses, shrubs, and perennials. Many uncommon or hard-to-find varieties, as twinflower, white baneberry, creeping snowberry, blazing star, tufted loosestrife, purple cinquefoil, mountain cranberry, pin-cushion moss, kidney-leaved violet. Catalog gives complete culture instructions for ladyslippers as well as concise culture notes on all plants listed. All plants are grown under authentic culture conditions.

Labeled collection of color slides of wildflowers available for group showings. For information on rental and listings, send SASE.

Panfield Nurseries, Inc., 322 Southdown Rd., Huntington, NY 11743. (516)-427-0112. Illustrated brochure. Open Mon.–Sat., 8 A.M.–4:30 P.M.

Native ferns, wildflowers, and

other plants, including laurel, viburnum, bayberry, inkberry, and holly. Native plants and trees especially for attracting birds and wildlife, such as chokeberry and winterberry. Woodland plant collections available, including a fern collection, wildflower collection, and ground-cover collection.

A demonstration woodland garden may be seen at the nursery.

Putney Nursery, Inc., Putney, VT 05346. (802)-387-5577. Color illustrated catalog. BAC and MC charges. Open every day, 8 A.M.–5 P.M.

Vermont-grown wildflowers and hardy ferns; many listings. Also culinary and aromatic herbs and perennials. Special collections of plants include "Shady Nook Fern Collection"; "Beginner's Wildflower Garden," with twenty different plants; "Woodland Trillium Collection"; and "Hardy Orchid Collection."

The Shop in the Sierra (Carl Stephens), Box 1-T, Midpines,

CA 95345. (209)-966-3867. Illustrated catalog, $1.00. MC charge. U.S. sales only. Open 9 A.M.–5 P.M.; weekends preferred.

Western native plants, wildflowers, and alpines; extensive listing. Very attractive, informative catalog, with sketches and descriptions. Annual listing of western native bulbs, such as brodiaea, calochortus, camassia, erythronium, iris, and trillium.

Stephens is in charge of landscaping for the Yosemite National Park concessioner.

Francis M. Sinclair, Rte. 1, Newmarket Rd., Exeter, NH 03833. (603)-772-2362. Price list. Visitors by appointment.

Hardy native plants, including bulbs, ferns, orchids, ground covers, vines, and numerous wildflowers.

Sunshine Seed Co., 310 N. Madison Ave., Wyoming, IL 61491. Price list, $1.00. Minimum order for plants, $15; no minimum for seeds.

Seeds and seedlings of native plants and wildflowers—concentrating on showy, outstanding species of the Midwest, Southwest, and West. Inventory, which changes constantly, includes prairie plants, cacti, lewisias, calochortus, aquilegia, and other rock plants.

"Our primary interest is scientific, and we tend to propagate obscure rare plants, such as milkweeds, and other ecologically interesting groups."

Thoreau Wildgarden, Myra Rd., Greenfield, ME 04423. (207)-827-7683. Catalog; send stamp. U.S. sales only. Visitors welcome; phone ahead.

Plants of wildflowers and ferns. Perennials *only*. New species added yearly. Good descriptions and cultural hints in catalog. No seeds, or annuals and biennials considered "weed" species, are listed.

"Most perennial wildflowers are generally rare and uncommon. Wildflower gardeners know this. People not familiar with them expect the impossible, such as planting them for miles along highways. All require specific soil, light, moisture, etc., and are *not* easy to grow.

"One of our major goals is to try to replace, in shady yards and woodlots, the native wild plants which have been bulldozed or otherwise cultivated out over the last three hundred years."

Did You Know . . .

—Many plants will root and grow in blocks of florists' foam.

—Vertical, "moss-wall" gardening offers marvelous dramatic effects.

—Water in which willows have steeped is a strong rooting stimulant.

—Some prairie grasses make fine lawns.

These are examples of the hundreds of subjects covered in *The Avant Gardener Handbook and Sourcebook of All That's New and Useful in Gardening.* Written by

Thomas and Betty Powell, expert gardeners and editors of the unique newsletter *The Avant Gardener*, this 263-page book is a complete guide to the latest gardening information $6.95, available from booksellers or from **Horticultural Data Processors**, Box 489, New York, NY 10028. If you're a gardener and don't have a copy of this book, you're missing something very worthwhile.

Vick's Wildgardens, Inc., Box 115, Gladwyne, PA 19035. (215)-525-6774. Illustrated catalog, 25¢. BAC charge. U.S. sales only. Open Mon.–Sat., 8 A.M.–4 P.M.

Nursery-grown wildflowers and ferns. Also wildflower and herb seeds and terrarium plants.

Gardens include twenty-eight

acres of plants, wildflowers, native and ornamental trees, greenhouses, and a shop offering unusual gift items, native terrariums, handmade vases and ceramic items, and books on wildflowers.

Woodland Acres Nursery (Frank and Marie Sperka), Rte. 2, Crivitz, WI 54114. (715)-757-3853. Catalog, 25¢ (credited). U.S. sales only. Visitors by appointment.

Hardy northern-grown wildflowers and ferns; many varieties. An everblooming fluorescent red bleeding heart, Dicentra Luxuriant, developed by the Sperkas from wild bleeding hearts over a period of sixteen years, is a special feature—"a field in bloom is a glorious sight to see."

Mrs. Sperka is author of an outstanding book on wildflowers, *Growing Wildflowers*, 320 pages with over two hundred illustrations. Autographed copies are available for $9.95 plus 60¢ for postage and handling.

"We have been at this location, in the heart of Nicolet Forest, for over thirty-six years. Carved the nursery and homesite out of the wilderness."

Woodstream Nursery, Box 510, Jackson, NJ 08527. Illustrated catalog; send stamp.

Native wildflowers. Many varieties, well described in the catalog. Numerous plants suitable for terrariums, such as round-lobed hepatica, partridgeberry, spotted wintergreen, rattlesnake plantain, and trailing arbutus.

Aquatic Plants, Water Gardens, Pools, and Fountains

Bee Fork Water Gardens (Otto Beldt), Bunker, MO 63629. Color illustrated catalog. Visitors welcome; write for appointment.

Hardy and tropical water lilies, bog plants, aquarium plants. Also pool supplies, pumps, fountains.

Hermitage Gardens, West Seneca Ave., Canastota, NY 13032. (315)-697-9093. Color illustrated catalog, $1.00 (credited). BAC and MC charges. Open Mon.–Sat., 10 A.M.–5 P.M.; Sun., 1 P.M.–5 P.M.

Fiberglass garden pools in many free-form shapes and sizes; fiberglass "rock" waterfalls (from nineteen inches to over seven feet high), bridges, and other pool components. Also pumps, fountains, lights, and related items. Several pool designs available as a package, with all materials and plans. Pools may be ordered directly from Hermitage or from regional distributors.

The gardens, in Canastota, have landscaped pools on display and a gift shop with many unusual items.

Paradise Gardens, Inc., 14 May St., Whitman, MA 02382. (617)-447-4711. Illustrated catalog, $1.00 (credited). Open Mon.–Sat., 8 A.M.–5 P.M.

Wide selection of garden pools —more than two dozen styles. Also special liners which can be

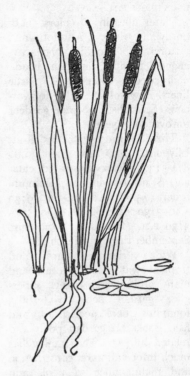

used to make any size pool. Pool supplies, including fountains, waterfalls, and pumps. Many water lilies and other aquatic plants.

Paul W. Stetson, president of Paradise Gardens, has been raising water lilies since he was a boy. "Years ago," he says, "only the wealthy could afford a water garden. Now anyone can make a showplace in his or her back yard for a minimal cost."

Slocum Water Gardens, 1101 Cypress Gardens Rd., Winter

Haven, FL 33880. (813)-293-7151. Color illustrated catalog, 25¢. Open Mon.–Sat., 8 A.M.–noon and 1 P.M.–4 P.M.

Water lilies in all colors—both hardy and tropical. Also lotus and victoria lilies, goldfish and scavengers, pumps, fountain heads, pool sweeps, filters, and plastic liners. Low-voltage lights for gardens. Specialist in water gardens for over forty years.

Three Springs Fisheries, Inc., Lilypons, MD 21717. (301)-874-5133. Color illustrated catalog, $1.00 (credited). Minimum order, $15. Open Mon.–Sat., 9:30 A.M.–3:30 P.M.; Sun., 12:30 P.M.–3:30 P.M. (Closed Sat. and Sun. September through March.)

Wide variety of hardy and tropical water lilies, lotus, and many other water plants. Fiberglass garden pools, waterfalls, fountains, pool accessories, and fish. Books on garden pools and related subjects. The catalog has much information on construction and maintenance of pools and culture of aquatic plants.

William Tricker, Inc., 74 Allendale Ave., Saddle River, NJ 07458. (201)-327-0721. Color illustrated catalog. 25¢. BAC and MC charges. Open Mon.–Sat., 8 A.M.–5 P.M. Also open Sun., 8 A.M.–5 P.M., May and June.

Water lilies and other aquatic plants. Pools, pumps, fountain heads; goldfish and other tropical fish. The world's oldest and largest water gardens; founded in 1895.

William Tricker, Inc., is also situated at 7125 Tanglewood Dr., Independence, OH 44131. (216)-524-2430.

Van Ness Water Gardens, 2460 N. Euclid Ave., Upland, CA 91786. (714)-982-2425. Color illustrated catalog, 50¢. BAC and MC charges. Open Tues.–Sat., 8 A.M.–5 P.M.

Water lilies, both tropical and hardy; lotus; papyrus; cattails; water iris; horsetails; and other bog plants. Pools and pool supplies. Good selection of related books.

Display water gardens are open to visitors. Oriental stone lanterns, garden statuary, as well as plants and pool supplies, are sold at the gardens in Upland.

Sedums and Sempervivums

Hollow Hills Succulent Farm, Rte. 2, Box 883, Carmel, CA 93921. (408)-624-8946. Illustrated price list, 25¢. Visitors welcome; phone ahead.

Over thirty varieties of sedums, and many sempervivums. Also numerous other succulents and cacti. Field-grown plants; most available in small, medium, and large sizes.

"Sempervivums (houseleeks)

and R. N. Payne), Rte. 3, Box 87, Dallas, OR 97338. (503)-623-4612. Descriptive price list, 25¢. Open every day, daylight hours.

Sedums and sempervivums—many species and hybrids imported from England and other European countries, not previously available in North America. Also new hybrids by Scrocki, Vaughn, and others. An excellent book on these plants, *Plant Jewels of the High Country*, by Helen E. Payne, with over one hundred color photographs, is available for $15.

In addition to display gardens, visitors can see a unique roof garden planted with sedums and sempervivums.

are grown on roofs from Norway to Ireland as a guard against evil spirits and lightning. They also are a remedy against the 'leeks' in the roof—hence the name."

Oakhill Gardens (Helen E.

"For the collector or the beginner we recommend using a small magnifying glass so that the intricate beauty of each sempervivum may be seen more clearly."

The Flower Garden

State University; six varieties of Fancifrills double impatiens; Blue Troll browallia; and Iowa heliotrope.

Ames Greenhouses, recently established, has a staff of plant-science specialists and is involved in development and propagation of new plant material.

Bluestone Perennials, Inc., 3500 Jackson St., Mentor, OH 44060. (216)-255-4644. Catalog. BAC and MC charges. Open Mon.–Sat., 8 A.M.–5 P.M., April 15 to June 15.

Many perennials, including aquilegia, aster, campanula, chrysanthemum, delphinium, dianthus, gaillardia, geranium, hedera, hollyhock, primula, scabiosa, statice, viola, and numerous other varieties. All started in liners, 1⅝ inches square by 2¼ inches deep, for customers to grow to full size. Economical prices.

Ames Greenhouses, Inc., Rte. 2, East 13th St., Ames, IA 50010. (515)-232-1985. Color illustrated brochure. Open Mon.–Sat., 8 A.M.–5 P.M.

Dormant roots and/or seeds of Melissa Hope hybrid delphiniums. Also other plants, including twelve varieties of Cyclone hybrid impatiens, developed at Iowa

Basic Guides for Flower Gardeners

Growing Flowering Annuals, G-91, 25¢, and *Growing Flowering Perennials,* G-112, 25¢. Order from the **Supt. of Documents,** Washington, DC 20402.

Garden Place, 6780 Heisley Rd., Mentor, OH 44060. (216)-255-3705. Illustrated catalog, 25¢. Open Mon.–Fri., 8:30 A.M.–5 P.M.

Over 1,100 different varieties of perennials, all field grown. General garden favorites and many old-fashioned varieties.

Garden Place is the retail outlet of Springbrook Gardens, a wholesaler, where forty-six acres with about 1 million perennials are open to visitors. The best blooms may be seen July through September. The gardens are operated by grandsons of the late Elmer H. Schultz, founder of Wayside Gardens.

Flowers, and gardens, are a perennial delight. Enjoy yours— and also the famous gardens and arboretums throughout the United States and Canada. Several hundred are described in *American Gardens—Traveler's Guide*, $1.50

from **Brooklyn Botanic Garden,** 1000 Washington Ave., Brooklyn, NY 11225.

Bulbs for All Seasons

The companies listed below offer a wide selection of bulbs, corms, tubers, and rhizomes. And following them are growers who specialize, for the most part, in one particular type.

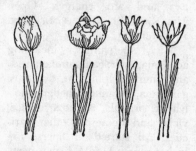

C. A. Cruickshank, Ltd., 1015 Mount Pleasant Rd., Toronto, Ont. M4P 2M1. (416)-488-8292. Color illustrated catalog. CGX charge. Open Mon.–Sat., 9 A.M.–5 P.M. (Closed Sat., June to September.)

One of the most extensive listings of bulbs of any firm in North America—more than seven hundred varieties. Canadian representatives for Van Tubergen, Ltd., leading Holland bulb growers for over fifty years. Specializes in rare bulbs, difficult or impossible to obtain elsewhere. Also a line of quality seeds, im-

ported orchids, garden supplies, and many books on gardening.

"This has been a small family business for over fifty-one years. It developed from a hobby interest and we stress top quality."

P. DeJager & Sons, Inc., 188 Asbury St., South Hamilton, MA 01982. (617)-468-1622. Color illustrated catalog. Open Mon.–Fri., 9 A.M.–5 P.M.

A complete stock of imported Dutch bulbs of all types. Also houseplants, seeds, and garden supplies. There is much cultural information in the catalog. The company has been in business for over a century.

French's Bulb Importer, West Proctor Rd., Box 87, Center Rutland, VT 05736. (802)-746-8162. Illustrated catalog. Minimum order, $6.00. BAC charge. U.S. sales only. Open by appointment, September to early November.

More than thirty-five types of bulbs imported from Holland and France. Bulbs for forcing. Also seed for greenhouse or indoor plants, many uncommon varieties.

John Messelaar Bulb Co., 150 County Rd., Rte. 1-A, Ipswich, MA 01938. (617)-356-3737. Color illustrated catalog. U.S.

sales only. Open Mon.–Sat., 9
A.M.–5 P.M.

Imported Holland bulbs of all
types. The company was founded
in the early 1940s by John Messelaar, who spent his youth in the
bulb fields of Holland.

John Scheepers, Inc., 63 Wall
St., New York, NY 10005. (212)-
422-1177. Illustrated catalogs.

Flowering bulbs of all types.
Extensive listings, color photos,
and good descriptions. Catalogs
include spring and fall editions, a
forcing catalog with bulbs for indoor and greenhouse growing,
and a catalog of hardy chrysanthemums and oriental poppies.
The company was founded sixty-
seven years ago.

Tulips Are Dutch Immigrants

Tulips, many gardeners are sur-
prised to learn, are natives of
Africa and Persia. It wasn't until
the late 1500s that they arrived in
Holland. But when they got there,
the practical Dutch took temporary
leave of their good senses. They
fell madly in love with the flowers.

According to The Netherlands
Flower Bulb Institute, one fancier
traded two loads of wheat, four
loads of rye, four fat oxen, eight
fat pigs, twelve fat sheep, two
hogsheads of wine, four barrels of
beer, two barrels of butter, a
thousand pounds of cheese, a suit
of clothes, a silver jug, and a bed
—all for a single, prized bulb. He
did keep a plot of ground in
which to plant it.

Tulips thrived in the sandy soil

and climate of the Netherlands,
and since those early days countless millions have been exported
to gardeners around the world.

Van Bourgondien Bros., Box
A, Babylon, NY 11702. (516)-
669-3500. Color illustrated catalog. AEX, BAC, and MC charges.
U.S. sales only. Open Mon.–Sat.,
7 A.M.–4 P.M.

Imported Dutch bulbs and domestic bulbs of all varieties.
Hardy lilies, perennials, wildflowers, houseplants, and small fruits
and vegetables. Many rare and
unusual items. In business over
125 years, the company has its
own growing operation in the
Netherlands.

Sven Van Zonneveld, Box 454,
Cassel Rd., Rte. 1, Collegeville, PA
19426. (215)-489-2216. Color illustrated catalog. Minimum
order, $15. U.S. sales only.

Imported Holland bulbs for
fall planting, including unusual
varieties of daffodils, tulips, and
lilies. Also fall-blooming and in-

door bulbs and Jan de Graaf hardy lilies. U.S. representative of John H. Van Zonneveld Co. of Holland, a bulb specialist for fifty-five years.

All About Bulbs

Spring Flowering Bulbs, Nr. G-136, is a fourteen-page illustrated guide to growing a variety of bulbs in the garden or forcing them for indoor bloom. The booklet is 30¢ from **Supt. of Documents,** Washington, DC 20402.

Bulbs, Handbk. 31, tells when and how to plant all kinds of bulbs and has illustrations of over sixty types. $1.50 from **Brooklyn Botanic Garden,** 1000 Washington Ave., Brooklyn, NY 11225.

Specialized Growers

AMARYLLIS

Amaryllis, Inc. (E. M. Beckman), Box 318, Baton Rouge, LA 70821. (504)-924-5560. Color illustrated catalog, $1.00. Minimum order, $10. Open to visitors, weekends, by appointment.

Named and registered varieties of amaryllis from leading Dutch and African growers, including Ludwig, Van Meeuwen, Van Waveren, and Hadeco. Also species amaryllis, seedlings, and seed.

"As an amaryllis grower and hybridizer, I have selected bulbs that you will enjoy growing as much as I have during the past twenty-five years."

CALADIUMS

Joyner's Caladiums, Rte. 3, Box 71, Lake Placid, FL 33852. (813)-465-2851. Illustrated brochure; send stamp. Minimum order, $5.50.

Over twenty-five varieties of caladiums, available in bulb sizes from one inch to over three inches. Also special collections available, by color. Excellent color illustrations of leaves.

Spaulding Bulb Farm, Sebring, FL 33870. Descriptive price list.

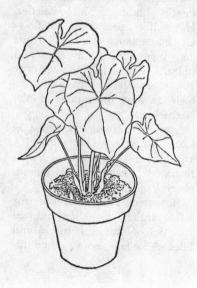

Minimum order, twenty-five bulbs.

Specializes in fancy-leaf cala-diums. Many varieties in shades of white, red, and pink. Information on culture is included.

DAFFODILS

Special prices on mixtures for naturalizing. Freshly cut daffodils are available from March 15 through April. A set of five postcards, with color photos showing over thirty varieties of daffodils, is 50¢. All the daffodils are grown in Virginia soil; the present owner is the third generation of growers.

Display gardens in Gloucester, Virginia, are open 10 A.M.–5 P.M., March 15 to April 15, and September 15 to October 31.

Grant E. Mitsch, Box 960, Canby, OR 97013. (503)-266-9161. Color illustrated catalog. Visitors are welcome at the gardens, at 22695 S. Haines Rd., in Canby, Mon.–Sat., during bloom season.

An extensive list of daffodils of all types; many Mitsch introductions and also those of other hybridizers. Good descriptions and cultural information. A daffodil specialist and hybridizer for some fifty years.

The Daffodil Mart (The Brent C. Heaths), Box 112, North, VA 23128. (804)-725-2427. Descriptive price list. Minimum order, $10. U.S. sales only.

Over three hundred varieties of daffodils—including over one hundred varieties and species of miniatures—for shows, gardens, and naturalizing. Many rarities.

DAHLIAS

Ackman's Dahlia Gardens, 9114 Oakview, Plymouth, MI 48170. (313)-453-1381. Price list. Visitors welcome anytime, August through October.

About two hundred varieties of dahlias, all types. Also dahlia seed.

Has been growing dahlias for over thirty years.

Bateman's Dahlias, 6911 S.E. Drew St., Portland, OR 97222. (503)-774-4817. Catalog. U.S. sales only. Open to visitors during bloom season; phone ahead.

Wide selection of standard and show-type dahlias. Both old and new varieties.

Connell's Dahlias, 10216 40th Ave. E., Tacoma, WA 98446. (206)-531-0292. Catalog. Visitors are welcome.

New and recent introductions. Listings of giant, large, medium and small, miniatures (four inches and under), balls, and pompons. Special collections are available.

The gardens are in bloom August to first frost.

Legg Dahlia Gardens, Rte. 2, Hastings Rd., Geneva, NY 14456. (315)-789-1209. Illustrated catalog. Open every day, 7 A.M.–7 P.M.

Specializes in dahlias collected from around the world. More than five hundred varieties; bloom range from one inch to twelve inches in diameter.

Tours through the three acres of the garden are held daily, August through October. All the plants are identified so visitors can jot down the names of their favorites.

E. Ray Miller's Dahlia Gardens, 167 N.E. 12th Ave., Hillsboro, OR 97123. (503)-648-2848. Catalog. Visitors welcome; phone ahead.

Specialist in large, exhibition-type dahlias. Hundreds of varieties, many imported.

"Dahlias originated in Mexico, and the original blooms were single. Now, through selective breeding, we have the beautiful blooms you see today. New varieties come from Japan, Africa, Australia, Holland, just to mention a few."

William P. Newberry Gardens, Rte. 2, Bland, VA 24315. (703)-688-4262. Price list; send SASE. Visitors welcome anytime.

Dahlias of exhibition quality: formal and informal decoratives; cactus; incurved; straight; reflexed; and fimbriated. Own new introductions yearly.

"We find it a challenge to grow the giants. The world of 'dahlia shows' is hungry for show-quality stock, and we strive to meet the demand."

Key to Dahlias

Here are some American Dahlia Society code classifications that are used in many catalogs.

Size of Flower

A	large, over 8 inches in diameter
B	medium, 6–8 inches
BB	4–6 inches
M	miniature, under 4 inches
Mba	miniature ball
Pom	under 2 inches
Dwf	low-bush varieties

Type of Flower

An	anemone
Ba	ball
SC	semi-cactus
STC	straight cactus
IC	incurved cactus
FD	formal decorative
ID	informal decorative
Coll	collarette
P	peony
S	single
Pom	pompon

Pennypack (Stanley Johnson), Cheltenham, PA 19012. (215)-379-0252. Illustrated catalog. Visitors by appointment.

Modern exhibition dahlia roots and green plants—named varieties. Numerous Pennypack introductions. Also dahlia seed.

Ruschmohr Dahlia Gardens (H. Dewey Mohr), 38 Vincent St., Box 236, Rockville Centre, NY 11571. (516)-766-1761. Catalog. Visitors welcome anytime.

Specialist in exhibition dahlias; own introductions as well as those of other growers. Also dahlia seed. Good cultural information

is in the catalog. Mohr has been raising dahlias since 1930 and has been a vice-president of the American Dahlia Society for the past thirty-six years.

S&K Gardens (Sam and Katherine Kordonowy), 401 Quick Rd., Castle Rock, WA 98611. Catalog; send stamp. Visitors welcome.

Over one thousand varieties of dahlias, all types. Complete cultural information is in the catalog. Dahlia growers for over thirty years.

Swan Island Dahlias, Box 800, Canby, OR 97013. (503)-266-7711. Color illustrated catalog, $1.50 (credited). Minimum order, $7.50. Open every day, 9 A.M.–4:30 P.M., in spring and again from August until frost.

Dahlias of all types; new introductions yearly. Excellent photos and descriptions are in the catalog. Dahlia growers for over forty years.

"Forty-five acres of dahlias in bloom during August and September. We also have an annual dahlia show Labor Day weekend at which we exhibit dahlia arrangements by professional florists."

White Dahlia Gardens, 2480 S.E. Creighton Ave., Milwaukie, OR 97222. (503)-654-4757. Illustrated catalog. Visitors are welcome at the gardens in Oak Grove, Oregon; phone ahead.

About two hundred varieties of dahlias, all types. A dahlia specialist since 1913.

"Some of the newest and some of the best varieties. Let others grow the rest."

Wilson's Dahlias, 24706 Warthen Rd., Elmira, OR 97437. (503)-935-1295. Price list. U.S. sales only. Visitors welcome.

About 350 varieties of dahlias, including own introductions.

"We sell only top-quality stock. If it does not measure up to our expectations and standards, it is not offered for sale."

Growing Dahlias is the title of an eight-page booklet that illustrates the various types of flowers and has information on culture and care. Order G-131, 25¢ from the **Supt. of Documents,** Washington, DC 20402.

DAYLILIES

Hundreds of seedlings, not offered by mail, are available at the garden; good for landscaping purposes.

Davidson Gardens, 1215 Church St., Decatur, GA 30030. (404)-373-6891. Price list. U.S. sales only. Open, daylight hours, during June.

Diploid and tetraploid plants. Own introductions plus cultivars of other hybridizers. Also tetraploid seeds from hand-pollinated crosses.

The peak blooming season in the gardens is usually the second and third weeks in June.

Double Daylilies (James F. Miles), 101 Roslyn Dr., Box 1041, Clemson, SC 29631. (803)-654-2410. Price list; send stamp. Visitors welcome; call ahead.

Named and American Hemerocallis Society-registered double-flowering daylilies developed by Miles. One of the largest and most outstanding displays of double-blossomed daylilies in the world.

Crochet Daylily Garden, R. 3, Box 18, Prairieville, LA 70769. (504)-673-8491. Price list. Minimum order, $10. Open Mon.–Fri., after 4 P.M.; Sat. and Sun., all day.

Outstanding daylily cultivars, both diploid and tetraploid, of prominent southern hybridizers. Also the best of the older cultivars. Many Crochet introductions; has been hybridizing daylilies since 1963, using the finest cultivars and seedlings.

Englerth Gardens, 2461 22nd t., Rte. 2, Hopkins, MI 49328. 616)-793-7196. Price list. Minimum order, $10. Visitors welcome; call ahead.

More than six hundred varieties of daylilies—the largest collection in Michigan. Also hostas and many spuria, Siberian, and Japanese iris. Plant growers for over forty-five years.

Hughes Garden, Rte. 3, Box 27-C, Mansfield, TX 76063. 817)-478-9851. Catalog. Open Mon.-Sat., 8 A.M.–6 P.M.

Daylily specialists for over twenty years. Many own originations plus new introductions from other hybridizers.

Learn How to Breed Plants

If you'd like to try plant breeding, here are two recommended booklets:

Home Plant Breeding, Handbk. 5, $1.50 from Brooklyn Botanic Garden, 1000 Washington Ave., Brooklyn, NY 11225. Tells how to create your own African violets, begonias, and many other plants. A down-to-earth introduction to a fascinating hobby.

Plant Breeding as a Hobby, C817. Order from Agricultural Publications Office, University of Illinois, 123 Mumford Hall, Urbana, IL 61801. Sent without charge to Illinois residents; we suggest others include 50¢ to cover costs.

Iron Gate Gardens (Van M. Sellers), Rte. 3, Box 101, Kings Mountain, NC 28086. (704)-435-9338. Illustrated catalog. Minimum order, $7.50. Open every day, daylight hours.

Extensive listing of outstanding tetraploid and diploid daylilies. Many introductions of Sellers, including "whites." Also hybridizations of other prominent breeders. The catalog also lists about seventy-five varieties of hostas, many rare.

Iron Gate Gardens, with about six acres of rare trees, shrubs, and perennials, is worth a special visit. All walkway areas are brick or cement, and intricate ironwork is used throughout the garden.

Lake Angelus Gardens (Howard J. Hite), 270 Waddington Rd., Birmingham, MI 48009. (313)-647-2391. Illustrated price list. Minimum order, $10. U.S. sales only.

Diploid and tetraploid daylilies; Hite hybrids. Seedlings and named and registered cultivars. Also hand-pollinated tetraploid seeds.

The gardens, at 370 Gallogly Rd., Pontiac, MI 48055, are open May 10 to October 25, every day, daylight hours. It is advisable to phone ahead: (313)-332-9780.

Lenington Gardens, 7007 Manchester Ave., Kansas City, MO 64133. (816)-358-6666. Catalog, 25¢ (credited). Visitors by appointment.

Many new or recent daylily introductions of Lenington and also of James E. March. George E. Lenington, a charter member of the American Hemerocallis Society, has been breeding daylilies for twenty-four years.

Louisiana Nursery (Ken Durio), Rte. 1, Box 43, Opelousas, LA 70570. (318)-948-3696. Catalog, $1.00. Minimum order, $15. U.S. sales only. Open every day, 8 A.M.–6 P.M.

Extensive collection of daylilies from leading breeders throughout the country. Many Durio introductions. Also many Durio introductions of Louisiana iris as well as from other Louisiana iris breeders.

The nursery, a family-owned and -operated business for twenty-seven years, has show gardens of daylilies and Louisiana iris. Also many hostas, magnolias, and an interesting cactus collection.

Mueller's Garden (A. Theodore Mueller), Rte. 1, Box 307, Cape Girardeau, MO 63701. (314)-334-1626. Price list.

Many listings of both daylilies and iris, from prominent hybridizers. A number of older varieties at moderate prices.

Saxton Gardens (S. E. Saxton), 1 First St., Saratoga Springs, NY 12866. (518)-584-4697. Illustrated brochure; send stamp. Visitors by appointment.

Daylilies; Saxton originations. Also daylily seed by named crosses, and lily bulbs. A daylily specialist since 1940 and a charter member of the American Hemerocallis Society, Saxton supplies daylily seed to many major seed companies.

Schoonover Gardens, 404 S Fifth St., Box 7, Humboldt, K 66748. (316)-473-2273. Descrip tive price list. Minimum order $9.00. Visitors are welcome.

Extensive list of daylilies, in cluding new Schoonover intro ductions and those of othe breeders. Numerous plants fo collectors, such as Edna Spaldin Memorial, a low-growing, green ish-yellow daylily hybridized b MacMillan (priced at $50). Als a list of sempervivums.

The gardens are in peak bloom from late June to early July.

C. G. Simon Nursery, Inc. Box 2873, Lafayette, LA 70502 Price list. The gardens, at 30 Carmel Avenue, are open Mon. Sat., 9 A.M.–5 P.M.

Many new Simon daylily intro ductions. Also several hundre varieties, of all types, from out standing hybridizers.

Starmont Daylily Farm (Ken neth & Ethel Peters), 1641 Shady Grove Rd., Gaithersburg MD 20760. (301)-948-3003. Cat alog, 30¢. Minimum order, $10 Open Mon.–Sat., 9 A.M.–5 P.M. Sun., 2 P.M.–5 P.M.

Over three hundred varieties o daylilies, including new cultivar and tetraploids. Own introduc tions and those of other hybrid izers.

Also available by mail ar cones from white, Austrian, and Himalayan pines; some cones are up to ten inches long.

Tanner's Garden, Rte. 1, Box 22, Cheneyville, LA 71325. (318)

297-4203. Price list. Visitors welcome; phone ahead.

Very extensive list of daylilies; own introductions as well as from other breeders. Well over eight hundred varieties listed.

"Visitors are always welcome. This year we are growing many new seedlings, both tetraploid and diploid, and would appreciate your comments and evaluation of them."

Tranquil Lake Nursery (Charles R. Trommer), 45 River St., Rehoboth, MA 02769. (617)-252-4310. Catalog, 10¢. Minimum order, $7.50. Visitors are welcome; phone ahead.

Many varieties of daylilies; own originations and new hybrids of several prominent breeders. Very extensive collection of double daylilies. Also eighty varieties of Siberian iris, about sixty varieties of Japanese iris, and several hundred varieties of peonies.

The nursery has around two thousand named varieties of daylilies and is probably the largest daylily and Siberian-iris specialty nursery in the Northeast. Iris are in bloom in June, and daylilies from mid-May to October.

Wheeler's Daylily Farm, 10024 Shady Ln., Houston, TX 77016. (713)-965-3532. Descriptive price list; send stamp.

Several hundred varieties of daylilies, including new introductions, doubles and tetraploids. Over twenty-five years' experience in hybridizing and growing.

Gilbert H. Wild & Son, Inc., Box 338, Sarcoxie, MO 64862. (417)-584-3514. Color illustrated catalog, $1.00 (credited). Minimum order, $6.00. Open Mon–Sat., 8 A.M.–4 P.M., May through September.

Extensive selection of daylilies, iris, and peonies. Many own originations. Listings are illustrated and well described, with name of hybridizer. In business since 1885.

Diploids . . . Tetraploids . . . It's Greek to Me!

You're right. These words do come from Greek. If you're not sure what they mean, here's a brief rundown.

Each cell of every plant (and animal, too) has a certain number of chromosomes, which carry the heredity traits passed on by its parents. Many plants have duplicate sets or pairs of chromosomes in their cells—with one of each set contributed by each of its parents. These plants are known as *diploids*.

A daylily, for example, in nature is a diploid, because its cells have twenty-two chromosomes in eleven sets. But if, by some method of plant breeding, this number of chromosomes can be doubled, the plant becomes a *tetraploid*. A tetraploid daylily has forty-four instead of twenty-two chromosomes per cell.

Tetraploidy often results in more-vigorous plants, with larger flowers. A common method of inducing it is by the use of the chemical colchicine.

Over one thousand varieties of glads. Also some four hundred varieties of dahlias, thirty-five types of cannas, many hard-to-find summer-flowering bulbs and tubers. The list also includes some seeds of unusual ornamental corn and Indian corn.

Visitors are welcome at the gardens and greenhouses, which, in addition to other plants, have an interesting collection of cacti and succulents.

Gruber's Gladiolus, 2910 W. Locust, Davenport, IA 52804. (319)-391-0787. Illustrated price list. U.S. sales only. Visitors welcome; phone ahead.

Several hundred varieties of glads. Most available in large, medium, or small sizes, or bulblets. Special prices on quantities.

Oscar W. Johnson (Idaho Ruffled Gladiolus Gardens), 612 E. Main St., Jerome, ID 83338. (208)-324-4726. Price list; send stamp. Open daily, 10 A.M.–5 P.M.; phone ahead.

Ruffled glads—new introductions and old varieties. A gladiolus hybridizer for many years.

George Melk & Sons, Rte. 2, Plainfield, WI 54966. (715)-335-4462. Color illustrated catalog. Minimum order, $6.00. Open Mon.–Fri., 8 A.M.–6 P.M.; Sat., 8 A.M.–noon.

Over one hundred varieties of glads in five different sizes of

Ed-Lor Glads (The Ed Fredericks), 234 South St., South Elgin, IL 60177. (312)-695-0495. Brochure and price list. Visitors welcome; phone ahead.

Own originations, new and recent, of miniatures, greens, and novelties. Has raised and exhibited glads for over twenty years.

Flad's Glads, 2109 Cliff Ct., Madison, WI 53713. (608)-255-5274. Illustrated catalog. Open Mon.–Sat., by appointment.

New originations of many breeders. Numerous miniatures. Special collections are offered.

Gladside Gardens, 61 Main St., Northfield, MA 01360. (413)-498-2657. Catalog; stamp appreciated. U.S. sales only. Open daily, 9 A.M.–5 P.M.; phone ahead.

bulbs. Melk introductions as well as those of other prominent hybridizers. Special prices for quantities. There are excellent descriptions in the catalog. Glad specialists for over fifty years.

The forty-five acres of gladiolus, in Plainfield, are at color peak in mid-August.

All-America Gladiolus Selection

If a gladiolus has an AAGS citation, a gardener is assured of its quality and beauty. It's the highest honor a glad can earn.

The non-profit All-America Gladiolus Selection organization maintains test gardens throughout the United States and Canada. Glads under trial are continually evaluated by expert judges. Only a very few outstanding glads pass the tests—and are awarded the All-America Gladiolus rating.

Noweta Gardens, St. Charles, MN 55972. (507)-932-3210. Color illustrated catalog, 50¢. Open Mon.–Fri., 8 A.M.–5 P.M.

Approximately 150–200 recent varieties and new introductions from Carl Fischer of Noweta, as well as those of other breeders worldwide. Special listing of "exotic seedlings," sold by number. Many varieties difficult to obtain elsewhere. Leading hybridizers of glads for over forty years.

Pleasant Valley Glads (Gary Adams), 163 Senator Ave., Box 494, Agawam, MA 01001. (413)-786-9146. Catalog. Minimum order, $7.00.

New introductions from prominent breeders as well as older varieties. Numerous miniatures. Available in various sizes. The listing includes the latest All-America glad selections.

Rich Glads, Marion, NY 14505. (315)-926-4273. Descriptive price list. Visitors welcome; phone ahead.

Ruffled glads, all Rich introductions. Many varieties, excellent descriptions.

Visitors are welcome at the growing field and the seedling test plot at 69 Newark Road in Marion. Glads are in bloom from August 1.

Winston Roberts (Modern Glads), Box 3123, Boise, ID 83703. Catalog. Minimum order, $8.00.

A gladiolus hybridizer for over forty years, Roberts offers many new introductions of his own, plus All-America winners and introductions of other breeders. The glads are in bloom late July through August.

Squires Bulb Farm, 3419 Eccles Ave., Ogden, UT 84403. (801)-392-8657 (phone after 5 P.M.). Catalog. Minimum order, $10. Visitors by appointment.

Over 150 varieties of glads listed, both large-flowered and miniature. New introductions from Squires as well as other hybridizers throughout the United States and Canada. Special prices for many medium and small bulbs.

Aril Iris Farm, Rte. 1, Box 3770, Ridgecrest, CA 93555. (714)-375-7955. Illustrated price list. Open every day, 7 A.M.–6 P.M., March through May.

Specializes in oncocyclus iris; species and their hybrids. Own introductions.

"Among the oncocyclus irises are some of the world's most beautiful flowers. They are native to semi-arid regions of the Near East that have hot, dry summers with most precipitation occurring from fall to early spring. Consequently they grow during the cooler part of the year and go dormant in the summer. An understanding of this is most important."

Avonbank Iris Gardens (Margaret and Lloyd Zurbrigg), 903 Tyler Ave., Radford, VA 24141. (703)-639-5593. Catalog. Visitors by appointment.

Features remontant iris; own originations plus a few from other breeders. Also extensive listings of non-remontants; intermediate, dwarf, and miniature bearded and spurias, Siberians, and Japanese.

"Few gardens in the United States feature remontants, but their number is increasing as the quality of the plants increases. Our catalog is considered to be of great interest, as it is unique in describing the growth habits of remontants in cold-climate gardens."

Baldwin's Iris, 1306 Monroe, Walla Walla, WA 99362. (509)-525-0809. Catalog. U.S. sales only. Open all day during bloom season.

Tall, median, and standard-dwarf bearded, and reblooming iris. More than 560 varieties listed, many new. Bargain selections of well-known favorites. There is a good description of every plant listed.

Peak bloom in the gardens is around May 20.

Bay View Gardens, 1201 Bay St., Santa Cruz, CA 95060. (408)-432-3656. Illustrated catalog, 20¢. Open weekends.

Bearded, Louisiana, Pacifica, Siberian, and spuria iris. Constantly expanding list of beardless. The listing of Pacificas is one of the most extensive of any grower.

Charjoy Gardens, 117 Acacia Dr., Lafayette, LA 70501. Catalog; send stamp. Minimum order, $10. U.S. sales only. Visitors by appointment.

Specializes in Louisiana iris; possibly the largest variety of Louisiana iris cultivars in the United States. Grows about one thousand new seedlings each year from own breeding program.

Cooley's Gardens, Inc., 301 S. James, Silverton, OR 97381. (503)-873-5463. Color illustrated catalog, 50¢ (credited). Open Mon.–Fri., 9 A.M.–5 P.M.

Bearded-iris specialists. Many outstanding introductions of hybridizers. Various collections available. Well-illustrated catalog with excellent descriptions. Iris growers for over forty-five years.

Cordon Bleu Farms, 418 Buena Creek Rd., San Marcos, CA 92069. (714)-744-3851. Illustrated catalog. The garden is always open to visitors.

Extensive listing of bearded iris —tall, border, intermediate, miniature tall, and standard dwarf. Beardless iris include spurias, Louisianas, Siberians, and Pacific Coast natives. Some species. Also many listings of the newest tetraploid hemerocallis.

The iris at the gardens are in bloom from mid-April through mid-May, with some cultivars in bloom almost any day of the year. Daylily bloom starts in early June, continues into late fall.

Darst Bulb Farms, 1519 Bennet Rd., Box 806, Mount Vernon, WA 98273. (206)-424-1014. Color illustrated catalog. Open Mon.–Fri., 8 A.M.–5 P.M.

Hybrid bulbous-iris bulbs; many Darst introductions and new miniatures.

"We are the only commercial hybridizers of bulbous iris, including miniatures, that we know of in the Western Hemisphere. The bulbs can be planted any month of the year with equally good flowering results."

Discovery Trail Gardens, 3897 Yellow Pine Dr., Rescue, CA 95672. (916)-677-1092. Price list, 25¢. Open weekends, April and May; phone ahead.

Arils, tall bearded, medians, and dwarfs. Specialists in Space Age—tall bearded with unusual elongations from beard area. Aril-bred introductions of Leo Clark; over forty space irises developed by the late Lloyd Austin. Home of Region 14 Aril Display Garden —two acres with some one thousand varieties.

Eden Road Iris Garden (Gordon Plough), Box 117, Wenatchee, WA 98801. (509)-884-7626. Color illustrated catalog, 50¢. Open Mon.–Fri., 10 A.M.–4 P.M.

Bearded iris of all types. Many new introductions of Plough as well as other hybridizers. Good descriptions in catalog. Twenty-four years as iris specialists.

"The garden is a veritable arboretum, with many rare and unusual trees, shrubs, and plants, and a bird sanctuary and wildlife refuge. You will find it an interesting place, with much to see besides iris."

Fleur de Lis Gardens (Chet W. Tompkins), Box 344, Oregon City, OR 97045. Price List. Visitors welcome.

Specialist in tall bearded iris; many originations by Tompkins plus other hybridizers. Special prices on older choice varieties.

Foster Iris, 850 Ora Avo Dr., Vista, CA 92083. (714)-727-0695. Price list. Open every day, 9 A.M.–5 P.M.

Specialists in aril iris (oncocyclus and regelia), species and hybrids, and aril-breds. Also standard dwarf, intermediate, and miniature talls, tall bearded, and Californicae. Many award-winning aril-bred introductions.

"Aril-bred are part aril species, part tall bearded or other bearded, and are easier to grow than the aril species."

N. Freudenburg, 310 E. Maple, Norfolk, NB 68701. Price list.

Extensive list of tall bearded iris. Also many dwarfs. Numerous "surplus" iris at moderate prices.

Gable Iris Gardens, 2543 38th Ave. S., Minneapolis, MN 55406. (612)-729-8855. Catalog. U.S. sales only. Visitors welcome; suggest phone ahead.

Dwarf, tall bearded, and Siberian iris. Also daylilies, hybrid peonies, oriental poppies, hardy phlox. Chemicals especially for treatment of iris and daylily diseases.

Granvil Gable, the oldest senior judge in Minnesota of the American Iris Society, was awarded the Distinguished Service Award for horticulture, in 1969, by the Minnesota State Horticultural Society.

Gene & Gerry's Gardens, 39 E. Patrick, Frederick, MD 21701. (301)-662-1580. Price list. U.S. sales only. Open to visitors anytime.

Many varieties of iris, including own hybrid introductions. Also daylilies.

Hamner's Iris Garden, 960 N. Perris Blvd., Perris, CA 92370. (714)-657-3501. Price list. U.S. sales only. Open Mon.–Fri., 10 A.M.–5 P.M.

Extensive list of iris, including aril-bred and spuria. Top-quality iris of new or recent introduction, including own originations. A selection of "beginners" specials at moderate prices.

Some Iris Terms

Standards: the three upright petals.

Falls: the three lower petals that hang down.

Beard: a fuzzy line running down the middle of a fall.

Crest: a small raised area on the middle of each fall.

Style arms: small, stiff segments just above the beard.

Harper's Orchard Gardens, Rte. 2, Moran, KS 66755. (316)-

939-4743. Illustrated catalog. Open every day, 9 A.M. to sunset.

Median, tall bearded, and spuria iris. Also lactiflora, hybrid, and tree peonies. Own introductions and from selected breeders. Features Kay See weatherproof garden markers and plant supports with a three-year guarantee. Allen Harper is a senior judge of the American Iris Society.

Visitors can buy fresh produce, fruit, and honey produced in the gardens.

A. H. Hazzard, 510 Grand Pre Ave., Kalamazoo, MI 49007. (616)-344-1721. Price list. Minimum order, $10. Open every day; phone ahead.

Japanese-iris specialist; over three hundred varieties. Also tall bearded and Siberian iris, Japanese anemones, and hardy primula.

"Japanese iris may safely be moved when in bud or full bloom, can be potted for exhibition, use on patios, or in the house."

Hildenbrandt's Iris Gardens, Star Rte., Box 4, Lexington, NB 68850. (308)-324-4334. Catalog. U.S. sales only. Visitors welcome anytime; phone ahead.

Extensive list of iris, including own border bearded and other median iris introductions. Also oriental poppies and peonies. Almost a thousand varieties of plants available.

"Our garden is an overgrown hobby. We have a 240-acre farm, with corn and alfalfa the main crops. We have several acres of gardens, with 1,100 varieties of iris and many other plants. Do most of the work ourselves."

Illini Iris (D. Steve Varner), N. State Street Rd., Monticello, IL 61856. (217)-762-3446. Price list. Minimum order, $10. Open Mon.–Fri., after 5 P.M., and all day Sat. and Sun.

Varner, an iris hybridizer for twenty-three years, has one of the largest collections of seedling and named iris in Illinois. He has won top awards for tall bearded and Siberian introductions.

Available at the nursery are over one hundred lilacs, hybrid and lactiflora peonies, tetraploid hemerocallis, clematis—as well as thousands of iris.

Imperial Flower Garden, Box 255-G, Cornell, IL 61319. (815)-358-2519. Catalog; send stamp. Visitors welcome anytime.

Tall bearded, dwarf, median, rebloomers, aril-bred, onco-bred, Siberian, Japanese, Louisiana, and spuria iris. Limited supply of Dykes Medal winners. Many rarities. Also oriental poppies. A grower for over thirty-five years.

The garden is in best bloom from mid-May to early June.

Iris Test Gardens (Ione and Austin Morgan), 1010 Highland Park Dr., College Place, WA 99324. (509)-525-8804. Illustrated catalog. U.S. sales only. Open every day except Sat., daylight until dark, during May bloom season.

Very extensive list of tall bearded iris. Gardens, with over eight acres of iris, have some 2,500 varieties plus many exceptional seedlings; have attracted visitors from all over the world to see new creations in tall bearded iris. Morgan, an iris grower since 1944, is an experienced judge for the American Iris Society, and held the post of regional vice-president.

J&J Iris Garden (Jack Boushay), Rte. 1, Box 329, Cashmere, WA 98815. (509)-762-3162. Catalog. Open evenings and weekends.

Tall bearded, border bearded, intermediate, standard dwarf, and miniature dwarf bearded iris. Features own new introductions and those of Rex and Alta Brown and Ken Shaver.

Boushay says he recently has become interested in stamp collecting and will be happy to trade iris for stamps. Drop him a card or a letter, letting him know what stamps you have available.

Jernigan Gardens, Rte. 5, Dunn, NC 28334. (919)-567-2135. Price list; send SASE. Open Mon.-Sat., 9 A.M.–noon and 2 P.M.–7 P.M.; Sun. afternoons; during bloom season.

Several hundred varieties of bearded iris, many uncommon. Also many varieties of daylilies and some unusual hostas.

Iris in bloom from late April to mid-May; daylilies are at peak bloom in June.

Dr. and Mrs. Currier McEwen, South Harpswell, ME 04079. (207)-833-5438. Price list. Visitors by appointment.

Outstanding hybridizer of Siberian and Japanese iris and daylilies. The list includes comprehensive descriptions. Originations include a rare yellow Siberian iris and the only registered tetraploid Siberians.

"Although I introduce both diploids and tetraploids in all three of the flowers noted above, my chief hybridizing efforts are directed toward tetraploids. My Siberians and daylilies have now reached their fifth generation of tetraploidy. In the case of the Japanese irises, the second generation was reached only in 1975, and thus far I have introduced only diploid and chimeral Japanese irises."

Melrose Gardens, 309 Best Road South, Stockton, CA 95205. (209)-465-8578. Illustrated catalog, 50¢. Minimum order, $7.50. BAC and MC charges. Open every day, 8 A.M.–5 P.M.

Wide variety of iris including tall bearded, dwarfs, median, Siberian, Japanese, Louisiana, spuria, remontant. Also daylilies and daffodils.

The bloom season at the gardens is March 15 through June 15.

Mission Bell Gardens (J. R. Hamblen), 2778 West 5600 South, Roy, UT 84067. (801)-825-7287. Catalog. Open every day, spring and summer, daylight hours.

About six hundred varieties of iris, many tall bearded and median; own originations as well as those of other hybridizers. New introductions yearly.

"At the gardens we grow a large number of 'guest' irises under seedling numbers and names. We also have a fine collection of spuria irises, but do not sell them. We are one of the National Spuria Display Gardens."

The Oscar of the Iris World

The highest award an iris can receive is the Dykes Medal—given annually by the American Iris Society to one outstanding iris.

Mohr Gardens, 1649 Linstead Dr., Lexington, KY 40504. (606)-277-4589. Price list; send stamp. Minimum order, $10. Open every day, 9 A.M.–5 P.M., May 10 to May 30.

Specializes in the newest accomplishments in tall bearded irises; also lists older AIS award winners. Many own introductions. Large selection of recent, named varieties that are overstocked are offered at low prices. The staff consists of Dr. H. C. Mohr, a professor of horticulture; Ken Mohr, a horticulturist; and David Mohr, a college student; all are iris breeders.

Moores Reblooming Iris Garden, 4233 Village Creek Rd., Fort Worth, TX 76119. (817)-536-0267. Price list; send stamp. U.S. sales only. Open weekends and weekdays after 4 P.M.

Specialist in reblooming iris; many uncommon and rare. Also large collection of once-blooming iris at reasonable prices. Starter collections are available.

Northwest Hybridizers, 16516 25th N.E., Seattle, WA 98155. (206)-362-9206. Price list. Visitors by appointment.

An organization of two iris hybridizers: Mrs. J. A. Witt, of Seattle, and John J. Taylor, 2329 Darrell Ln., Missoula, MT 59801. Offers new introductions not usually available elsewhere; species iris, chiefly Californicae and Sibericae, and aril-breds, hybridized by Taylor, and miniature tall bearded, by Witt.

Pilley's Gardens, Box 308, Wilderville, OR 97543. (503)-479-8623. Catalog. Visitors by appointment.

Many varieties of tall bearded, border, intermediate, and standard iris. Also daylilies, diploids and tetraploids.

Powell's Gardens, Rte. 2, Princeton, NC 27569. (919)-936-4421. Catalog, 50¢. U.S. sales only. Open Mon.–Sat., 10 A.M.–6:30 P.M.; Sun., 2 P.M.–6:30 P.M.; March 1 to August 1.

About five hundred iris and daylily cultivars; own new introductions and the newest of other hybridizers. Also sedums, sempervivums, hostas, and many other perennials. The state's largest perennial growers.

"Our gardens, which include a rock garden, Japanese garden, iris garden, and a 'hen' garden, are a great pleasure for visitors. But my first love is iris."

Riverdale Iris Gardens, 7124 Riverdale Rd., Minneapolis, MN 55430. (612)-561-1748. Catalog. U.S. sales only. Visitors are welcome during the growing season; phone ahead.

Upward of five hundred varieties of iris are listed in the catalog; specialist in dwarf and median iris; many older varieties not available elsewhere. Exclusive introducer of new varieties from several hybridizers.

Over one thousand varieties are growing in the garden. Unusual species are tested for adaptability to northern climates.

Schliefert Iris Gardens, R.F.D., Murdock, NB 68407. (402)-234-4172. Catalog, 25¢. Visitors welcome; phone ahead.

Nebraska's largest iris grower; many own introductions plus those of other prominent breeders. Extensive listings of all types. All the American iris winners of the Dykes Medal since 1929 are available. (*All* Dykes Award-winning iris can be seen in the gardens in Murdock.)

Schreiner's Gardens, 3625 Quinaby Rd., N.E., Salem, OR 97303. (503)-393-3232. Color illustrated catalog, 50¢. Visitors are welcome during the bloom season in May; phone ahead.

Specialist in new hybrid iris. Outstanding collection of newest award winners and selected new genetic developments from own hybridizing plots. Established in 1925; iris have won many awards throughout the world.

Several sets of color slides of iris are available for rental for group showings.

Dr. Raymond G. Smith, 3821 Sugar Ln., Bloomington, IN 47401. (812)-896-2353. No sales literature; send SASE for inquiry. Visitors by appointment.

Reblooming iris rhizomes of own origination. Has devoted over twenty-five years to hybridizing rebloomers.

Southern Meadows Garden (James S. Tucker), Box 230, Centralia, IL 62801. (618)-532-7898. Catalog. Open 8 A.M.–8 P.M. during the bloom season.

Iris and daylilies; many new varieties of each, introduced by Tucker and other hybridizers.

Species Specialties (Earl & Marge Roberts), 5809 Rahke Rd., Indianapolis, IN 46217. (317)-786-7839. Price list; send SASE. Minimum order, $10. Open every day, 10 A.M. to dark.

Specialist in wild species iris collected from around the world; probably the largest collection in the United States. Also new tall bearded, median, and dwarf iris. Many daylilies; over 250 varieties of sempervivums, sedums, hostas, and miniature rock-garden plants. Roberts was awarded the American Iris Society's Hybridizers Medal in 1975 and has won many other awards in international competitions.

"This is not a true commercial garden. We are both hybridizers and enjoy our hobby very much. Each year, we introduce several new iris and daylilies. Our sales are a runoff of our hybridizing hobbies."

Summerlong Iris Gardens, Rte. 2, Box 163, Perrysville, OH 44864. Price list. Visitors by appointment.

Specializes in cold-climate reblooming iris—own introductions plus introductions of other growers. Limited quantities available.

"These iris bloom at normal time, at the end of May or early June, then repeat bloom, according to variety, anytime from late July to frost."

Plantsmen—Not Companies

Many of the sources listed in this book are not large commercial growers. Dr. Currier McEwen, iris hybridizer, is an example. Although "retired," he is still active in medicine—the only rheumatologist in Maine north of Portland.

This is one of the reasons why we stress: *please do not write for catalogs or price lists unless you have a definite interest.*

Tell's Garden, Box 331, Orem, UT 84057. (801)-225-6145. Price list, 15¢.

Siberian, median, aril, and spuria iris. Also daylilies. New introductions of both. Also some iris seed available.

Valley's End Iris Gardens (The Heins), 32375 Dunlap Blvd., Yucaipa, CA 92399. Catalog; send stamp.

Border bearded, intermediate, standard dwarf, and miniature dwarf bearded iris. Hybridizers listed; good descriptions. Specially priced collections and assortments.

Wilder Iris Garden (Dr. R. W. Wilder), Box 362, Stanhope, IA 50246. (515)-826-3602. Catalog. Visitors welcome anytime; phone ahead.

Extensive list of iris, featuring many new introductions and some of the older, hard-to-find varieties. From prominent hybridizers, including many Wilder originations. Dr. Wilder has specialized in iris for twenty-eight years and has been a judge of the American Iris Society for a number of years.

Peggy Williams Gardens, 3136 N. Haltom Rd., Fort Worth, TX 76117. (817)-831-1417. Brochure-price list. Minimum order, $10. Open every day, 7 A.M.–7 P.M.

About four hundred varieties of iris, sixty varieties of cannas, and around one hundred varieties of daylilies. Has been hybridizing these plants for over twenty-five years, with new introductions annually. Mrs. Williams is an iris judge and an organic gardener.

A number of other plants, including begonias and perennials, are available at the gardens.

Iris Information

Growing Iris in the Home Garden is an eight-page basic guide, 35¢ from the **Supt. of Documents,**

Washington, DC 20402. Ordering number is G-66.

A more comprehensive booklet, *What Every Iris Grower Should Know*, is $1.10 from the **American Iris Society**, 2315 Tower Grove Ave., St. Louis, MO 63110.

And if you're seriously interested in growing iris, consider a membership in the American Iris Society. Among its benefits is a quarterly publication with more than one hundred pages devoted to iris.

LILIES

Numerous special lily collections. Also imported Dutch bulbs, wildflowers, hardy native orchids, clematis, hostas, native ferns, chrysanthemums, phlox, iris, and other perennials. Lily seeds. Many rare, unusual items. Very informative catalog with much information about culture.

Blackthorne Gardens has been awarded the Gold Medal of the Massachusetts Horticultural Society for horticultural excellence.

Gaybird Nursery (Ed Robinson), Wawanesa, Man. RoK 2Go. Descriptive list.

Extensive list of hardy lilies. New and recent originations of Robinson, including martagon hybrids. Also hybrids of Patterson and other breeders. Some species lilies.

Honeywood Lilies (A. J. Porter), Parkside, Sask. SoJ 2Ao. (306)-747-3296. Descriptive price list. Minimum order, $15. Visitors by appointment.

Blackthorne Gardens, 48 Quincy St., Holbrook, MA 02343. (617)-767-0308. Color illustrated catalog, $1.00.

Very extensive listing of lilies of all types; many own originations.

Hardy Asiatic lilies, including Porter, Patterson, Barber, and Simonet hybrids. There are detailed descriptions in the list. Porter has done extensive breeding of lilies, as well as of various small fruits, with emphasis on hardiness in severe climates. He received the H. E. Wilson Memorial Award of the North American Lily Society in 1971.

Laurie's Garden (Lorena M. Reid), 41886 McKenzie Hwy., Springfield, OR 97477. (503)-896-3756. Price list of lilies and price list of iris; send stamp for each. Visitors are welcome; phone ahead.

Lilies, including Asiatic, martagon, candidum, American species hybrids, trumpets, aurelians, oriental hybrids. Many varieties of iris, including Japanese, Louisiana, Siberian, spuria, and other species iris.

McCormick Lilies, Box 700, Canby, OR 97013. (503)-266-9596. Color illustrated catalog, 25¢. Visitors by appointment.

Hybrid Jagra lilies; all new varieties. Also native bulbs and hardy miniature cyclamen. Offers a spring booster food and a specially formulated lily fertilizer.

"Founded in 1927, we offer personalized service. We take the time to answer letters, not just a 'form letter' reply."

Oregon Bulb Farms, Box 529, Gresham, OR 97030. (503)-663-3133. Color illustrated brochure. BAC and MC charges. U.S. sales only.

World-famous lily hybridizers —featuring Jan de Graaf Jagra hybrids.

Piedmont Gardens (Formerly Stone & Payne), 533 Piedmont St., Waterbury, CT 06706.

(203)-754-3535. Price list. Visitors by appointment.

Hybrid lilies, chiefly Asiatics; most are own originations. Also about twenty-five varieties of rare and uncommon hostas, and numerous native wild plants. A partnership of lily hybridizers who started as amateurs and soon became internationally known for hybrid lilies.

Color slide lectures are offered to groups in near areas. Slides are also available for rental.

Five Rules for Success with Lilies

In their handbook *Let's Grow Lilies,* the North American Lily Society says Rule Number 1 for success with lilies is *good drainage.* It's also Rule Number 2 . . . and Rule Number 3, etc.

A copy of this handbook is available for $2.00 from the **North American Lily Society**, Box 40134, Indianapolis, IN 46240.

Rex Bulb Farms (John M. Shaver), Box 145, Newberg, OR 97132. (503)-538-4089. Color illustrated catalog. Open Mon.–Fri., 9 A.M.–4 P.M.

Specializes in lilies of all types; originations of prominent hybridizers. Special moderately priced collections. Also lily seed, both hybrid and species. There are detailed descriptions in the catalog. A color slide collection with lecture information is available; reservations should be made as far in advance as possible.

Riverside Gardens (A. E.

Delahey), Rte. 5, Saskatoon, Sask. S7K 3J8. (306)-374-0494. Descriptive price list. Minimum order, $7.50. Visitors by appointment.

Very hardy lilies, with stock of all registered Patterson lilies. Lilies all are completely winterhardy, surviving at temperatures as low as —45° F.

Julius Wadekamper—Lilies, Rte. 2, Box 141A, Rogers, MN 55374. (612)-497-2377. Illustrated catalog. Visitors welcome; phone ahead.

Specializes chiefly in Asiatic lilies, but also some species and trumpet lilies. Lists about a hundred cultivars and species. Features own originations and is exclusive introducer of lilies of several prominent hybridizers. Lists hybridizations of Gontarek, Porter, Hickling, Windus, Feldmaier, Simonet, Kroell, and Koehler. Wadekamper, who has served as president of the North American Lily Society, grows about ten thousand seedlings and also tests seedlings from many hybridizers in the United States, Canada, and Germany for future introduction.

Lilies Take Harvard Tests

The famous Arnold Arboretum, in Jamaica Plain, Massachusetts, which is sponsored by Harvard University, has the most extensive lily test garden in the world. Several hundred varieties and species are always under evaluation.

You can be pretty sure a Harvard-grad lily is tops!

CHRYSANTHEMUMS

Baumer, Inc., 9900 N. Michigan Rd., Carmel, IN 46032. (317)-873-4647. Illustrated brochure. BAC and MC charges. Minimum order, $7.50. U.S. sales only. Open Mon.–Sat., 8:30 A.M.–5:30 P.M.; Sun., 11 A.M.–4 P.M.

Rooted cuttings of florists' varieties of mums (football and spray types) and carnations (large double and miniature varieties). Instructions for growing mums and carnations in hobby greenhouses will be sent on request. Baumer is successor to Baur-Steinkamp & Co., a hybridizer of carnations and mums for over fifty years, developers of Indianapolis varieties of mums.

Greenhouses, in Carmel, have two acres of foliage plants, bedding plants, carnations, and mums.

Dooley Gardens, Rte. 1, Hutchinson, MN 55350. Descriptive price list. Visitors are welcome at the trial fields, September and October.

Rooted cuttings of garden mums. Own introductions, University of Minnesota and Canadian introductions, plus others.

Several hundred varieties may be seen in bloom at the trial gardens.

Mums Are Heavy Drinkers

Because chrysanthemums have shallow root systems, they need large amounts of water to grow and flower properly. Apply enough water, USDA horticulturists recommend, to *thoroughly soak the top six inches* of soil. Don't water again until the soil is dry and the plants begin to wilt slightly.

Fleming's Flower Fields, 3100 Leighton Ave., Box 4607, Lincoln, NB 68504. (402)-466-1355. Illustrated catalog. U.S. sales only. Open every day, 8 A.M.–6 P.M.

Hardy mums; many own introductions, new University of Nebraska introductions as well as from other breeders. Emphasis on new "Modern Mums." Also lists hibiscus, dianthus, and miniature roses.

"Primary aims of our chrysanthemum breeding have been the development of exhibition-quality mums with good plant habit, and the improvement of cushion mums by increasing size and quality of flowers."

Flowerland, 816 English St., Racine, WI 53402. (414)-632-0143. Price list.

Extensive list of mums: early-English-garden-exhibition, extra-large-flowered, and hardy garden varieties. Bloom dates are indicated.

Huff's Gardens, Inc., 618 Juniatta, Box 187, Burlington, KS 66839. (316)-364-2933. Catalog. Visitors are welcome anytime, June through December.

Rooted cuttings of over 950 varieties of mums; all types; one of the largest selections available from one source. Many varieties listed are no longer offered by other dealers. Third generation of family specializing in mums.

Visitors may see blooming stock plants in the fall and use them as a check list for varieties wanted the following year.

Plant Pronouncer a Good Investment

Chrysanthemum is one of the relatively few botanical names that most people can pronounce correctly. But even experienced gardeners may stumble over *Aponogeton, Boussingaultia, Glycyrrhiza,* or *Zantedeschia.*

There are several good books that have pronouncing guides. A favorite of ours is *Wyman's Gardening Encyclopedia,* by Dr. Donald Wyman (The Macmillan Co., 1971). The book also has more than 1,200 pages, with a wealth of garden information. It's a very worthy investment.

Glycyrrhiza, incidentally, is an easy one. Just say "gly-ki-RY-za." Or, if you prefer, "licorice."

King's Chrysanthemums, 3723 East Castro Valley Blvd., Castro Valley, CA 94546. (415)-582-7172. Color illustrated catalog, $1.00 (credited). Open Sat. & Sun., 9 A.M.–5 P.M., October to mid-November. Other times by appointment.

Large show flowers a specialty. Many King introductions including dwarf cushion early bloomers. Also bonsai-type mums from Japan, and imported cascade and hanging-basket types. Exclusive U.S. agents for H. Woolman, Ltd., of England, long famous for fine show flowers.

The Lehman Gardens, 420 10th St., S.W., Faribault, MN 55021. (507)-334-8404. Illustrated catalog. Open every day, 9 A.M.–5 P.M., September and October.

Over one hundred varieties of garden mums, many own introductions. Known for northern-grown and early-blooming garden mums. In business over forty-five years.

Five acres, with over fifty thousand mums in bloom during the fall season.

Sunnyslope Gardens, 8638 Huntington Dr., San Gabriel, CA 91775. (213)-287-4071. Color illustrated catalog.

Mums of all types. Many own award-winning introductions as well as those from other breeders. Numerous imported varieties. There are good descriptions and cultural information in the catalog.

Visitors are welcome at the annual mum show, October and November.

If You're a Beginner

The *Beginners Handbook,* $2.25 from the **National Chrysanthemum Society, Inc.,** 394 Central Ave., Mountainside, NJ 07092, will be helpful. Check the listing of the society for other publications written by chrysanthemum authorities.

Thon's Garden Mums, Inc., 4815 Oak St., Crystal Lake, IL 60014. (815)-459-1040. Color illustrated catalog. U.S. sales only. Open Mon.–Fri., 8 A.M.–5 P.M.

Specializes in garden mums; about 180 varieties. Many own introductions. Also some of the better English exhibition and spider varieties. The list includes Cheyenne Series, bred by USDA in Wyoming; they are extremely winter-hardy in most areas and bloom quite early. A specialty is various collections of different types of mums, such as cushions, English exhibitions, spiders, and daisies. A sixteen-page booklet, *Growing Garden Mums,* will be sent on request.

"The chrysanthemum, dating back several thousand years, from a small, single daisy, to today's large exhibition varieties, is probably one of the best known flowers to our civilization today. Its ease of growth and reproduction, its brilliant color in the fall, when all other flowers have faded, make mums a most desirable addition to the garden."

Tom's Garden Mums, Box 42, Ashton, NB 68817. Descriptive price list.

Extensive list of mums, including exhibition, cushions and doubles, spiders, pompons, spoons and buttons, cutflowers and decoratives, and footballs. Height and bloom date indicated.

HOSTAS

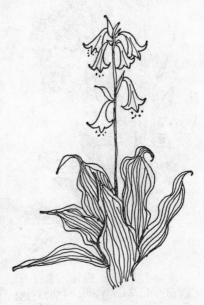

Gray & Cole Nursery, Inc., 1269 Boston Rd., Rte. 125, Haverhill, MA 01830. (617)-372-4780. Price list; send stamp. Minimum order, $12. Open every day, 9 A.M.–5 P.M., April–December 24.

About fifteen old hosta species; no new hybrids.

A wide variety of nursery stock, including many rare and dwarf plants, and numerous rhododendrons, is available at the nursery in Haverhill.

Minks' Fairway Gardens, 114 The Fairway, Albert Lea, MN 56007. (507)-373-5290. Price list. Minimum order, $10.

Specialists in hostas; cultivars and species; numerous Minks originations. Also Skyline diploid and tetraploid daylilies, including Minks introductions, and over thirty varieties of astilbes.

Savory's Greenhouses, 5300 Whiting Ave., Edina, MN 55435. (612)-941-8755. Price list. Minimum order, $10. U.S. sales only. Visitors by appointment.

Over one hundred varieties of hostas, with frequent new introductions. A family operation for over thirty years. There are detailed descriptions in the catalog.

"This hardy herbacious perennial group has done more than any other to enhance the shaded portion of the garden by supplying background plantings, outstanding accent points, borders and ground covers of infinite variety of sizes, leaf textures, coloration, and flower variations."

Alex J. Summers, 14 I. U. Willets Rd. West, Roslyn, NY 11576. (516)-627-2686. Price list. Minimum order, $20. Visitors by appointment.

Largest collection of hostas in the United States. Large- and small-leaf varieties; many rarities. Also a listing of Japanese ferns.

Brand Peony Farm, Box 36, Faribault, MN 55021. (507)-334-6373. Illustrated catalog. Visitors are welcome; phone ahead.

Minnesota's oldest nursery specializing in peonies, founded in 1868. Many varieties, including own originations. There are detailed descriptions in the catalog. Also features lilacs and iris.

Annual peony show—the public is welcome—is usually June 10 through June 20.

Gratwick Tree Peonies, 1912

PEONIES

York Rd., Pavilion, NY 14525. (716)-584-3440. Illustrated brochure.

Tree peonies. Grafted, named varieties of Japanese and lutea hybrids; also Gratwick-Daphnis hybrids. Very informative catalog.

Visitors are welcome at the Tree Peony Festival, in late May, when three thousand plants are on display in the gardens.

"In America, though still a rarity, the tree peony is fast becoming the outstanding aristocrat of flowering plants—a treasure no 'self-respecting' gardener can be without. Few plants can vie with the magnificent size of its bloom —up to twelve inches across."

Lienau Peony Gardens (Clarence Lienau), 9135 Beech Daly Rd., Detroit, MI 48239. (313)-937-3147. Catalog. Open 10 A.M.–9 P.M., June 5 to June 20.

Some two hundred varieties of peonies; all types except tree forms. Also numerous listings of oriental poppies. Lienau, a peony grower for over thirty years, has won all commercial-class awards of the American Peony Society since the inception of this award.

An annual peony show is held

at the three-acre gardens at 45875 Ford Rd., Plymouth, Michigan, in June.

David Reath Hybrid Peonies, 100 Central Blvd., Vulcan, MI 49892. (906)-563-9321. Illustrated catalog. Visitors by appointment.

Tree and herbaceous peony hybrids. Reath originations as well as those of Saunders and Daphnis. The catalog has comprehensive descriptions of plants and culture. Two-year-old tree-peony grafts as well as older specimen plants available.

Display garden in bloom in June.

Louis Smirnow, 85 Linden Ln., Brookville, NY 11545. (516)-626-0956. Color illustrated catalog, $1.00 (credited). Minimum order, $10. Open Fri.–Sun., 9 A.M.–5 P.M.

Oldest grower and dealer in peonies in the United States. Specializes in Japanese, European, and lutea tree peonies; many own introductions. Also herbaceous and hybrid peonies and peony species. Very informative catalog.

"Will be glad to explain growing habits of peonies to visitors, show them how to graft, and other things they may be interested in."

Relief for Allergic Gardeners

Miseries caused by ragweed pollen, dust, mold spores, and other airborne particles may be prevented by wearing a Micropore Pollen Mask. Manufactured by the 3M Company, the face-fitting mask is molded of non-woven synthetic fiber, and filters particles of five microns and larger. (Ragweed pollen ranges in size from twenty-two to twenty-four microns.)

The masks are available from most drugstores and pharmacy departments. Readers who would like more information may write to 3M Home Health Care Products, 3M Company—223-3S, St. Paul, MN 55105.

PRIMROSES

Far North Gardens, 15621 Auburndale Ave., Livonia, MI 48154. (313)-422-0747. Illustrated catalog, 50¢. Visitors by appointment.

Plants, transplants, and seed of Barnhaven Silver Dollar primroses; northern-grown for hardiness. Exclusive distributor in the United States for the Barnhaven strain. Also seeds of many varieties of rare flowers and wild and rock plants collected from around the world.

Louis A. Hindla, 986 Church St., Bohemia, NY 11716. (516)-589-2243. Price list; send stamp.

Numerous primroses, including polyanthus varieties, Pacific giants, doubles. Some own originations.

Skyhook Farm (Mrs. Barbara

Kittell), Clay Hill Rd., Johnson, VT 05656. (802)-635-7119. Descriptive price list; send stamp.

Primroses, including denticulatas, auriculas, polyanthus, candelabras, woodland, and species.

"Queen of the flowers" is the title Sappho of Lesbos gave to the rose in 610 B.C. The oldest flower known to man, the rose is perhaps the universal favorite. And the ultimate achievement, for many gardeners, is growing that "one perfect rose."

Armstrong Nurseries, Inc., 1265 S. Palmetto, Ontario, CA 91761. (714)-984-1211. Color illustrated catalog. BAC and MC charges. U.S. sales only. Open Mon.–Fri., 8 A.M.–5 P.M.

Bare-root roses of all types; many varieties of each. Also standard and dwarf fruit trees, grapes, and flowering bulbs.

A rose specialist since the 1890s, Armstrong has originated or introduced more than 170 patented varieties, with many All-America Rose Selections winners. An AARS rose test garden is maintained at the nurseries.

Arp Roses, Inc., Box 3338, Tyler, TX 75701. (214)-592-3104. Price list.

Patented and unpatented roses, including Speaker Sam and other Arp introductions. Also pecan, black walnut, and Japanese persimmon trees. The company,

"All plants are Vermont-hardy and will flourish if given a rich, humus-filled soil, good drainage, and a compost mulch to conserve moisture and keep a cool root run."

ROSES

started in 1916, is now operated by a grandson of the founder.

The Conard-Pyle Co. (Star Roses), West Grove, PA 19390. (215)-869-2426. Color illustrated catalog. BAC and MC charges. Open every day, 9 A.M.–6 P.M.

Largest rose grower east of the Mississippi; specializing in roses since 1897. Many varieties. Also chrysanthemums, hollies, delphiniums, and other perennials. Memorial Rose Garden and rose fields are open to the public May through September.

Star roses are grown on land that was part of the original William Penn grant. The deed of Penn's grandson specifies an annual payment of "one red rose." This payment is celebrated every year the first Saturday after Labor Day.

The All-America Rose Selections Testing Program

A rose that wears the green and white oval metal seal identifying it as an AARS winner is sure to be a beauty in your garden.

For more than thirty-five years the All-America Rose Selections testing program has been held at trial gardens throughout the country, situated so that all types of soil and climate are represented. Roses entered in the tests are grown in each of the gardens for two years, and during this time receive four ratings from official judges.

Less than 4 per cent of the roses entered survive the fierce competition—and become AARS winners.

Dynarose, Ltd., Brooklin, Ont. LoB 1Co. (416)-655-3143. Catalog. Open March 15 to May 15 and October 1 to November 30; phone ahead.

Canadian-grown roses of all types: hybrid teas, floribundas, grandifloras, polyanthas, climbers, bourbon and hybrid perpetuals, rugosas (including species and hybrids), modern shrubs, hybrid musks, species, and old roses. Many introductions by Adam J. Golik.

The fields are open for inspection the third and fourth weekends in July.

Jackson & Perkins Co., Box 1028, Medford, OR 97501. (503)-776-2000. Color illustrated catalog. Open weekdays, 8 A.M.–11 A.M. and 1 P.M.–4 P.M.

World's largest rose grower; has over 10 million roses growing at a time; many AARS winners. Also offers flowering bulbs, vegetable seeds, perennials, strawberries, and lilacs.

Tours are held from August 15 through December 15. The rose test garden is of special interest during late spring and summer.

Joseph J. Kern Rose Nursery, Box 33, Mentor, OH 44060. (216)-255-8627. Catalog. Visitors by appointment, June to October.

Some five hundred varieties of roses, many rare and unusual. The largest collection of old roses available to the public. Among the listings are "Paul Neyron," 1869, a hybrid perpetual; "White Bath," 1810, a moss rose; and "Duchesse de Brabant," 1857, a tea rose and favorite of Teddy Roosevelt.

Soak Your Roses

Unless you've had a heavy rainfall, give your roses a thorough watering every week, advises The American Association of Nurserymen. Roses need about an inch of water a week—enough to soak their roots. To check the amount, just stick your finger in the ground to about an inch depth. If there's moisture there, the roses have enough water. And avoid frequent light sprinklings. They do more harm than good.

Kimbrew-Walter Roses, Rte. 1, Box 138, Wills Point, TX 75169. (214)-865-6281. Color illustrated catalog. Open Mon.–Fri., 8 A.M.–5 P.M.

Many varieties of roses, patented and unpatented. Latest AARS winners available. The roses are shipped bare-root.

Visitors are welcome at the rose fields, in bloom from mid-June through October.

McDaniel's Miniature Roses, 7523 Zemco St., Lemon Grove, CA 92045. (714)-469-4669. Price list. Open Mon.–Sat., 9 A.M.–5 P.M.; phone ahead.

Miniature roses including bush, tree, hanging-basket, and climbers. About 250 varieties available.

"With condominiums, apartment living, and mobile homes, people want flowers that are small and showy for their limited space. The miniature rose is becoming one of the most popular flowers."

Miniature Plant Kingdom, 4125 Harrison Grade Rd., Sebastopol, CA 95472. (707)-823-3023. Catalog, 25¢. Open Mon.–Fri., 10 A.M.–4 P.M.; Sat. by appointment.

Several hundred varieties of miniature roses; many old types unavailable elsewhere.

Visitors are welcome at the show garden, with two thousand plants in bloom.

Mini-Roses, Box 4255, Station A, Dallas, TX 75208. (214)-946-3487. Catalog. Visitors by appointment.

Pot-grown miniature roses; bush, climber, hanging-basket, and "special effect" varieties. About two hundred listings. The nursery maintains an active breeding program, with around twenty introductions to date.

Nor'East Miniature Roses, 58 Hammond St., Rowley, MA 01969. (617)-948-2408. Color illustrated catalog, MC charge. Open every day, daylight hours (but best to call ahead).

Exclusively devoted to producing and growing quality miniature roses. Many uncommon varieties. Collections of various types at special prices.

The display garden, in a delightful rural setting in Rowley, has tens of thousands of blooming miniatures. A number of rarities, not cataloged, may be purchased there.

"Miniature roses as a class are hardier than hybrid teas. Here in Rowley where the winters can get really tough, we merely rake a foot-deep layer of oak leaves into the beds, and have no winter kill. Miniatures are also more resistant to disease and produce bloom continuously."

Carl Pallek & Son Nurseries,

Box 137, Virgil, Ont. LoS 1To. (416)-468-7262. Catalog. Visitors welcome; phone ahead.

Roses, including hybrid-tea, grandiflora, floribunda, climbing, miniature, and a selection of very hardy types.

"We have about four hundred varieties of the best rose cultivars from all over the world, with many new additions each year. Our rose fields are in bloom from about mid-July till early October."

Rose-Growing Supplies

Uncle Charlie's Rose Products, Inc., Rte. 1, Finchville, KY 40022, has a wide selection of insecticides, fertilizers, sprayers, and other items for rosarians. Send $1.00 (credited) for an illustrated catalog.

"Pixie Treasures" Miniature Roses, 4121 Prospect Ave., Yorba Linda, CA 92686. (714)-993-6780. Illustrated catalog, 25¢. BAC and MC charges. Open Mon.–Sat., 9 A.M.–5 P.M.; Sun. by appointment.

Miniature roses; emphasis on new varieties, including "Tiny Treasures," ranging from three to six inches tall.

Visitors are welcome at the propagating greenhouse and miniature-rose garden with five hundred plants, tiny tree roses, and roses in containers and hanging baskets. (Also, to amuse the children, pure-bred dairy goats.)

Roses by Fred Edmunds, 6235 S.W. Kahle Rd., Wilsonville, OR 97070. (503)-638-4671. Color illustrated catalog. Open weekdays, 8 A.M.–4:30 P.M., by appointment.

Many varieties and types of roses, including uncommon foreign introductions. Also gloves, especially designed for rose growers, in sizes for men and women. Cut holly is shipped for Christmas.

In 1976, Edmunds' floribunda, Cathedral, with apricot buds and salmon-tinted blooms, won an AARS award. He says, "Quite by chance three years ago we picked Cathedral when it was still being tested to plant around our house because it was such a fabulous rose and its rich color looked so good against weathered cedar siding."

Sequoia Nursery (Moore Miniature Roses), 2519 E. Noble Ave., Visalia, CA 93277. (209)-732-0190. Color illustrated catalog. Open Mon.–Fri., 9 A.M.–4 P.M.

Pot-grown miniature roses, including tree and "shorty" tree roses and varieties suitable for hanging baskets. Collections are available at special prices. Information about breeding miniatures is given in the booklet *The Story of Moore Miniature Roses,* $1.50 postpaid.

P. O. Tate Nursery, Rte. 3, Box 307, Tyler, TX 75701. (214)-593-1020. Color illustrated brochure. U.S. sales only.

Rose specialist with almost fifty

years of experience. Varieties include hybrid-tea, grandiflora, floribunda, climbers. Also AARS winners.

Thomasville Nurseries, Inc., 1842 Smith Ave., Box 7, Thomasville, GA 31792. (912)-226-5568. Illustrated catalog. U.S. sales only. Open Mon.–Sat., 8:30 A.M.–5:30 P.M.; Sun., 2 P.M.–5 P.M.

Rose specialists since 1898. Many varieties, both old and new. Also daylilies, azaleas, camellias, and liriopes.

The public rose garden, including AARS test plants, is open mid-April to November; camellias are in bloom during the winter, native azaleas in spring, and daylilies in spring and summer.

Rosebush Winterizer

A fiberglass frame, designed to slip over most roses and still allow room for several inches of mulch, is available from **F&R Farrell Co.**, 6810 Biggert Rd., London, OH 43140. The winterizer has a three-year absolute guarantee. Literature about it is sent without charge.

Tillotson's Roses, 802 Brown's Valley Rd., Watsonville, CA 95076. (408)-724-3537. Illustrated catalog, $1.00. The gardens are always open to visitors.

Old, rare, and unusual roses, many associated with history; popular in restoration projects. Also selected new roses including extremely hardy varieties developed by Iowa State University. Excellent catalog with much interesting lore about roses.

"Growing the old, rare, and unusual roses is an adventure. If you watch and study and understand them, you will make your own discoveries. They are not look-alikes and act-alikes, but very individual and fascinating to know."

Melvin E. Wyant, Rose Specialist, Inc., Johnny Cake Ridge, Mentor, OH 44060. (216)-255-2553. Color illustrated catalog. BAC and MC charges. Open every day, daylight hours.

Roses of all types, including a number of hybrid teas unavailable elsewhere. About three hundred varieties of hardy three-year-old roses budded onto multiflora japonica roots.

"We have been growing roses for more than fifty years in this severe climate of northern Ohio."

Reading for Rosarians

Write to **All-America Rose Selections,** Box 218, Shenandoah, IA 51601, for the booklet *Roses Are for You,* which describes various types of roses and their uses, and lists public rose gardens throughout the United States.

Handbook for Selecting Roses is a buyer's guide, updated yearly, to currently available roses. For a copy, send 25¢ plus SASE to the **American Rose Society**, Box 30,000, Shreveport, LA 71130. Roses are rated on a scale from 5.9 and lower (Questionable Value) to 10.0 (Perfect Rose).

Basics of rose culture are included in the twenty-four-page illustrated booklet *Roses for the Home*, Nr. G-25, 30¢ from the **Supt. of Documents**, Washington, DC 20402.

Roses, Handbk. 48, $1.50 from **Brooklyn Botanic Garden**, 1000 Washington Ave., Brooklyn, NY 11225, is a mine of information on planting, pruning, hybridizing, and exhibiting roses.

You'll learn all about hybrid roses in the four-lesson correspondence course *Rose Gardening*, $2.50 from **Pennsylania State University**, 307 Agricultural Administration Bldg., University Park, PA 16802.

VIOLETS

Capitola Violet Gardens, 3645 Gross Rd., Santa Cruz, CA 95060. Catalog, 15¢. Visitors welcome.

About two dozen varieties of hardy violets. Wide range of colors and plants, suitable for sun or shade. Numerous fragrant types and English violets. There are detailed descriptions in the catalog.

Nelson Coon, Waterview Gardens, Vineyard Haven, MA 02568. (617)-693-0282. Price list. Visitors welcome; phone ahead.

Several varieties of rare Parma violets, unavailable elsewhere in the United States. Limited stock.

Coon, a well-known horticulturist and garden writer, recently completed a book on violets, both wild and cultivated types. He has also written a number of other books, including the very helpful *Dictionary of Useful Plants*. A brochure describing his books will be sent on request.

The Indoor Garden

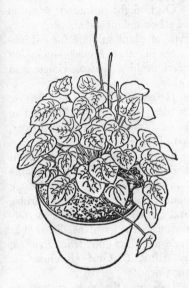

Following are sources for many different types of indoor plants. Specialists—in orchids, gesneriads, and so on—are listed later. But some growers are difficult to categorize, which means you'll have to do some cross checking. And also look in the index for additional sources of specific plant groups.

Alberts & Merkel Bros., Inc., 2210 S. Federal Hwy., Boynton Beach, FL 33435. (305)-732-2071. Illustrated brochure and price list, 50¢. Open Mon.–Sat., 8 A.M.–4:30 P.M.

Tropical plants, including orchids, bromeliads, flowering gingers, gesneriads, anthuriums, aralias, palms, peperomias, philodendrons, and other foliage plants.

Many rarities. Third generation of horticulturists operate the business, founded in 1890.

Arant's Exotic Greenhouses, Rte. 3, Box 972, Bessemer, AL 35020. (205)-428-1827. Illustrated catalog, $1.50 (credited). Minimum order, $15. MC charge. Open Tues.–Sat., 9 A.M.–5 P.M.

Hundreds of varieties of tropical ferns, over two hundred different bromeliads, many orchids, and a great number of other houseplants.

Edelweiss Gardens, 54 Robb-Allentown Rd., Robbinsville, NJ 08691. (609)-259-2831. Descriptive price list, 35¢. Open Mon.–Sat., 10 A.M.–4 P.M.

Several hundred types of tropical plants: bromeliads, cacti, orchids, gesneriads, footed ferns and other ferns, begonias. Many plants suitable for terrariums. Also plant foods and tree-fern products. Special collections of related groups of plants.

Greenland Flower Shop, Rte. 1, Box 52 (Stormstown), Port Matilda, PA 16870. (814)-692-8308. Catalog, 25¢. U.S. sales only. Open Mon.–Sat., 9 A.M.–6 P.M.

Over 225 different rare and exotic houseplants, including numerous terrarium subjects. Also cacti and succulents. The plants, in 2¼-inch pots, are moderately priced.

Visitors to the shop can see propagation areas, large plants used for propagation, some rare collectors' items, and sand terrariums.

Greenlife Gardens (Dr. and Mrs. Ira Slade, Jr.), Rte. 3, Box 613, Griffin, GA 30223. (404)-228-3669. Illustrated price list, 30¢. Minimum order, $10. U.S. sales only. Open Mon.–Sat., 10 A.M.–5 P.M.; Sun., 2 P.M.–6 P.M.

About 150 varieties of unusual house and basket plants including begonias, ferns, pileas, peperomias, ivies, herbs, and others. The Slades began organic growing of medicinal and culinary herbs in 1966 and soon became full-time growers, specializing in propagating unusual varieties.

Many unique hanging baskets are sold at the greenhouse, where visitors are welcome—"especially children, so we can introduce them to the world of plants."

Harborcrest Nurseries, 4634 W. Saanich Rd., Victoria, B.C. V8Z 3G8. (604)-479-1333. Illus-

trated catalog, 25¢. Open every day, 9 A.M.–4 P.M.

Over eight hundred varieties of houseplants—"almost every type of plant suitable for cultivation in the home"—including cacti, orchids, African violets, and others.

Hewston Green, Box 3115, Seattle, WA 98199. Descriptive price list, 50¢. Minimum order, $10. U.S. sales only.

Tropical plants, including cacti and succulents, flowering plants and vines, ferns and other foliage plants, indoor trees and shrubs, and numerous miniatures for terrariums. Each plant listed has code identifications from *Exotica,* by Alfred B. Graf (Roehrs Co., 1975).

"We are the only source we know of for *Caladium humboldtii,* and we have an excellent selection of *Streptocarpus* 'Nymph' hybrids. While maintaining a stock of standard foliage and small plants, we are constantly searching for new introductions."

Jerry Horne, 10195 S.W. 70th St., Miami, FL 33173. (305)-270-1235. Price list. Minimum order, $10. Visitors by appointment.

Rare and unusual tropical plants imported from around the world. Aralias, bromeliads (especially variegated varieties), ferns (many footed ferns such as aglaomorphas and davallias), and unusual foliage plants, as alocasias, anthuriums, calatheas, heliconias, musas, palms, and cycads.

"Ours is a small, family-run

business where my wife and I do most of the work. Our prices are reasonable and many of the plants we ship are in the four- to eight-inch pot size—not tiny seedlings or sporelings, which do not ship well and are delicate to care for."

International Growers Exchange, Inc., Box 397-V, Farmington, MI 48024. Illustrated catalog, $3.00 (credited).

Very large collection of tropical and hardy plants and bulbs from breeders and nurseries throughout the world. Among the thousands of offerings are gesneriads, orchids, bromeliads, hardy perennials, begonias, dahlias, hostas, aquatic and bog plants, wildflowers, carnivorous plants. Many rarities. Sales agents for many of the world's leading growers.

Kartuz Greenhouses, 92 Chestnut St., Wilmington, MA 01887. (617)-658-9017. Color illustrated catalog, $1.00. Minimum order, $10. Open Tues.–Sat., 9 A.M.–5 P.M.

Tropical plants, with emphasis on many uncommon gesneriads and begonias. Kartuz, a prominent plant breeder, offers his own originations plus outstanding varieties from other hybridizers. Also a number of other tropical plants, and numerous miniatures suitable for terrariums.

Kuaola Farms, Ltd., Box 1140, Hilo, HI 96720. (808)-959-6522. Price list. Open Mon.–Fri., 7 A.M.–3 P.M.

Anthurium plants, bare-root or potted. All plants shipped are either in flower or in bud.

A number of other tropical plants may be purchased at the nursery, which is just a few minutes from the Hilo Airport and easily accessible to tourists.

Lauray of Salisbury, Undermountain Rd., Rte. 41, Salisbury, CT 06068. (203)-435-2263. Catalog, 50¢. Open daily; phone ahead.

Very many uncommon gesneriads, begonias, fuchsias, cacti, and succulents.

Also available at the greenhouse, but not by mail, are ferns, orchids, tuberous begonias, and roses.

"We're a small, family-run greenhouse—but in our busy season it really runs us!"

LaVonne's Greenhouse, 463

2nd Ave., Box 131, Riddle, OR 97469. Catalog; send stamp.

Seeds for houseplants, and also for tropical shrubs and other exotics, that can be grown indoors or in greenhouses. Among the wide selection are begonias, geraniums, freesias, ferns, many herbs, gesneriads, acacias, and many tree seeds suitable for bonsai. All listings include scientific names and good descriptions.

Lehua Anthurium Nursery, 80 Kokea St., Hilo, HI 96720. (808)-935-7859. Descriptive price list; send SASE. Visitors by appointment.

Plants and seeds of many tropicals such as anthuriums, gingers, tree ferns, bamboo, guavas, bougainvillaeas, dracaenas. Many uncommon varieties.

"We are basically a small nursery growing plants that are tropical in nature, that can be grown indoors, that are not easily available elsewhere, and that do not grow too big or too fast."

Loyce's Flowers, Rte. 2, Box 11, Granbury, TX 76048. (817)-326-4326. Descriptive list, 50¢.

Specializes in hoyas, bougainvillaeas, and tropical hibiscus. Plants are described in detail, and complete cultural information is included.

"So far as I can find out, I have the largest listing (over eighty) of hoyas available anywhere—the result of collecting these beauties for about twenty years. Very few people can grow just one hoya—they love them and want more and more."

Maile's Anthurium, Ltd., 41-1019 Kakaina St., Waimanalo, HI 96795. (808)-395-5155. Price list. Minimum order, $8.00. Visitors by appointment.

Tropical plants, including anthuriums, orchids, dracaenas, palms, gingers, bougainvillaeas, philodendron hybrids, ferns. Large specimen plants are available on request.

McComb Greenhouses, Rte. 1, New Straitsville, OH 43766. (614)-394-2239. Illustrated catalog, 35¢. Open every day, 8 A.M.–5 P.M.

Extensive variety of houseplants, including begonias, geraniums, vines and creepers, mosses and ferns, cacti and succulents, bromeliads, herbs, and many others. A number of rarities. Most of the plants are illustrated in the catalog.

Merry Gardens, Box 595, Camden, ME 04843. Price list, 50¢. Minimum order, $10. Open Mon.–Sat., 9 A.M.–4 P.M.

Lengthy list of unusual and rare indoor plants, including begonias, fuchsias, hederas, cacti, ferns, and geraniums. Plants are illustrated in the booklet *The Merry Gardens Pictorial Handbook of Rare Indoor Plants,* which has 341 photos of indoor plants, along with botanical and common names and a key to culture. Price is $1.00, postpaid.

A large collection of unusual indoor plants, all labeled and priced, can be seen at the gardens —which also have attractive display areas all seasons of the year.

Merryspring—the Garden Spot of Maine Mary Ellen Ross, a nationally known horticulturist, and her husband, C. Ervin Ross, specialize in rare plants at Merry Gardens. But they also conceived the idea—now a reality—of a horticultural park on the Maine coast, near Camden.

Merryspring, a sixty-six-acre park, is devoted to the culture of flowers, shrubs, and trees in an unspoiled, natural setting, both to preserve their kind and to display them for nature lovers. A brochure on Merryspring is available on request from Merry Gardens —and a visit there is a "must" if you're in the area.

Shadow Lawn Nursery, 637 Holly Ln., Plantation, FL 33317. (305)-587-4792. Illustrated catalog, 26¢ (stamps or coin). Visitors by appointment.

Seeds of rare and unusual plants, suitable for indoor and greenhouse growing. Many aroids, anthuriums in all colors, dieffenbachias, aralias, bromeliads, several of the rarer crotons, ferns, bamboos, dracaenas, crossandras, many flowering trees and vines, and numerous others. Plants also available; send SASE for the list.

The nursery has a botanical garden, with over a thousand different plants and trees, which has been opened to the public through the Federated Garden Clubs.

Southern Gardens, Box 547, Riverview, FL 33569. Illustrated catalog, 25¢. (The catalog will be sent without charge if this book is mentioned.)

Succulents, cacti, aralias, and other rare plants. Also seeds of tropical trees, shrubs, and vines— many very rare—suitable for indoor or greenhouse growing.

Mary Walton, 1013 Park Dr., West Memphis, AR 72301. Descriptive price list; send two stamps.

Hundreds of listings of various houseplants, such as rhizomatous, fibrous, rex, and wax begonias, many types of geraniums, hoyas, philodendrons, ferns, cacti and succulents, African violets and other gesneriads. Small plants and freshly cut leaves.

World Gardens, Dept. G, 845

Pacific Ave., Willows, CA 95988. (916)-934-4701. Catalog, 35¢.

Unusual tropical seeds and plants. Many types of gingers, anthuriums, palms, bromeliads, orchids. Rare plants include bat-flower, autograph plant, jade vines, and white bird-of-paradise. Good descriptions. Culture in-structions are sent with each order. Three separate catalogs are mailed during the year, with the winter catalog listing just seeds (all three are included for the 35¢ payment).

"If customers want plants not listed in catalogs, we try to locate them."

Houseplant Basics

House Plant Primer, Handbk. 70, $1.50 from **Brooklyn Botanic Garden,** 1000 Washington Ave., Brooklyn, NY 11225. A guide for beginners to easy-to-grow kinds and their care.

Care of House Plants, $2.50 from **Colorado State University,** Bulletin Rm., Fort Collins, CO 80523. A home study course that covers all the fundamentals.

Insects and Related Pests of House Plants, G-67, 25¢ from the **Supt. of Documents,** Washington, DC 20402. Tells how to recognize and control the most common in-sects that attack your plants.

Data on Soilless Mixes

Technical information about two of the widely used mixes for container plants is given in the following booklets:

Cornell Peat-Lite Mixes, IB-43, 25¢ from **Cornell University,** Mailing Rm., Bldg. 7, Research Park, Ithaca, NY 14850.

U.C. Type Soil Mixes, Leaflet Nr. 89, from **University of California,** Public Service, University Hall, Berkeley, CA 94720. Sent without charge to California resi-dents. We suggest others include 25¢ to cover costs.

Specialized Growers

BEGONIAS

Antonelli Brothers, 2545 Capi-tola Rd., Santa Cruz, CA 95062. (408)-475-5222. Illustrated cat-alog. BAC and MC charges. Open daily, 9 A.M.–5 P.M.

Specialists, for over forty years, in tuberous begonias. Numerous Antonelli introductions. Rose forms, double rose forms, giant double ruffleds, miniatures, hang-

Also hundreds of varieties of geraniums, herbs, and indoor and tropical plants. There are good descriptions in the catalog. Growers since 1894.

"A tour through the greenhouses is a rewarding experience, as expressed by many of our visitors, 'like entering a real botanical garden.' Many of the mature specimens, such as bougainvillaeas, jasmines, allamandas, ferns, camellias, acacias, and a ponderosa lemon tree have been growing for over fifty years."

Paul P. Lowe, Mt. Vernon Springs, NC 27345. (919)-742-3796. Descriptive price list, 25¢. Minimum order, $10. U.S. sales only.

Over two hundred varieties of begonias, including several exclusive Lowe hybrids. Specializes in the odd, rare, and unusual types. No semperflorens or tuberous begonias. The list is updated regularly, with many new hybrids added each year.

ing-basket types, and many others. Also over forty varieties of ferns, and listings of gladioli, dahlias, fuchsias, and gloxinias.

Dutch Bulb Import Co. (Van Sciver's Dutch Gardens), Box 12, Tannersville, PA 18372. (717)-629-0573. Illustrated brochure. Open every day except Thurs., noon–9 P.M.

Imported tuberous begonias of many types. Also a wide variety of other Dutch bulbs.

Begonias are in bloom in display gardens in Tannersville from July to frost. Spring bulbs are in bloom from late April to June.

Logee's Greenhouses, 55 North St., Danielson, CT 06239. (203)-774-8038. Color illustrated catalog, $1.50. Minimum order, $10. Open Mon.–Sat., 9 A.M.–4 P.M.

Indoor-plant specialists, featuring some six hundred varieties of begonias—the largest commercial collection in the United States.

Don't Sneeze Near These Seeds!

If you've ever opened a package of begonia seeds and wondered where they were, it's understandable. Begonia seeds are among the tiniest of all. Some varieties average more than 2 million seeds per ounce.

Routh's Greenhouses, Rte. 65, Louisburg, MO 65685. (417)-752-3762. Descriptive price list, 25¢. U.S. sales only. Visitors welcome anytime except Sunday morning; phone ahead.

About 250 varieties of begonias. Also about one hundred varieties of African violets. All the plants are well described in the list. A begonia collector and specialist for nineteen years.

Vetterle's Begonia Gardens, Box 1246, Watsonville, CA 95076. (408)-722-5633. Illustrated catalog. Visitors welcome; phone ahead.

Tuberous begonias of many types and colors. Special collections are available. Good cultural information is in the catalog.

The gardens have fifteen acres of begonias in bloom from early July until October.

Mrs. Rosetta White, 1602 N.W. 3rd St., Abilene, KS 67410. (913)-263-2795. Price list; send stamp. U.S. sales only. Visitors welcome 9 A.M.–5 P.M.

Several hundred varieties of begonias, especially rex and miniatures. A selection of larger types. Many very uncommon.

"When I saw all the different varieties of begonias, I made up my mind to grow them all. It wasn't long before I had a business going, and it keeps getting bigger each year."

Wilson's Greenhouse (Mrs. Wilbur Wilson), Rte. 1, Box 165, Ozark, MO 65721. Descriptive price list; send stamp. The greenhouse is open "by chance or appointment."

Extensive list of begonias; angel wings, hirsute (hairy leaves), and other rare and odd types. Also about two hundred varieties of African violets. Freshly cut leaves and cuttings.

BROMELIADS

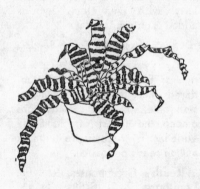

Beach Garden Nursery, 2131 Portola Dr., Santa Cruz, CA 95062. (408)-476-4087. Descriptive brochure; send SASE. Minimum order, $15. MC charge. Open Mon.–Sat., 9 A.M.–5 P.M.; Sun., 10 A.M.–5 P.M.

Bromeliads of all types. Many listings of aechmea, billbergia, cryptanthus, guzmania, neoregelia, nidularium, tillandsia, and vriesia. Numerous collectors' items. "Living pictures"—plants mounted on driftwood—a specialty. A general guide to care and culture of bromeliads sent with each order.

Nursery has display gardens with bromeliads in bloom in a natural setting.

Cornelison's Bromeliad Nursery, 225 San Bernardino St., North Fort Myers, FL 33903. (813)-995-4206. Illustrated price list; send stamp. Open Mon.–Fri., 10 A.M.–4 P.M.

Over 125 varieties of bromeliads, most imported from South America and Europe. Seedlings and mature plants. Many rarities.

Exoticus Tropical Plants (Robert Richfield), 108 Blossom Rd., Westport, MA 02790. (617)-675-2578. Price list. Minimum order, $10. Open Wed.–Sun., 9 A.M.–5 P.M.

Large variety of bromeliads including many aechmea, billbergia, cryptanthus, guzmania, neoregelia, nidularium, quesnelia, tillandsia, and vriesia. Imported and grown from seed. Many hybrids, seedlings, and specimen plants. Also some orchid species.

"Exoticus is devoted to the growing of quality stock. Our plants are all greenhouse grown and well established by the time they are ready for shipping."

Fuchsia Land (Mike Kashkin), 4629 Centinela Ave., Los Angeles, CA 90066. (213)-822-8900. Bromeliad catalog and succulent catalog; send a stamp for each. U.S. sales only. Open every day, 9 A.M.–5:30 P.M., February to November.

Some one thousand varieties of bromeliads, collected on annual trips to South American rain forests. Many new introductions every year. Succulent catalog describes over two hundred species; concentrates on the more unusual and choice varieties.

Fuchsias, begonias, ferns, geraniums, and other rare and unusual plants, not offered by mail, are available at the nursery.

"Many of our customers await our return from our annual safari to South America to purchase new and rare plants for their collections. We collect them ourselves, in the jungles. They are unique and gorgeous!"

Kent's Bromeliads, 4314 W. Slauson Ave., Los Angeles, CA 90043. (213)-776-0557. Catalog, 50¢. Minimum order, $20. Visitors by appointment.

Largest collection of bromeliads in the United States— second largest in the world. Hundreds, including many rarities, are listed in the catalog.

Blooming plants may be seen at the growing area, 703 Polemo Dr., Vista, CA 92083. Phone: (714)-758-2396.

"Our bromeliad collection is a labor of love and is an ongoing and thriving thing. There will always be new plants, both personally collected and imported— many 'unknown' and 'unnamed' species and natural hybrids."

Kerry's Nursery, 16245 S.W. 304th St., Homestead, FL 33030. (305)-247-5990. Price list, 15¢. Minimum order, $20. Visitors by appointment.

Many varieties of aechmea, billbergia, canistrum, cryptanthus, dyckia, guzmania, neoregelia, nidularium, tillandsia, vriesia, and others.

Marz Bromeliads, 10782 Citrus Dr., Moorpark, CA 93021. (805)-529-1897. Price list, 35¢ (credited). Minimum order, $7.00.

Bromeliad grower and importer for over fifteen years; grows from seed and offset. More than 250 different bromeliads, including Hummel hybrids. Landscape bromeliads, cold-hardy to Philadelphia. Introduced own select variety of *Aechmea orlandiana,* named "Charlie." Also rare hoyas and caudates—succulent bonsai.

"We are a small firm and intend to stay that way so we may continue to give personal service to our customers."

North Jersey Bromeliads, Box 181, Closter Dock Rd., Alpine, NJ 07620. (201)-767-3790. Price list, 25¢. Minimum order, $15. BAC charge. U.S. sales only. Open every day, 10 A.M.–6 P.M.

Very extensive list of bromeliads, some 1,500 varieties. Mature plants and seedlings. Also creative arrangements on driftwood and other materials. A culture sheet is sent with each shipment.

"Started as a collection five years ago, the company is growing expediently with the new-found interest for bromeliads. Most of our bromeliads have been raised in our greenhouses. We will be glad to answer any specific questions."

Seaborn Del Dios Nursery (Bill Seaborn), Rte. 3, Box 455, Escondido, CA 92025. (714)-745-6945. Price list, $1.00 (credited). Open every day, 9 A.M.–5:30 P.M.

Very extensive collection of bromeliads—over 850 species. Some rarities, hybrids, and mutations. Also palms, cycads, and other tropical plants, some extremely rare.

Seaborn, who has been collecting rare plants for twenty-nine years, recently completed a book on bromeliads with several hundred pictures in full color.

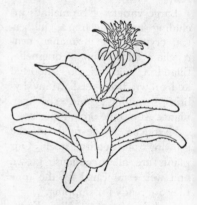

Grow a Pineapple

The most familiar bromeliad is the pineapple. To start a plant from a store-bought pineapple, cut off most of the top leaves, slice off all but a small section of fruit, and scoop out the pulp. Let it dry, dust with a rooting powder, and plant it. Keep the soil moist but not soggy. In time, a new pineapple may develop in the center of the leaf rosette.

Velco's Bromeliad Nursery, 2905 Washington Blvd., Marina Del Rey, CA 90291. (213)-821-2493. Price list, $1.00 (credited). Minimum order $25. Open every day, 9 A.M.–4:30 P.M.

Extensive list of bromeliads, many types and varieties. Also fern-wood totems, boards and plaques, and cork bark.

Walther's Exotic House Plants, Rte. 3, Box 30, Hwy. 9-W, Cats-kill, NY 12414. (518)-943-3730. Illustrated brochure, $1.00 (credited). Minimum order, $15. Open daily, 10 A.M.–6 P.M.

Specialist in tillandsias mounted on cork bark, hand-carved plaques, and sculptures. Also many other tropical plants, including succulents, ferns, gesneriads, begonias. Hanging baskets, terrariums, handmade ceramics, and pottery.

CACTI AND OTHER SUCCULENTS

Abbey Garden, 176 Toro Canyon Rd., Carpinteria, CA 93013. (805)-684-5112. Illustrated catalog, $1.00. Minimum order, $10.

Very extensive listing of cacti and other succulents—about half are rare and not generally available. The catalog, which has some 138 photos, contains much cultural information. Abbey Garden supplies collectors, botanists, universities, and botanical gardens throughout the world.

Barnett Cactus Garden, 1104 Meadowview Dr., Bossier City, LA 71010. (318)-746-7121. Descriptive price list; send stamp. Open Sat. and Sun. by appointment.

Cacti and other succulents, many collected from Mexico. Numerous varieties of echinocereus, echinocactus, mammillaria, and notocactus. Special collections are available.

Helen & John Braniff, Box 31,

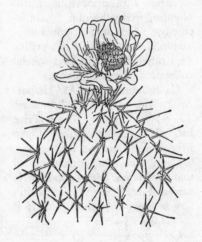

Egg Harbor City, NJ 08215. Illustrated catalog, 50¢. Minimum order, $6.00.

Many varieties of cacti and other succulents. Plants are available in 2½–6-inch pot sizes; some specimen or rare varieties from one foot to over three feet. Also a cactus/succulent plant-of-the-

month club. There are good illustrations of varieties in the catalog.

Cactus by Mueller, 10411
Rosedale Hwy., Bakersfield, CA
93308. (805)-589-2674. Catalog,
50¢ (credited). Open every day
except Tues. and Wed. 10 A.M.–5
P.M.

Many uncommon lithops, cono-
phytum, and titanopsis. Also varieties of eriocactus, ferocactus,
gymnocalycium, echinopsis hybrids, and others.

Cactus Gem Nursery, 18435
Rea Ave., Box 327, Aromas, CA
95004. Price list.

Varieties of ariocarpus, astrophytum, coryphantha, echinocereus, ferocactus, numerous
mammillaria, agave, haworthia.
Also other succulents and special
collections of related plants.

**Cactusland (Chas. M. Fitzpat-
rick),** Rte. 3, Box 44, Edinburg,
TX 78539. (512)-383-2296. Price
list. U.S. sales only. Open
Mon.–Sat., 7 A.M.–5 P.M.

Cacti and other succulents of
many varieties. Many moderately
priced. Fitzpatrick has the world's
largest private cactus garden; it
covers twenty acres.

**Collector's Succulents (Cath-
ryn Mangold),** 548 Crestline
Dr., Los Angeles, CA 90049.
(213)-472-4929. Price list, 50¢
(credited). Minimum order, $10.
Open Sun., by appointment.

Specializes in lithops, conoph-
ytum, and other mesembryanthemums; crassula; and haworthia.
Very extensive list. Also lithops
seeds.

"My nursery is a small, personally operated extension of my
hobby, which is raising interesting
succulents."

*Take a Look at My
Coleocephalocereus Fluminensis!*

A quick way to impress your
friends is to grow a few cacti and
other succulents. Then you can talk
like this:

You must see my *Echinocactus
horizonthalonius.* And my *Grap-
topetalum paraguayense* is really
thriving. Just traded a small *Le-
maireocereus marginatus* for an
Astrophytum myriostigma. If you'd
care for a *Neobuxbaumia euphor-
biodes,* I've got one to spare. I
sure hope my *Zygocactus truncatus*
blooms for Christmas.

[Might be a good idea to bone
up on basic Latin before you roll
off these names.]

Desert Dan's Cactus, W. Summer Ave., Minotola, NJ 08341.
(609)-697-2366. Illustrated catalog, 50¢. Open Sat. and Sun., by
appointment.

About one thousand varieties of
cacti and other succulents; many
rarities. Also a selection of unusual grafted cacti.

Desert Plant Co., Box 880,
Marfa, TX 79843. (915)-729-
4943. Illustrated catalog, $1.00.

Native cacti of the Southwest,
such as Texas Night Blooming
Cereus, Devil's Head, Texas
Rainbow, Eagle Claw, Little Chi-
lie. Good photos and descriptions
of plants. Some rarities.

A. Hugh Dial, 7587 Deer Trail, Yucca Valley, CA 92284. (714)-365-3743. Price list, 50¢. Open every day, 8 A.M.–4 P.M.; phone ahead.

Exotic and rare agaves, yuccas, aloes, and other succulents. Very extensive listings. A grower for over fifty years.

Fernwood Plants (Roger Weld), Box 268, Topanga, CA 90290. (213)-455-1176. Catalog, 50¢. Minimum order, $10. Open every day, 8 A.M. to dusk.

Cacti and other succulents, with emphasis on the rare and unusual. Echeverias, aloes, mesembryanthemums, epiphytic cacti, and many others.

"A visit to our nursery would be beneficial, as it's not possible to list everything. Everyone who has been here has commented on its beauty and uniqueness."

Grigsby Cactus Gardens, 2326 Bella Vista, Vista, CA 92083. (714)-727-1323. Illustrated catalog, $1.00 (credited). Minimum order, $10. Open Thurs.–Sat., 8 A.M.–4 P.M.

Cacti and other succulent plants, including many rarities. Specimen plants available. Plants are illustrated and well described. Cactus growers for over twelve years—gardens cover four acres.

Helen's Cactus (Helen Winans), 2205 Mirasol, Brownsville, TX 78520. (512)-542-5117. Price list; send stamp. Minimum order, $6.00. Visitors by appointment.

Cacti, collected and grown from seed. Various other succulents including some rare African species.

"A small business, one person owner and operator. Visitors are welcome, but better to call first."

Henrietta's Nursery, 1345 N. Brawley, Fresno, CA 93711. (209)-237-7166. Illustrated catalog, 35¢. Minimum order, $12.

One of the world's largest collections of cacti and other succulents—over one thousand varieties. Also seed, fertilizers, special vitamins for cacti and succulents, and many related books.

Jack's Cactus Garden (Jack Feldman), 1707 W. Robindale St., West Covina, CA 91790. (213)-338-8331. Price list, 25¢. U.S. sales only. Visitors by appointment.

Many varieties of echeverias, aloes, crassulas, as well as other succulents. A selection of cactus seeds. A family-owned and -operated business since 1957.

Prickly Pear Cactus for Dinner

Pads of prickly pear cactus, commonly called nopals, can be used just like green peppers (and they're a lot cheaper), according to an article by home economists in *Progressive Agriculture in Arizona*. A generous serving supplies about half the daily recommended allowance of vitamin C.

To prepare, scrape off stickers, peel off outer skin, and parboil until tender. They're great on pizza, say the authors.

K&L Cactus Nursery, 12712 Stockton Blvd., Galt, CA 95632. (209)-745-2563. Illustrated catalog, 50¢. Minimum order, $10. Open Mon.–Fri., 9 A.M.–5 P.M.; Sat. and Sun. by appointment.

Cacti and other succulent plants, including many rare Mexican cacti and grafted cacti imported from Japan. Seeds of twenty-four varieties.

Specimen-size Mexican cacti and holiday cacti are sold at the nursery.

"Each year, we try to add at least fifty new types of cacti and succulents to our catalog listing, and we're trying to add the same number of new photos. We've always found it hard to buy a plant without seeing a photo or picture of it first."

Kirkpatrick's, 27785 De Anza St., Barstow, CA 92311. (714)-252-3254. Price list; send stamp.

Minimum order, $10. Visitors by appointment.

Rare, hard-to-obtain cacti and other succulents for advanced collectors and botanic gardens. Brazilian cacti a specialty. Also cactus seeds and numerous related books.

Loehman's Cactus Patch, 8014 Howe St., Box 871, Paramount, CA 90723. (213)-633-1704. Illustrated catalog, 30¢. Minimum order, $7.50. Open Sat. and Sun., 11 A.M.–5 P.M.

Many varieties of cacti and other succulents, some quite rare. Collections at special prices. Limited selection of seeds and specimen plants.

"Our company is still small enough to be personal. Questions are answered as quickly and as completely as possible."

Modlins Cactus Gardens, 2416 El Corto, Vista, CA 92083. (714)-727-1761. Price list, 25¢. Open every day except Monday and Tuesday; phone ahead.

Extensive listing of mammillarias; also many other cacti, including grafts, and other succulents. The list indicates height and diameter in metric measurements. [A good idea for other companies to follow. The coming generation of gardeners is now learning metrics in kindergarten.]

New Mexico Cactus Research, Box 787, Belen, NM 87002. (504)-864-4027. Catalog. Visitors by appointment.

Seeds of cacti and other succulents—over three thousand varie-ies. Most are exclusive with the company, or rare and uncommon. Ships seeds to seventy countries throughout the world.

Singers' Growing Things, 6385 Enfield Ave., Reseda, CA 91335. (213)-343-8304. Illustrated catalog, 50¢ (credited). Minimum order, $10. Visitors by appointment.

Specializes in succulent plants and caudiciforms; one of the largest collections in the world. Cycads, many euphorbias, cotyledons, cyphostemmas, pachypodiums. A recent introduction is seedling plants of *Adansonia digitala,* the baobab tree. Culture notes are included in the catalog.

"Our specialty is African and Mexican succulent plants with curious shapes, infrequently seen, and exciting for any person, collector and novice alike. The plants are usable as bonsai plants, can be grown indoors, and make wonderful conversation pieces. Easily grown with minimum care."

Ed Storms, 4223 Pershing, Fort Worth, TX 76107. (817)-732-7112. Illustrated catalog, 35¢. Minimum order, $7.50.

Specialist in mesembryanthemums, particularly lithops; one of the most extensive selections of these plants available. Storms, an international authority on lithops, has written the book *Growing the Mesembs,* which has habitat information gathered on a trip to South Africa plus tips on growing the plants in home and greenhouse environments. Has ninety-six color photos of lithops plus photos of other mesembs; the price is $3.50.

"Whether you call them 'Stone faces,' 'Living stones,' 'Flowering-stones,' or (preferably!) lithops, they are undoubtedly the jewels of the plant world. Resembling the pebbles and stones among which they grow in habitat, their subtle colors of gray, brown, rust, green, and pink, combined with their fantastically intricate markings, make them a source of continuous pleasure."

Dick Wright, Rte. 3, Box 21, De Luz Rd., Fallbrook, CA 92028. (714)-728-2383. Illustrated price list, 25¢. Open daily, 9 A.M.–5 P.M.

Features echeverias; many varieties with detailed descriptions are in the list. Also euphorbias, aloes, and other succulents. Many new hybrids and novelties.

Cacti for Cold Climates

Contrary to some beliefs, not all cacti are tropical plants. Some, in fact, are hardy in winters where temperatures may dip to a bone-chilling −40°. These cold-climate cacti and other succulents are a specialty of Ben Haines Co., 1902 Lane, Topeka, KS 66604. The price list is 40¢.

An excellent book about these hardy plants is *Handbook of Cold Climate Cacti and Succulents,* $3.25 postpaid. Written by Ben Haines, the sixty-five-page book has photos, descriptions, and cultural information.

Cactus Info

Succulent Plants, Handbk. 43, $1.50 from **Brooklyn Botanic Garden,** 1000 Washington Ave., Brooklyn, NY 11225, describes native American cacti, South African "flowering stones," and others; tells how to grow hardy and tender succulents; includes an illustrated dictionary.

The **Abbey Garden Press,** Box 3010, Santa Barbara, CA 93105, has one of the most extensive listings of cactus and succulent books available. Titles range from *Cactus Growing for Beginners* to *Genera of the Mesembryanthemaceae.* Send a stamp for a copy of their list.

CARNIVOROUS PLANTS

Armstrong Associates, Inc., Box 94, Kennebunk, ME 04043. (207)-985-3161. Color illustrated catalog, 25¢ (credited).

Full line of carnivorous plants, from venus fly-traps to cobra lilies. Also rare terrarium plants and living lichens. Terrariums and miniature greenhouse kits. Special collections of related plants.

A display of all the plants may be seen at Mapes Garden Center in Kennebunk; open Mon.–Sat., 9 A.M.–5 P.M. Garden seminars and slide shows are held weekly in the spring.

Peter Pauls Nurseries, Canandaigua, NY 14424. (315)-394-7397. Illustrated brochure; send SASE. Open first Saturday and second Sunday of each month except August; phone ahead.

Some fifty species of carnivorous plants including hybrid sundews and pitcher plants; also seeds of twenty species. Many varieties. An excellent guide to growing carnivorous plants is *The*

World of Carnivorous Plants, by Pietropaolo. The book, illustrated with sixty-eight photos, is $6.30 postpaid.

Pitcher Plant a New Insecticide?

The carnivorous pitcher plant paralyzes its insect victim until it's ready to digest it. Paralysis is caused by two amine-based compounds in the plant, and Mississippi State University scientists think this may be a clue to a new type of insecticide.

Sun Dew Environments, Box 503, Boston, MA 02215. (617)-254-0587. Brochure-price list sent without charge; color illustrated catalog, 50¢. Retail plant shop at 1155 Commonwealth, Allston, MA; open Mon.–Sat., 10 A.M.–6 P.M.

Wide variety of carnivorous plants; many rare and unavailable elsewhere. All the plants are commercially propagated. Numerous books on carnivorous plants, and growing supplies. The

talog has photos and descrip-
ons of plants along with cultural
formation.

In addition to carnivorous
ants, the retail shop also sells

orchids, gesneriads, cacti and
other succulents, and a wide variety of common and uncommon
foliage plants.

EPIPHYLLUMS

California Epi Center, Dept.
, Box 2474, Van Nuys, CA
404. Catalog, 35¢. Minimum
rder, $10.

More than 150 hybrid epiphyl-
ms in a complete selection of
lors and bloom sizes. A special
tarter collection" is available.
he catalog has cultural instruc-
ons for the novice.

"We hope eventually to spe-
alize in the hybrids that have a
nall bloom, as these bloom heav-
y and 'off season' (i.e., early in
e blooming season), and are
mewhat more suitable for lim-
ed spaces, as they grow more
owly than plants with large
looms."

Cox's Epiphyllum Nursery, 90
IcNeill St., Encinitas, CA 92024.
714)-753-3048. Illustrated cata-
g, 35¢. Minimum order, $7.00.
pen every day, 11 A.M.–5 P.M.

Rooted and unrooted cuttings
f epiphyllums; many varieties,

including miniatures. Special collections for beginners.

"If you like beautiful, vivid, iri-
descent flowers, unlike any others
you have ever seen, and if you are
very busy or want to go fishing
for a week, then epiphyllums are
for you. They are very easy to
grow and will tolerate more neg-
lect than any other type of plant
and still reward you with large,
vivid blooms in the spring."

Hawks Nursery, 2508 E. Vista
Way, Vista, CA 92083. (714)-
758-1282. Catalog, 40¢. Open
daily, 9 A.M.–5 P.M.

Very extensive list of epiphyllums; over seven hundred named
varieties are in the catalog, including many new hybrids. Both
rooted and unrooted cuttings.

Ferns, various cacti, and several hundred epiphyllums not
listed in the catalog are available
at the nursery.

FUCHSIAS

Hidden Springs Nursery, Rte.
, Rockmart, GA 30153. (404)-
45-4268. Illustrated catalog, 20¢
credited). Minimum order, $10.
isitors by appointment.

Rooted cuttings of some seventy-five varieties of fuchsias.
Propagated from acclimatized
stock and tested for heat resist-
ance. Some varieties hardy in the

Atlanta, Georgia, area; many suitable as houseplants. New varieties are introduced yearly.

Culture of fuchsias, as well as background about Hidden Springs Nursery (a group of three families and friends), is covered in a ten-page, color illustrated booklet, *Fuchsias in the South,* $1.95 postpaid. In it, author Hector Black writes:

"We earn our livelihood with our nursery and a small whole-wheat bakery. We cultivate our land by organic methods. We are very interested in conservation and alternate sources of energy. Our practical life together is an attempt to make it a reflection of our deeper beliefs."

Wileywood Nurseries, Inc., Box 2628, Lynnwood, WA 98036. Catalog, $1.00 (credited). Minimum order, $12.50. MC charge. U.S. sales only.

Some 290 varieties of fuchsia both hanging-basket and uprig types, and some fuchsia specie Also unusual rock-garden plan and ferns, philodendrons, a various perennials.

The nursery, at 17474 Both Way, S.E., in Bothell, Washin ton, is open Sat. and Sun., A.M.–7 P.M.

GERANIUM

Carobil Farms, Church Rd., Rte. 1, Brunswick, ME 04011. (207)-725-6778. Catalog, 35¢. Open daily, 9 A.M.–5 P.M.

Over four hundred varieties of geraniums, including miniature and dwarf, dwarf tetraploid, ivy leaf, fancy leaf, regal, species, and many European types. Carobil handles new introductions from plant breeders looking for national distribution.

Cook's Geranium Nursery, 712 N. Grand, Lyons, KS 67554. (316)-257-5033. Catalog, 35¢. Open every day, 8 A.M.–6 P.M.

Geraniums of all types—doub zonals, single zonals, rega scented, fancy and ivy leaves, sp cies, dwarfs. Many own intr ductions and numerous unusu and rare types.

"We conduct an extensiv breeding program to produce ne and better varieties, to improv old varieties by selection, to bui up a stronger, more disease-resis ant, better, and larger-bloomir plant."

Wilson Brothers Floral C Inc., Roachdale, IN 4617 (317)-596-3455. Color illustrate catalog. BAC and MC charges. Open every day, 8:30 A.M.–5 P.M.

Geranium growers for over fifty years. All types, including many unusual varieties. Also extensive list of African violets and many uncommon houseplants, flowering and foliage. Special collections of geraniums and African violets.

The greenhouses are situated in Raccoon, Indiana, about forty miles west of Indianapolis.

Is it a Geranium, a Pelargonium, or a Saxifrage?

The geraniums referred to here are those familiar, colorful plants on windowsills and gardens that most people call "geraniums." But the correct botanical name is *Pelargonium*. The true botanical geranium, often called crane's-bill, is a hardy herbaceous plant that usually blooms in spring. And that popular hanging-basket plant, with its long runners and little plantlets attached, called a "strawberry geranium," is neither geranium nor

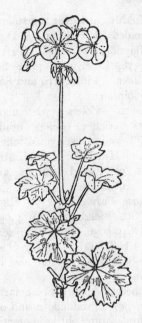

pelargonium. It's a *Saxifraga stolonifera*.

Sources for botanical geraniums include The White Flower Farm and Wayside Gardens (plants) and J. L. Hudson (seeds).

GESNERIADS

Al's Violets (Albert G. Krieger), 1063 Cranbrook Dr., Jackson, MI 49201. (517)-782-1158. Descriptive price list; send SASE. U.S. sales only. Visitors by appointment.

Extensive collection of achimenes, episcias, African-violet varieties and species (most with hybridizer's name), sinningias, and streptocarpus. Many miniatures suitable for terrariums. Plants and freshly cut leaves and stolons.

Annalee Violetry, 29–50 214th Pl., Bayside, NY 11360. (212)-224-3376. Descriptive price list; send SASE. Visitors, Fri. and Sat., by appointment.

African violets, particularly newest varieties, trailers, miniatures, and variegated-foliage types. Hybridizers indicated. Plants or rooted clumps and freshly cut leaves.

Louise Barnaby, 12178 Highview St., Vicksburg, MI 49097. (616)-649-9036. Price list; send SASE. U.S. sales only. Open Tues.–Sat., 9 A.M.–4 P.M., by appointment.

Numerous African-violet starter plants, new introductions and old favorites. Many have potential for show plants. An African-violet grower for over twenty-five years.

Buell's Greenhouses, Inc., Box 218, Weeks Rd., Eastford, CT 06242. (203)-974-0623. Descriptive list, 25¢ plus SASE. Open Mon.–Sat., 8 A.M.–5 P.M.

Gesneriads of all types: gloxinias; miniature African violets, including trailers; over five hundred varieties of standard-size African violets, including trailers; over fifty varieties of columneas; forty varieties of episcias; twenty varieties of aeschynanthus; and many others. Numerous miniature gesneriads, many suitable for terrariums.

Mr. Albert H. Buell, a gesneriad specialist, is internationally known for his hybrid gloxinias.

Greenhouses, in Eastford, have some 150,000 African violets and a multitude of exotic gesneriad relatives.

David Buttram, Box 193, Independence, MO 64051. (816)-373-4679. Descriptive price list, 25¢. U.S. sales only. Minimum order, $6.00.

New varieties of African violets, especially selected for ease of growing by amateurs. Complete line of growing supplies including Jungle Growth products, insecticides, soil mixes, plant foods, and plastic and self-watering pots.

"I am certified as a judge by the African Violet Society of America and Saintpaulia International. Will be glad to answer any questions."

Chrysler's Gesneriad House, 140 Petworth Crescent, Agincourt, Ont. M1S 3M5. (519)-293-3423. Descriptive price list, 15¢. Visitors by appointment.

Gesneriads, including African violets, aeschynanthus, codonanthe, columnea, diastema, dry-

nonia, gloxinia, episcia, nautiloc-
lyx nematanthus, sinningia, and
treptocarpus. Some own origina-
ions. Clumps, leaves, or rooted
uttings. Included with each or-
ler is a stamped, addressed post-
ard so customers can report how
heir orders arrived.

"Each year, we try to include
ome new plants as well as bring
back some older varieties. All of
our plants are grown under
luorescent lights with lots of
T.L.C. They are also used to
being talked to."

Doris Drennen, 1415 Central
Ave., Sandusky, OH 44870. Descriptive price list, 20¢.

Extensive list of African violets
from many prominent hybridizers. Starter plants, rooted leaves,
and freshly cut leaves. Also other
gesneriads, including episcias, columneas, and nematanthus.

L. Easterbrook, Greenhouses,
10 Craig St., Butler, OH 44822.
(419)-883-3931. Catalog, $1.25.
Minimum order, $15. Open every
day except Thursday and Sunday,
9 A.M.–noon and 1 P.M.–5 P.M.

One of the largest gesneriad
collections in the United States;
many own originations as well as
those of other hybridizers. Also
cacti and other succulents, begonias, hoyas, gingers, various
other tropical plants, herbs, and
bonsai stock. Everything required
in growing supplies.

Fischer Greenhouses, Oak
Ave., Linwood, NJ 08221.
(609)-927-3399. Illustrated plant
catalog and illustrated supplies

catalog, 40¢ for both. Open daily,
8 A.M.–5 P.M.

Hybrid African-violet introductions, including "Fischer Bal-
let," plus many from other
breeders. Also miniature African
violets, episcias, and other gesneriads. Supplies include a wide
selection of indoor growing
needs; fluorescent tubes and
stands, timers, trays, pots, plant
foods, misters.

**Green Thumb Home Nursery
(Mrs. Leland Kincaid),** Box 43,
Ramsey, WV 25912. (304)-658-
4724. Descriptive price list, 50¢
(credited). Open Mon.–Sat., 3
P.M.–5 P.M.

Over nine hundred varieties of
African violets; plants and freshly
cut leaves; many unusual crosses.
Also episcias, columneas, and
nematanthus. Mrs. Kincaid, who
grows all her plants in her home,
says:

"An African violet is as individual as a person. Some people
think African violets are hard to
grow. The trouble is that they are
starting off with diseased stock.
Nothing is as easy to grow as a
healthy African violet."

**Heavenly Violets (Mrs. Mary
V. Boose),** 9 Turney Pl., Trumbull, CT 06611. (203)-268-4368.
Price list, 20¢. Visitors by appointment.

Many varieties of African violets; some new hybrids by Cora
and Newell Mallette. Freshly cut
leaves. Currently the only source
for Irene Fredette originals. Also
freshly cut episcia stolons. Offers

a rooting service. Mrs. Boose, an African Violet Society of America judge, has won numerous awards for her plants.

Plants, as well as freshly cut leaves, are available at her home, plus plastic pots, soils, and fertilizers.

The House of Violets (Ralph & Charlyne Reed), 936–40 Garland St. S.W., Camden, AR 71701. (501)-836-3016. Price list; send stamp. U.S. sales only. Open Mon.–Sat., 9 A.M.–5 P.M.; Sun. by appointment.

African violets; starter plants; own introductions as well as from many other hybridizers. Also Aquamatic and Moist-Rite self-watering planters.

Theo Jensen, 4090 W. Barnes, Rte. 2, Millington, MI 48746. Price list, 20¢.

Extensive list of African violets; freshly cut leaves. Various collections are available at special prices.

Klinkel's African Violets, 1553 Harding St., Enumclaw, WA 98022. (206)-825-4442. Descriptive price list, 25¢ (credited). Open 10 A.M.–4 P.M.; phone ahead.

Miniature and semiminiature African violets, about three hundred varieties. Also standard and variegated-leaf types. Hybridizers are indicated. Both plants and freshly cut leaves.

Visitors are welcome but, because of lack of space, must be limited to four at a time.

Knowlton's African Violets, 715 W. Housatonic St., Pittsfield, MA 01201. (413)-442-3251. Price list; send stamp. Visitors are welcome every day after 1 P.M.

African violets of all types—more than five hundred varieties. Freshly cut leaves. (Plants and growing supplies are available at home in Pittsfield.)

"Bought my first African violet at a show in Albany, New York, in 1956. Now have thousands."

Louise's Greenhouse (Louise Pitts), Box 767, Sour Lake, TX 77659. (713)-287-3387. Price list, 20¢. Visitors by appointment.

Over a thousand varieties of African violets. Freshly cut leaves.

Plants and cuttings of African violets and other gesneriads, as well as soils and fertilizers, are sold at the greenhouse.

Lyndon Lyon Greenhouses, 14 Mutchler St., Dolgeville, NY

13329. (315)-429-3591. Illustrated catalog; send stamp. Open every day, 8 A.M.–6 P.M.

Many outstanding Lyon hybridizations of African violets and other gesneriads, such as columneas, dwarf and miniature sinningias, hypocyrta, and achimenes.

Numerous exotic plants, not listed in the catalog, are available at the greenhouse.

Park Nursery, 1200 St. Clair Ave., St. Paul, MN 55105. (612)-698-5557. Illustrated price list; send stamp. U.S. sales only. BAC charge. Open Mon.–Sat., 8 A.M.–5 P.M.

African violets, hundreds of varieties, all hybridized by Vernon Lorenzen. Lorenzen, who has been breeding violets since age eleven, has introduced many top winners, such as "Dora Baker," "Mrs. Greg," and "Yuletide."

African violets, plus unusual gesneriads, various exotic tropical plants, special organic potting mix, and growing supplies are available at the nursery.

The Plant Room, 6373 Trafalgar Rd., Hornby, Ont. L0P 1E0. (416)-878-4984. Catalog, 35¢. Minimum order, $8.50. Open Mon.–Fri., 10 A.M.–4 P.M.; other times by appointment.

Freshly cut leaves of African violets, including miniatures, and variegated miniatures and standards. Also extensive list of other gesneriads, miniature roses, dwarf and miniature geraniums, begonias, and various flowering and foliage plants. Many books on indoor plants.

San Francisco Plant Co. (Mrs. Alberta Flora), Box 575, Daly City, CA 94014. (415)-992-9998. Illustrated brochure, 25¢. U.S. sales only.

All types of African violets; excellent selection of miniatures. Plants are well described, and hybridizers are listed.

Schmelling's African Violets, 5133 Peck Hill Rd., Jamesville, NY 13078. (315)-446-1539. Leaf list, 25¢. *Cultural Circular,* 25¢. Minimum order, $6.00. U.S. sales only. Visitors by appointment.

Leaf cuttings of some 250 new and most popular varieties of African violets. Also Magic Starter Kits for propagating leaves, plant mixes, organic potting soil, pots, and other supplies. Over twenty-five years of practical experience with African violets.

Tinari Greenhouses, 2325 Valley Rd., Box 190, Huntingdon Valley, PA 19006. (215)-947-0155. Color illustrated catalog, 25¢. Open Mon.–Sat., 8 A.M.–5 P.M. Sun., 1 P.M.–5 P.M. (closed Sun., June through September) at greenhouses in Bethayres, PA. (215)-947-0144.

African violets of all types. Specialists and hybridizers for more than thirty years. Also many types of fluorescent light units, growing supplies, and books.

At the greenhouses, groups of the many varieties grown are assembled in one area so that visitors can better become acquainted with them. A gift shop offers unusual pottery, planting aids, and lighting equipment.

Vincent Greenhouses, 96 Paul Molbert Rd., Judice, Duson, LA 70529. (318)-873-8437. Price list; send SASE. Visitors by appointment (call before 7 A.M.).

Rooted cuttings of a wide variety of African violets. Also Flora light-garden carts, self-watering pots, insecticides, and fertilizers.

The Violet House, 1480 S. Jersey Way Denver, CO 80222. (303)-756-2950. Price list plus culture list, 35¢. Visitors by appointment.

Over a thousand varieties of African violets, including own hybridizations. Also other gesneriads, gesneriad seed, house and terrarium plants, bonsai and flower-arranging supplies, and growing supplies. African-violet specialist for over thirty years.

"Plants' reactions to stimuli are fascinating. My plants have always responded to my touch and voice—especially a fern, which waves its fronds when I speak softly or in time to music, droops fronds when my big dog barks. People today are so busy they don't pause to truly *look* at their plants or see their reactions."

L. Volkart's African Violets, Rte. 1, Box 216, Russellville, MO 65074. Price list, 20¢. Visitors welcome, Mon.–Sat.

Freshly cut leaves of African violets. Introductions from leading hybridizers plus superior selections of older varieties. Also other gesneriads.

Wood's African Violets, Proton Station, Ont., NoC 1Lo. (519)-923-6123. Brochure-price list, 15¢. Minimum order, $7.00. Open every day, 10 A.M.–7 P.M.

African violets; originations of Ernest Fisher as well as other hybridizers. Rooted clumps, freshly cut leaves. Numerous growing supplies including Fisher's formula for African-violet soil mix.

Visitors from the United States who plan to purchase plants should notify three days in advance so that necessary permits may be obtained.

Photograph Your Flowers

In just a few minutes of movie time, gloxinia buds turn into magnificent flowers, and a midget cucumber growing under lights twines itself around a neighboring geranium. Time-lapse photography is a fascinating garden hobby.

Time-lapse devices, which work with motor-drive 8mm movie cameras or 35mm still cameras with motor or spring film advance are available from both **American Science Center, Inc.** (5700 Northwest Hwy., Chicago, IL 60646) and **Edmund Scientific Co.** (555 Edscorp Bldg., Barrington, NJ 08021). The price is around $200.

You'll find a lot of helpful hints on taking pictures of flowers in the pamphlet *Kodak Tips on Taking Flower Pictures.* It's 15¢, from photo dealers or by mail from **Eastman Kodak Co.,** Dept. 454, Rochester, NY 14650.

Orchid plants for home growing—cool, warm, and intermediate temperatures. Many orchids
suitable for terrariums. Species
and botanical orchids, including
outdoor-growing lady-slippers, not
normally available. Also supplies
and orchid books. A color illustrated booklet on orchid growing
is $1.50 postpaid.

Bates Orchids, 7911 U. S. Hwy.
301, Ellenton, FL 33532.
(813)-722-2297. Catalog. AEX,
BAC, and MC charges. Open
Mon.–Sat., 8 A.M.–4:30 P.M.;
other times by appointment only.

Species and hybrid orchids,
many varieties, available in flats
and community pots. Seed flasking and reflasking services. Orchid-growing supplies.

"We plan to increase our species collection so that we may
offer many of the hard-to-get jungle orchids at a reasonable price
to everyone. This will also help
eliminate the need to strip the
environment of orchids."

The Beall Co., Box 467, Vashon Island, WA 98070.
(206)-463-9151. Catalog. AEX,
BAC, and MC charges. Open
Mon.–Fri., 8 A.M.–4 P.M.

Specializes in odontoglossum
and oncidium intergenerics. Also
cattleyas, paphiopedilums, phalaenopsis, and many others, including some species orchids. In
business some seventy years.

"We are known throughout the
world for our advanced hybridization of art-shade Cattleyas and

**Armacost & Royston of Santa
Barbara, Inc.,** 3376 Foothill Rd.,
Box 385, Carpinteria, CA 93013.
(805)-684-5448. Color illustrated
catalog, $2.00 (credited). Mini-
mum order, $12.50. BAC charge.
Open every day, 8 A.M.–4:30 P.M.

Many varieties of cattleya,
paphiopedilum, phalaenopsis, and
species orchids. Orchid books and
growing supplies. Founded in
1918, one of the largest orchid
breeders in the United States.

Bailey Orchids Victoria, 1055
Trans Canada Hwy., Victoria,
B.C. V8Z 1L1. (604)-479-1777.
Price list, 25¢. Open Mon.–Sat.,
9 A.M.–5 P.M.; phone ahead.

unusual bi-generics of the Oncidium alliance."

Black River Orchids, Inc., Box
110, 77th St., South Haven, MI
49090. (616)-637-5085. Price
list. BAC and MC charges. Open
Mon.–Sat., 9 A.M.–5 P.M.

Orchid species—many ex-
tremely rare—from all parts of
the world. Also hybrid orchids
and a complete line of growing
supplies. Orchid growers for over
twenty-five years, with the largest
orchid collection in Michigan.

"Our place is listed as an at-
traction of interest for tourists in
the area. We have thousands of
visitors each year."

Carter & Holmes, Inc., Box
668, Newberry, SC 29108.
(803)-276-0579. Price list. Minimum order, $10. Open Mon.–
Fri., 8 A.M.–5 P.M.; Sat., 8 A.M.–
noon.

Hybrid and meristem cattleyas
as well as many other varieties.
Orchid specialists for over thirty
years.

In addition to orchids, the
greenhouses have ferns, bromeliads, and other house and foliage plants, plus a full line of
growing supplies.

"Visitors are welcome at the
greenhouses. Highly trained personnel, informal and friendly at-
mosphere, and free growing advice to all comers."

Coastal Gardens, 137 Tropical
Ln., Corpus Christi, TX 78408.
(512)-882-9896. Price list. Minimum order, $15. Visitors by ap-
pointment.

Exotic and unusual orchids
from around the world. Also own
hybrids and unique miniature
plants suited to terrariums. Many
growing supplies.

Clark Day, Jr., Orchids, 19311
S. Bloomfield Ave., Cerritos, CA
90701. (213)-865-8270. Price list.
Minimum order, $15. Open every
day, 10 A.M.–5 P.M.

Cattleyas, miniature cymbidiums, cymbidium divisions,
awarded paphiopedilums, and
paphiopedilum seedlings.

Everglades Orchids, 751½ S. E.
Ave. F, Belle Glade, FL 33430
(305)-996-9600. Price list. Minimum order, $10. Open Mon.–
Fri., 10 A.M.–5 P.M.

Specialists in miniature cymbidiums and oncidium-alliance
intergenerics. Among rarities are
Oncidium staceyi, from Bolivia,
and hybrids.

John Ewing Orchids, Inc., Box
384, Aptos, CA 95003. (408)-
222-4422. Color illustrated catalog, $1.00 (credited). Open (at
nursery, 487 White Rd., Watsonville, CA) Tues.–Sat., 9 A.M.–5
P.M.

Specialist in phalaenopsis—
seedlings, mature plants, flasks of
seedlings. Laboratory for seed
sowing and green pod culture of
customer's crosses. Also many
award-quality pinks, yellows,
candy stripes, novelties, and species.

"We feel Phalaenopsis (the eas-
iest of all orchids) has a great
future for producing many varied
beautiful flowers that can easily

be grown in the home or greenhouse and can be appreciated by everyone."

Fennell Orchid Co., Inc. (The Orchid Jungle), 26715 S.W. 157th Ave., Homestead, FL 33030. (305)-247-4824. Illustrated catalog. AEX, BAC, DC, and MC charges. Open every day, 8:30 A.M.–5:30 P.M.

Orchids from seedlings to mature plants. Many new hybrids and introductions. Also bromeliads, anthuriums, ferns, and other tropical plants. Company founded in 1888—pioneers in promoting home orchid growing.

"We grow, almost exclusively, rare plants not available many other places—this is our specialty."

Finck Floral Co., 9849-M Kimker Ln., St. Louis, MO 63127. (314)-843-4376. Illustrated price list. Minimum order, $10. Visitors by appointment.

Phalaenopsis plants, *Cattleya* divisions, and mericlones of rare, selected, and awarded varieties. Also oncidiums, miltonias, and others. Orchid growers for over thirty years.

Fox Orchids, Inc., 6615 W. Markham, Little Rock, AR 72205. (501)-663-4246. Price list, 25¢. Open Mon.–Fri., 7 A.M.–noon and 1 P.M.–4 P.M.; Sat., 8 A.M.–noon.

Cattleyas, oncidiums, dendrobiums, miltonias, species, meristem seedlings, and others. Full line of orchid-growing supplies.

Orchids, cacti, and many other unusual tropical plants are for sale at greenhouses (closed the week before Mother's Day and the week before Easter).

"Visitors welcome. Coffeepot always on. No phone on Saturday, just come on out. And don't phone after hours, as it bothers the dog."

Arthur Freed Orchids, Inc., 5731 S. Bonsall, Malibu, CA 90265. (213)-457-9771. Illustrated catalog. Minimum order, $10. Open Mon.–Sat., 10 A.M.–4 P.M.

Over twenty vanda varieties, including many unusual intergeneric hybrids. Orchids are available as mature flowering plants and also as seedlings that are three, two, and one year from flowering. In the past thirty years, Freed's "Living Jewels" orchids have received over five hundred awards.

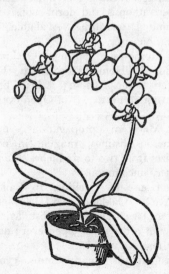

"All of our varieties are ideal houseplants which do *not* require greenhouse care."

Greenbrier Orchids, 4711 Palm Beach Blvd., Fort Myers, FL 33905. (813)-694-1539. Price list; send stamp. BAC and MC charges. U.S. sales only. Open Mon.–Sat., 8 A.M.–6 P.M.

Very extensive list of species orchids. Also over thirty varieties of imported tropical ferns.

"Our goal is to become a source for species orchids that, while not necessarily rare, are not usually stocked by the large orchid houses."

Herb Hager Orchids, 30th & Capitola Rd., Box 544, Santa Cruz, CA 95061. (408)-475-2425. Descriptive price list. Minimum order, $10.

Phalaenopsis: whites, multifloras, semialbas, striped, miniatures, novelties, and others. Also renanthopsis and doritaenopsis in limited quantities. Available in various sizes.

Homosassa Springs Orchids, Box 8, Homosassa Springs, FL 32647. (904)-628-2381. Price list. Minimum order, $10. Open every day, 8 A.M.–5 P.M.

Meristem propagations, numerous listings, ranging in pot sizes from two to six inches. Many very uncommon.

House of Orchids, 10 Bailey Ave., Oakland, NJ 07436. (201)-337-4734. Price list. Minimum order, $10. Open every day after 10 A.M.

Cattleyas, cypripediums, cym-bidiums, and other orchids, many uncommon varieties. Also ferns and anthuriums. An orchid specialist for over forty years.

Ilgenfritz Orchids—Great Lakes Orchids, Inc., Box 1114, Monroe, MI 48161. (313)-242-5995. Color illustrated catalog, $1.00 (credited). Minimum order $10. BAC and MC charges. Open Tues.–Sun., 10 A.M.–4 P.M.

Specializes in species orchid plants from all over the globe. Also hybrids (seedlings and mature plants) and full line of orchid supplies. Many books on orchid culture.

Jones and Scully, Inc. (Orchidglade), 2200 N.W. 33rd Ave., Miami, FL 33142. (305)-633-9000. Color illustrated catalog, $3.00. Minimum order, $15. AEX, BAC, and MC charges. Open Mon.–Fri., 8 A.M.–4 P.M.; Sat., 8 A.M.–noon.

Very extensive list of orchid species and quality hybrids, ranging in price from a few dollars to several hundred, and in size from small seedlings to mature plants. Special "Plant-A-Month Plan," tailored to suit individual preferences and budgets. Also wide variety of orchid supplies and many related books. The cattleya "Imperial Collection" is one of the most outstanding cattleya exhibition and breeding clones in the world.

"Our 160-page catalog, *Recommendations,* is a valuable listing of hundreds of different orchids, along with more than 300 color plates. Our staff, 'The Orchid People,' offer customers unequaled experience in commercial orchid growing and hybridization."

Kensington Orchids, Inc., 3301 Plyers Mill Rd., Kensington, MD 20795. (301)-933-0036. Price list. Open every day, 8 A.M.–5 P.M.

Many varieties of orchids, hybrids, seedlings, and mature plants. Cattleyas, phalaenopses, paphiopedilums, dendrobiums, miltonias, oncidiums, cymbidiums, meristems, and species. Orchid books and full line of growing supplies. Ships plants all over the world.

Lager & Hurrell Orchids, 426 Morris Ave., Summit, NJ 07901. (201)-273-1792. Catalog, $2.00 (credited). Open Mon.–Sat., 9 A.M.–4 P.M.

One of the largest existing orchid collections—plants for both the beginner and the professional. Full line of orchid-growing supplies. Oldest orchid firm in the world—founded in 1896.

"In 1931 Lager & Hurrell pioneered a new concept and issued a booklet entitled *Orchids as House Plants,* exploding the time-worn theory that orchid growing was impossible without a greenhouse. Orchids are incredibly fantastic as a plant family, offering a multitude of possibilities for the home grower."

Ann Mann's Orchids, Rte. 3, Box 202, Orlando, FL 32811. (305)-876-2625. Illustrated price list, 25¢. Minimum order, $10. Open Sat., and Sun., 9 A.M.–5 P.M., by appointment.

Orchid plants and seedlings. Specializes in art-shade cattleyas and species. Also numerous bromeliads and palms. Planting and cultural information included.

Rod McLellan Co., 1450 El Camino Real, South San Francisco, CA 94080. (415)-871-5655. Color illustrated catalog, 50¢ (credited). Minimum order, $10. BAC and MC charges. Open every day, 8 A.M.–5 P.M.

World's largest orchid firm. Listings include cymbidiums, cattleyas, paphiopedilums, miltonias, phalaenopses, and many novel hybrids. Complete line of growing supplies.

Daily guided tours at 10 A.M. and 1:30 P.M. at McLellan's "Acres of Orchids" in South San Francisco and also at 2352 San Juan Rd., Watsonville, CA 95076. The Watsonville phone number is (408)-728-1797.

Orchids by Hausermann, Box

363, Elmhurst, IL 60126. (312)-543-6855. Color illustrated catalog, $1.25. Orchid range, at 2N134 Addison Rd., Villa Park, IL 60181, open Mon.–Sat., 7 A.M.–4:30 P.M.

Orchid plants from around the world (over seven hundred varieties). Many newly awarded orchids not available elsewhere. There are good descriptions and cultural data in the catalog. Wide selection of growing supplies and many books on orchid culture.

An open house is held the last weekend in February every year; the public is welcome.

Orchid Imports (S. M. Howard), 11802 Huston St., North Hollywood, CA 91607. (213)-762-8275. Illustrated catalog. Minimum order, $10. Visitors by appointment.

Importer, for over twenty years, of species orchids from Mexico, Colombia, Ecuador, Brazil, and Southeast Asia. Many uncommon and hard-to-find species. Offers a beginner's collection of easy-to-grow-and-bloom species, complete with cultural instructions. Will conduct a search for any species orchids not stocked.

Penn Valley Orchids, 239 Old Gulph Rd., Wynnewood, PA 19096. (215)-642-9822. Color illustrated catalog, $1.00. Visitors by appointment.

Orchid plants (species and hybrids) of many genera, but specializes in paphiopedilums—seedlings and mature plants.

"Paphiopedilum seedlings are offered by relatively few people.

We are very small in size but none surpass us in quality of stud plants or number of paph crosses made each year. Our successes in producing outstanding paph hybrids are known throughout the world."

Joseph R. Redlinger—Orchids, 9236 S.W. 57th Ave., Miami, FL 33156. (305)-661-4821. Illustrated price list. Open every day, 7 A.M.–7 P.M., by appointment.

Specialist in orchid-culture flasks and seedlings. Also meristem-culture flasks and clones. Extensive collection of awarded breeding stock, especially cattleya, dendrobium, oncidium, phalaenopsis, and vanda. Grower for over twenty-five years; ships worldwide.

S&G Exotic Plant Co., 22 Goldsmith Ave., Beverly, MA 01915. (617)-927-2379. Illustrated catalog, 50¢ (credited). BAC and MC charges. Visitors by appointment.

Many rare and unusual orchid species, imported from around the world. Also orchid-growing supplies, bark mix, terrestrial mix.

A separate brochure on greenhouse insulation claims to cut 58 per cent of heat loss in glasshouses. The catalog has excellent cultural information.

Santa Barbara Orchid Estate, 1250 Orchid Dr., Santa Barbara, CA 93111. (805)-967-1284. Illustrated price list. BAC and MC charges. Open Mon.–Sat., 8 A.M.–4:30 P.M.; Sun., 11 A.M.–4:30 P.M.

Over a hundred genera and

more than a thousand species. Specializes in cymbidiums, dendrobiums, paphiopedilums, lycastes, and other botanical and outdoor-growing orchids. Flasks of seedlings. Largest group of botanicals, species, and genera on the West Coast.

Shaffer's Tropical Gardens, 1220 41st Ave., Capitola, CA 95010. (408)-475-3100. Price list. BAC and MC charges. Open Mon.–Sat., 9 A.M.–5 P.M.; Sun., 11 A.M.–5 P.M.

Many varieties of phalaenopsis, cymbidium, miltonia, ascocentrum, and odontoglossum. Growing supplies and books on orchid culture. Orchid specialists since 1937.

Fred A. Stewart, Inc., 1212 E. Las Tunas Dr., Box 307, San Gabriel, CA 91778. (213)-287-0015. Color illustrated catalog, $1.00 (credited). Minimum order, $10. Open Mon.–Sat., 8 A.M.–5 P.M.; Sun., noon–5 P.M.

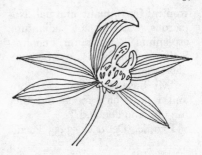

Specializes in cattleyas, cymbidiums, paphiopedilums, and phalaenopses. A complete line of orchid supplies, equipment, and publications. Internationally known for work in orchid hybridizing and culture.

Group tours are offered, with one week advance notice; tours include an introduction to various types of orchids, a view of lab and bottle houses, cultural procedures, and packing and shipping. The company also holds classes on orchid culture in May and October.

Orchid-growing Supplies

Rheinfrank & Associates, 5414 Sierra Vista Ave., Los Angeles, CA 90038. (213)-465-4146. Illustrated catalog. Open Mon. and Wed.–Fri., 9 A.M.–4:30 P.M.; Sat., 9 A.M.–noon.

Orchid-growing supplies, including insecticides, fertilizers, fungicides, flasking kits, culture mediums, bark mixes, pots, watering devices, and other equipment. Books on orchid culture. Also saran and polypropylene shading cloths and fabrics for greenhouses and outdoor beds.

TROPICAL FERNS

Bolduc's Greenhill Nursery, 2131 Vallejo St., St. Helena, CA 94574. (707)-963-2998. Price list; send SASE. Open Sat. and Sun., 10 A.M.–4 P.M., by appointment.

More than seventy varieties of

tropical ferns, many unusual. Numerous varieties of adiantum, asplenium, cyrtomium, nephrolepis, polystichum, polypodium, and others.

"My business is really a hobby and I have only ferns—but they are much in demand."

Exotiks, Dept. G., 3333 Pacific Ave., San Pedro, CA 90731. (213)-547-3490. Price list, 25¢. Open weekends, 10 A.M.–5 P.M. Other times, by appointment.

Specializes in platyceriums and polypodiums; many varieties of each. Also numerous other tropical ferns.

Special Techniques with Plants Indoors

BONSAI

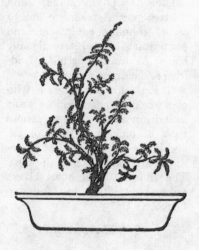

Bonsai (say "bone-sigh") translates from Japanese as "tray planting." In Japan this graceful art of growing dwarf trees by careful pruning and wire restraints has been practiced for centuries. Many of these beautiful little trees are several hundred years old and have been passed down from generation to generation in families.

Brussel's Bonsai Nursery, 305 Colonial Rd., Memphis, TN 38117. (901)-685-9977. Illustrated catalog, 25¢ (credited). U.S. sales only. Visitors by appointment, weekends, and Mon.–Fri., after 5 P.M.

Bonsai imported from Japan; domestic starter plants; bonsai containers, statuary, and tools.

"The art of bonsai lies not in what the plant is but in what it suggests. A bonsai may be only a few inches tall but still have the exact features of a towering forest tree or a lonely, windswept pine. There are many different styles of bonsai, but like their counterpart in nature no two are exactly identical."

Heirob Bonsai Nursery, Willowemoc Rd., Livingston Manor, NY 12758. (914)-439-4580. Illustrated catalog; send stamp. AEX, BAC, CB, DC, and MC charges. Open Thurs.–Mon., 9 A.M.–5 P.M.; other times by appointment.

Specimen bonsai imported from China and Japan—one of the largest collections in the United States. Also starter plants, containers, tools, turntables, training wire, and other accessories. Several kits, with trees, containers, planting medium, and necessary tools.

Hortica Gardens, Box 308, Placerville, CA 95667. (916)-622-7089. Brochure, 25¢ (credited). Visitors by appointment.

Plants suitable for bonsai training (and also for gardens). Unusual and slow-growing dwarf conifers, azaleas, dwarf rhododendrons, lavenders. Special bonsai collections for beginners. Bonsai tools. A booklet, *Pruning and Pinching Tips,* is available for 50¢. Pinched plants are sold with minor shaping or shaped as requested, which can often be transformed into "instant bonsai."

Hortica Gardens is operated by Don and Pauline Croxton, a husband-and-wife team. Don Croxton frequently gives talks and demonstrations on bonsai.

Sarasota Bonsai Gardens, Rte. 2, Fruitville Rd., Sarasota, FL 33578. (813)-371-3818. Color illustrated catalog. AEX, BAC, CB,

DC, and MC charges. Open every day, 9 A.M.–5 P.M.

Bonsai trees, many imported from Japan and China; some over 150 years old. Also bonsai pots, tools, ornaments, turntables, and related supplies.

Tinytrees Nursery Co., 5212 N. Peck Rd., El Monte, CA 91732. Price list; send SASE.

Seeds suitable for bonsai, such as bristlecone pine, dwarf pomegranate, Japanese elm, cork oak, and tea crab. All seeds come with planting instructions.

Western Arboretum, Box 2827, Pasadena, CA 91105. (213)-449-5517. Illustrated catalog, $1.00 (credited).

Some four–five hundred varieties of trees, shrubs, and ornamentals suitable for bonsai and general horticulture. Features yearlings and one-gallon size, with emphasis on root growth. One of the largest selections of bonsai stock in the United States. Very wide selection of authentic containers and pottery; tools, planting mix, fertilizers, and many books on bonsai.

Booklets

If you'd like an introduction to bonsai, send for the twenty-page booklet *Growing Bonsai,* G-206, 40¢ from the **Supt. of Documents,** Washington, DC 20402.

Traditionally, bonsai have been considered outdoor plants. But many plant materials can be

adapted to indoor growing. Information about these plants, their culture, and how to train them can be found in the handbook *Indoor Bonsai,* $1.50 from **Brooklyn Botanic Garden,** 1000 Washington Ave., Brooklyn, NY 11225.

TERRARIUM PLANTS AND SUPPLIES

A. E. Allgrove Nursery, 281 Woburn St., Wilmington, MA 01887. (617)-658-4869. Illustrated catalog, 50¢. U.S. sales only. Visitors by appointment.

Woodland terrarium plants, bonsai plants, wildflowers. Many uncommon and rare. Also terrarium, bonsai, and saikei supplies of all types. Partridgeberry bowls. Very informative catalog with information on planting terrariums and shaping bonsai. Recommended for all gardeners with these interests.

"Twenty years dealing in nostalgic New England plants for woodsy dish gardens, terrariums, bonsai, and the wildflower gardener."

Council Oak Products, Box 3777, South Bend, IN 46628. (219)-234-4638. Illustrated catalog, 50¢.

Natural accessories—petrified wood, weathered wood, driftwood, decorator stones, nuts, and pods—for accents for terrariums, bonsai, saikei, and dish gardens. Also live mosses and lichens, coniferous seeds. The catalog has detailed planting instructions, as well as suggestions for use of accent materials.

"Picture the beauty of a small army of British soldier lichens standing guard over a tiny valley in a woodland scene greened by a patch of live moss snuggling next

to a driftwood log. Accents make the difference between an ordinary assortment of green plants and a living replica of Nature in miniature."

Open Season, Box 225/B, Ashland, OR 97520. (503)-482-4116. Illustrated price list.

Terrarium tool kit, including five planting tools and instructional booklet. Also tweezers, twenty-four inches long, with exclusive tip-locking mechanism for terrarium plantings.

Rainbow Sand, 301 W. Louden St., Philadelphia, PA 19120. (215)-324-1744. Price list plus samples, $2.00 (credited).

Very fine grit sand, non-toxic to plants, in eighteen colors; for dish gardens and terrariums. Samples of all colors are sent with the price list.

For More Information

Terrarium Topics, a newsletter published by the Terrarium Association, is filled with how-to information. For information on ordering copies, see the listing of the association under "Plant Societies."

A good introductory booklet, *Terrariums,* C-1086, is 50¢ from the University of Illinois, Agricultural Publications Office, 123 Mumford Hall, Urbana, IL 61801; thirty-two pages, many illustrations.

Gardening Aids, Equipment, and Supplies

Bloom 'N Vine, Box 1442, Dept. G-1, Savannah, GA 31402. (912)-234-1465. Illustrated catalog, 25¢ (credited). BAC and MC charges. Open Mon.–Sat., 10 A.M.–5 P.M.

Plant ladders, jute-crate hangers, wrought-iron scroll stands, wall brackets, and other plant stands, hangers, and accessories. All original designs, made by Savannah craftsmen.

Home Plant Displayers, Inc., 51 E. 42nd St., New York, NY 10017. (212)-661-2237. Illustrated catalog. MC charge.

Many types of plant stands including floor-to-ceiling poles with adjustable clamps and arms, floor stands with adjustable arms that hold up to twelve large plants, wall arms for three pots, hanging wall holders with spotlights. Also pole extensions and other accessories.

Riverside Studio, Hancock, ME 04640. (207)-422-6738. Illustrated catalog, 35¢ (credited).

Unusual brass and aluminum fixtures for mounting plant pots on walls or suspending from ceilings. Variety of sizes and shapes, including a mobile that holds three pots. Swivel hooks and extension rods permit flexibility of arrangements.

Sundials & More, Box H, New Ipswich, NH 03071. (603)-878-1000. Color illustrated catalog, 25¢. BAC and MC charges. Open Mon.–Fri., 9 A.M.–4:30 P.M.

Sundials—domestic and from around the world, in bronze, brass, pewter, and cast and carved iron, steel, stone, and acrylic. Also leaded-glass hanging gazebos for plants or dried arrangements, hand-hammered copper weathervanes, various pots and hanging planters, wild-bird seeds, and bird supplies.

Tara Eden, Inc., Box 17, Roslyn, NY 11576. Illustrated brochure.

The Plantrac system for hanging plants. The basic system consists of a rack that may be suspended or attached to the ceiling, swivel hooks that move along it, and holders and tiering rings that attach to the hooks. Racks, in several sizes, can be used for many arrangements, such as one rack hung below another, tiers of hanging pots, or pots at varying levels.

Tonia, Inc., 97 Hawthorn Dr., Box 2665, Atherton, CA 94025. (415)-323-0797. Illustrated brochure. Visitors by appointment.

Handcrafted wire hanging baskets, plant stands, topiary forms, gazebos, and other wire items. Also makes custom designs and restores or repairs antique wire planters and wire furniture.

Topiary, 41 Bering St., Tampa, FL 33606. (813)-257-6241. Illustrated brochure. Visitors by appointment.

Topiary frames for 6–9-inch containers. Unique designs include various animals, birds, fish, spheres, and cones. Owners Mia Hardcastle and Carole Guyton, who are also housewives, will make custom frames to order.

"We feel our approach makes topiary accessible to many more people than the more traditional approach. Also, it is almost 'instant.' A wire frame with viny plant material is complete in a few months."

The Village Greenhouse, 2027 Skyline Rd., Ruxton, MD 21204. Illustrated price list.

Unusual plant containers, such as sandstone birds, stoneware baskets, frogs, hanging spheres with three openings, small turtles in brown stoneware, tiny red clay pots $1\frac{1}{4}$ inches in diameter, and Mexican pots. Also plant hangers, decorative miniatures, and figurines.

Decorate with Flower Posters

Attractive wall charts of various plants, reproduced from original watercolors, may be ordered from The Shop in the **New York Botanical Garden,** Bronx Park, Bronx, NY 10458. Other floral posters and gardening items are also illustrated in The Shop's brochure, which is sent without charge.

Pots, Planters, and Self-watering Systems

Aqua-Pots, Inc. (Rose-Marie Dunn), 2625 Cascade Pl. West, Tacoma, WA 98466. (206)-564-2385. Illustrated brochure; send SASE.

Patented Aqua-Pots, in several sizes, which supply constant source of water and nutrients to plants; can be used for patio tubs, too. Also covers for clay pots, designed to protect furniture.

John Caschetto, 396 Clark St., Bridgeport, CT 06606. (203)-372-7431. Illustrated catalog.

Fertil Pots—peat pots in a variety of sizes and shapes; round, square, and in strips. Also round plastic pots, plastic flats, and plastic hanging baskets.

Flor-L-Pot (Albert Hazewinkel), 11550 Larch St., Minneapolis, MN 55433. (612)-755-

950. Brochure plus plastic ower-pot samples, $1.00.

Plastic flower pots, sizes 2¼–16 nches, round and square. Azalea ots, bulb pans, hanging pots. Also moisture meters.

Green Planter System, Inc., 14 Kenneth Ave., North Bellmore, NY 11710. (516)-781-4176. Illusrated brochure.

Patented Green Planter feed ubes for automatic irrigation of otted plants, window boxes, or reenhouse benches. Can also be sed in root systems of garden lants such as roses.

Golden Earth Enterprises Peerless Potman), 338 Red-vood, Box 336, Brea, CA 92621. 714)-990-0681. Illustrated cata-og, 25¢. Minimum order, $10.

Plastic pots in various colors, square or round, with bottom or side drain holes, in sizes 2–14 inches. Also exclusive molded-fiber plant containers, 8–16 inches. Plastic saucers, planter boxes, hanging baskets, and wires.

Mardon Gardens, 637 Quaker Rd., East Aurora, NY 14052. (716)-648-1755. Illustrated brochure.

Water Genie—automatic watering wicks for potted plants. From garden dealers or direct by mail.

Millstone, Inc. (Plantamation), 716 S. Main St., Seaman, OH 45679. (513)-386-2255. Illustrated brochure.

Plantender—automatic start-stop watering devices for large potted plants. Operated by sensing device that controls water flow from a reservoir. Available from garden dealers or order direct.

Ordev Mfg. Co., Inc., 6781 Ward Rd., Niagara Falls, NY 14304. Illustrated brochure.

Ordev plant supports for indoor and patio plants. The tip-proof plastic base, placed in the bottom of the pot, is connected to an aluminum rod; aboveground sections are redwood-stained hardwood. Supports can be easily adjusted or lengthened with connecting aluminum fasteners. Also a trellis kit with the same features.

Practical Products, Box 246, South Salem, NY 10590. Price list.

Plastic pots in many sizes;

standard, azalea-type, square, bulb pans. Also hanging pots, plastic flats, and plastic saucers. Special prices for quantities.

The Violet House, 15 S.E. 4th Ave., Gainesville, FL 32601. (904)-377-8465. Price list. Minimum order, $7.50.

Plastic pots; round standard, round tub, and square; sizes up to eight inches in diameter. Also plastic water reservoirs for pots,

plastic saucers with hanger hanging baskets, metal nursery cans, and galvanized flats.

About Pot Sizes

Standard pot	depth equals top diameter
Azalea or ¾ pot	depth equals ¾ of top diameter
Square pot	depth equals top width
Bulb pan	depth equals ⅓ of top diameter

Indoor Light Gardening

Fluorescent lights make gardening an anyplace, 365-days-of-the-year activity. With them you can raise orchids in a basement, begonias in an attic, or salad greens in the kitchen.

An added plus in these energy-short times: fluorescent tubes give more light per watt than incandescent bulbs. So gardeners are putting them to dual use—to grow plants and to light living areas. Many manufacturers are producing light-garden units that equal fine furniture and are a complement to any room.

Sources for indoor light-gardening supplies are listed below.

And check the Indoor Light Gardening Society of America for many booklets on this subject.

Aladdin Industries, Inc., Box 10666, Nashville, TN 37210 (615)-748-3166. Illustrated catalog. AEX and BAC charges.

Furniture-styled light-garden stands, shelves, and carts. Also controlled-environment light-garden chambers. Available from retail dealers or direct from the company.

Alprax Enterprises, Ltd., Box 2636, Schenectady, NY 12309 (518)-356-2800. Color illustrated catalog, 50¢. BAC and MC charges. Open Mon., Tues., Wed., and Fri., 10 A.M.–4 P.M.

Phytarium, a controlled-environment plant-growth chamber that includes fluorescent tubes and automatic control watering, heating, venting, and carbon dioxide release. Available in several sizes or in kit form. Also

Plant Survival Kits, with automatic watering and capillary feeding, light stands, plant shelves and poles, and other light-garden accessories.

Floralite Co., 4124 E. Oakwood Rd., Oak Creek, WI 53154. (414)-762-1770. Illustrated brochure; send stamp. Open by appointment.

Lumen-liter Plant Center (lighted plant stands), and Starlite Plant Lamp for indoor growing. Also plant-growth tubes, timers, trays, and other growing supplies.

The Green House, 9515 Flower St., Bellflower, CA 90706. (213)-925-0870. Color illustrated brochure. Minimum order, $20. BAC and MC charges. Open Mon.–Sat., 10 A.M.–5 P.M.; Sun., 1 P.M.–5 P.M.

Manufacturers and sellers of Gro-Cart line of light-garden plant stands. Several models. Also plant-growth fluorescent tubes.

For sale at The Green House in Bellflower (but not by mail) are many varieties of African violets and houseplant supplies. The Green House, founded in 1946 by Carol Green, in a 14×14-foot greenhouse, has now expanded to a two-thirds-acre site, with three full-time employees and four subcontractors producing components for Gro-Carts.

"In this ready-cooked, quick-frozen, bite-sized, cellophane-wrapped world, it's nice to live and work in a live environment, growing African violets."

House Plant Corner, Ltd., 506 Gay St., Box 5000, Cambridge, MD 21613. (301)-228-9300. Illustrated catalog, 25¢. Open Mon.–Thurs., 7 A.M.–5:30 P.M.

The largest selection, according to the company, of light-garden fixtures and stands available. These range from carts, table-top models, mini-lights, and wall fixtures, to spotlights. Other supplies of all types, such as plant holders and brackets, pots, window shelves, fertilizers, humidifiers, moisture meters, sprayers, light meters, foggers, imported watering cans—just about everything needed by indoor gardeners. Also a listing of orchids, African violets, bromeliads, and other tropical plants.

"We have been in business since long before indoor gardening became 'vogue'—over twenty-nine years. Many items are exclusives and sold only by us. The president of the corporation is a woman—Dolores Anderson Daringer—who is an active indoor gardener. We always weigh suggestions from customers concerning good new products and attempt to stock difficult-to-find items."

H. L. Hubbel, Inc., Zeeland, MI 49464. (616)-772-2147. Color illustrated catalog. BAC and MC charges.

"Indoor Furniture Gardens"—wood tables, shelves, and other furniture equipped with plant growth lights. Modern and traditional styles in various sizes and colors.

Indoor Gardening Supplies, Box 40551, Detroit, MI 48240. (313)-464-8873. Illustrated catalog. BAC charges.

Very large selection of indoor gardening needs. Many types of light fixtures and wood and metal plant stands. Plant growth lights and standard fluorescent tubes in various sizes. Numerous books on indoor gardening. Quantity discounts on lamps to groups and clubs.

Indoor Garden Sales, Box 28, Lowell, MA 01853. (617)-454-7108. Illustrated catalog plus brochures, 50¢. BAC charge.

All types of light fixtures, major brands of fluorescent and incandescent lamps. Timers, trays, plastic pots, and other accessories for indoor and greenhouse gardening. Included with each catalog is a Gro-Lux instruction manual. All items are sent postpaid.

Interior Products of Rockford, Inc., Box 2116, Rockford, IL 61111. (815)-654-1770. Illustrated brochure. BAC and MC charges.

Light-garden units designed as furniture. Wall and corner shelves and room dividers; various sizes; waterproof finishes in walnut grain and several colors.

JD-21 Lighting Systems, 1840 130th N.E., Bellevue, WA 98005. (206)-885-2195. Illustrated brochure.

Shadegro—a fluorescent light fixture with an engineered, mir-rorlike reflector system that provides optimum distribution of light on the growing area. Available either as a hanging or a stand unit.

Mailex, 4365 Greenberry Ln., Annandale, VA 22003. Illustrated brochure; send SASE.

Unique wood-crafted light-garden units, including a floral display cart, tea cart, hanging corner unit, and various shelves. Assembled units are available and also plans and working drawings for home construction using stock lumber.

Shoplite Co., Inc., 566 Franklin Ave., Nutley, NJ 07110. (201)-661-2447. Illustrated catalog, 25¢. Open Mon.–Fri., 9 A.M.–5 P.M.; Sat., 9 A.M.–noon.

Many hard-to-find items for light-gardeners. Wide variety of light units, stand and table models. Also parts for custom fluorescent installations: ballasts, starters, lamp holders, reflectors, switches, leg supports for fixtures, plant trays. Plant growth lights and standard fluorescent tubes including circular tubes and miniature tubes.

Tube Craft, Inc., 1311 W. 80th St., Cleveland, OH 44102. (216)-281-8011. Illustrated brochure. BAC and MC charges. Open Mon.–Fri., 8 A.M.–4:30 P.M.

Flora Cart fluorescent light carts and table units. Also humidifiers, trays, plastic tents, watering aids, and other light-garden accessories.

Which Plant Lights Are Best?

Few light-gardeners agree on the best type of lighting. There are a number of special plant growth fluorescent tubes that some gardeners swear by, while others prefer standard tubes—cool or warm white.

To help you decide, the following lamp manufacturers will send you brochures about their plant lights:

Duro-Test Corp., North Bergen, NJ 07047;

General Electric Co., Lamp Division, Nela Park, Cleveland, OH 44112;

Sylvania Lighting Products Division, 100 Endicott St., Danvers, MA 01923;

Westinghouse Electric Corp., Lamp Division, Bloomfield, NJ 07003;

Verilux TruBloom, 35 Mason St., Greenwich, CT 06830.

If You're Thinking About a Greenhouse . . .

You have many choices. All the companies listed here, unless otherwise indicated, have "hobby size" models—ranging from inexpensive, vinyl-covered, portable models to permanent buildings. Factors to consider are the price you want to pay, your climate, the size you need, and how you plan to use it. In almost every case, price per square foot decreases as size increases.

Catalogs, brochures, and other literature are available from these companies on request.

Aluminum Greenhouses, Inc., 14615 Lorain Ave., Cleveland, OH 44111. (216)-251-5572.

Everlite greenhouses, aluminum frames with glass. Freestanding and lean-to models. Freestanding models from about 7½×8½ feet. Accessories are included in the purchase price.

Archway Green Houses, Box 246, Duck Hill, MS 38925. (601)-565-2526.

Arch-style greenhouses, yellow-pine-treated frames, fiberglass panels, aluminum storm doors. From 8×10 feet. Available in kit form, or delivered and installed.

Casaplanta, 9489 Dayton Way, Beverly Hills, CA 90210. (213)-275-3893.

Arch-style greenhouses, plastic-tube framework, vinyl-covered. From 4×6 feet. Additional units are easily attached for expansion. Also small, indoor units or "working" terrariums.

Clover Garden Products, Inc., 412 8th Ave., Box 874, Smyrna, TN 37167.

Arch style, steel tubing frames, fiberglass of Monsanto Copolymer covers. From 12×12 feet.

Dome Greenhouses, Box 666, Aptos, CA 95003. (408)-427-1146.

Geodesic-dome styles, redwood or steel frames, glass or fiberglass panels. From about nine feet in diameter.

Early Garden Greenhouses, Inc., Mendenhall, MS 39114.

Arch-style greenhouse 8×9 feet, wood frame, plastic covering. In kit form. Also furniture-styled indoor-light-garden units.

Edward Owen Engineering, Snow Shoe, PA 16874. (814)-387-4284.

Edward Owen Safety greenhouses. Aluminum frames, double-strength glass. Freestanding models from about 6½×8½ feet.

Enclosures, Inc., 80 Main St., Moreland, GA 30259. (404)-253-9944.

Gothic-arch and traditional-style freestanding greenhouses, from 10×10 feet. Steel framework; Ceylon plastic covering. The company has installed some solar-heated models; it is hoped that, in the not too distant future, solar heating will be available for hobby greenhouse owners.

Feather Hill Industries, Box 41, Zenda, WI 53195. (414)-275-6770.

Nature Bubble—a unique, bubble-type-window greenhouse unit made of plastic.

Garden of Eden Greenhouse Center, Inc., 875 E. Jericho Tnpk., Huntington Station, NY 11746. (516)-427-3367.

Greenhouses of many types styles, and prices from various manufacturers. A very helpful booklet, *All You Need to Know About Greenhouses,* offers guidelines for prospective buyers. Many accessories are listed, including "Plantation Staging Tables," in various sizes, open grating, weatherproof finish.

Many greenhouses are on display at the center in Huntington Station.

Gothic Arch Greenhouses, Box 1564, Mobile, AL 36601. (205) 432-7529.

Arch-style greenhouses, redwood frames, fiberglass panels. Both freestanding and lean-to models. Sizes start at about 6×8 feet.

Hansen Weatherport, 313 N Taylor, Gunnison, CO 81230 (303)-641-0480.

Lightweight, portable, arch-style greenhouses. Steel frames with polyethylene covering. Sizes from 10×12 feet.

Hydro-Growth Greenhouses, Inc., 21675 W. Doral Rd., Waukesha, WI 53186. (414)-784-2500.

Arch-type units, fiberglass framing, in various sizes; include automatic equipment for hydroponic gardening.

Lord & Burnham, Irvington, NY 10533.

Wide range of greenhouses; freestanding, lean-to, straight and curved eaves, window units. Various types of construction. Size of freestanding units ranges from about 8½×6½ feet.

Maco Home Greenhouses, Box 109, Scio, OR 97374.

Arch-type freestanding and lean-to models. Aluminum framing with vinyl or fiberglass panels. Freestanding models from about 5×10 feet.

McGregor Greenhouses, 1195 Thompson Ave., Santa Cruz, CA 95063. (408)-476-5390.

Freestanding and lean-to models; redwood frames with fiberglass covering. Sizes start at about 4×6½ feet.

National Greenhouse Co., Box 100, Pana, IL 62557.

Freestanding and lean-to models; glass with aluminum framing. From about 7½×8½ feet.

J. A. Nearing Co., Inc. (Janco Greenhouses), 10788 Tucker St., Beltsville, MD 20705. (301)-937-3300.

Wide variety of greenhouses, including freestanding, lean-to, and window models. Aluminum frames with glass. Freestanding models from about 10×11 feet.

Pacific Coast Greenhouse Mfg. Co., 430 Hurlingame Ave., Redwood City, CA 94063. (415)-366-7672.

Freestanding and lean-to models with redwood frames, glass or fiberglass covering. Sizes from about 3×6 feet. Designed for easy expansion.

Redfern Greenhouses, 57 Mt. Hermon Rd., Scotts Valley, CA 95066. (408)-438-0515.

Freestanding and lean-to greenhouses. Redwood frames with fiberglass or Twinglas coverings. Sizes from about 6×9 feet.

Peter Reimuller, The Greenhouseman, 980 17th Ave., Santa Cruz CA 95062.

Variety of lean-to and freestanding models in various shapes and sizes. Redwood frames with vinyl or fiberglass panels. Sizes from about 6½×8 feet.

Reliable Greenhouses, 171 Washington St., Norwell, MA 02061. (617)-878-5500.

Baco greenhouses; aluminum frames with glass. Freestanding and lean-to models. Sizes from 6×8 feet.

Semispheres, Box 26273, Richmond VA 23260. (804)-321-9283.

Geodesic-dome styles; wood frames, Plexiglas panels. Also vinyl covers available for small models. Sizes from about eight feet in diameter.

Sturdi-Built Manufacturing Co., 11304 S.W. Boones Ferry Rd., Portland, OR 97219. (503)-244-4100.

Redwood frames, glass or fiberglass panels. Lean-to and freestanding. Many styles, including A-frames. Models from about 8×9 feet.

Texas Greenhouse Co., 2717 St. Louis Ave., Fort Worth, TX

76110. (817)-926-5447.

Freestanding and lean-to models. Aluminum or redwood frames, glass or fiberglass panels. Freestanding models from about 9×10 feet.

Turner Greenhouses, Box 1260, Goldsboro, NC 27530. (919)-734-8345.

Aluminum frames, plastic and fiberglass panels. Lean-to and freestanding models. Sizes start at 8×10 feet.

Vegetable Factory Greenhouses, Box 2235, Grand Central Station, New York, NY 10017. (212)-686-0173.

Freestanding and lean-to models. Aluminum frames with double-walled acrylic panels.

Sizes from about 8×8 feet.

Verandel Co., Box 1568, Worcester, MA 01601.

"Stairhouse" model, aluminum frame with glass to cover basement entrances or hatchways.

Water Works Gardenhouses, Box 905, El Cerrito, CA 94530. (415)-525-8240.

Redwood frames with fiberglass panels. Models from 8×12 feet. Optional hydroponic and climate-control systems.

Jack C. Williams Co., 21519 92nd Ave. West, Edmonds, WA 98020. (206)-776-9202.

Freestanding and lean-to models. Aluminum frames with glass. Sizes from about 8×12 feet.

Want to Build Your Own Greenhouse?

Greenhouse Specialties Co., 9849 Kimker Ln., St. Louis, MO 63127, has the supplies you'll need: fiberglass, aluminum flashings, ridge rolls, sealing strips, caulking compound, fans, shutters, heaters, and other accessories. Also steel greenhouse frames and plastic coverings. Send $1.00 (credited) for a price list, a sample of special acrylic fiberglass, and a set of greenhouse plans.

Hydroponic Gardening Supplies

Burwell Geoponics Corp., Box 125, Rancho Santa Fe, CA 92067. Illustrated brochure, 40¢ (credited).

"Hydropod" hydroponic garden units for greenhouse or outdoor use. Also "Plantqbator," a miniature hydroponic unit with wick watering and a sealed heating unit for starting seeds and cuttings. Accessories such as nutrients, pumps, electrical controls, nutrition test kits, plastic liners, pumps, interval timers, and instructional books.

ECOREF, Box 1600, Palo Alto, CA 94302. Illustrated catalog, 25¢.

Hydroponic equipment, including Hypalon rubber tray liners, nutrient tank frames, pumps, contols, nutrients. Many books on hydroponics. Hypalon liners can be custom-fabricated to specifications, and plans are available for construction of systems using the liners.

"ECOREF is a contraction of Ecology Reference Service, and it stands for our commitment to offer the best hydroponic systems at the lowest prices."

Environmental Dynamics, 12615 S. La Cadena Dr., Colton, CA 92324. (714)-781-9258. Illustrated catalog. BAC and MC charges. Open Mon.–Sat., 10 A.M.–6 P.M.

Hydroponic kits and supplies of all types. Also materials for greenhouse construction; heating, cooling, and ventilating systems; greenhouse instruments; growing accessories; and many related books.

"Our definition of hydroponics: growing plants by feeding them a solution of water and nutrients, thereby eliminating the need for soil as a food source . . . and all the toil that goes with soil!"

Hydro-Gardens, Inc., Box 9707, Colorado Springs, CO 80932. (303)-495-4784. Catalog and price list, 50¢. BAG and MC charges.

Nutrients, tanks, pumps, control panels, and other hydroponic supplies. Also greenhouses (window units and freestanding models) for hydroponic installations. A book, *Hydroponics—a Growing Business,* by Tim Carpenter, general manager of Hydro-Gardens, is $2.95 plus 25¢ for postage.

Hydro-Gardens is the largest blender of custom-formulated hydroponic nutrients in the world and has a complete testing laboratory for fertilizers, water, soils, and plant tissues.

Modular Hydroponic Gardens, Box 8121, Fountain Valley, CA 92708. Illustrated brochure, 25¢.

Hydroponic gardening kits that include planter, nutrient tank, nutrients, testing supplies, and instruction manual.

Hydroponics, 941-GS, is an introduction to this method of gardening that is rapidly gaining in popularity. Price is 50¢ from **Colorado State University,** Bulletin Rm., Fort Collins, CO 80523.

Tools, Gadgets, and Other Equipment

Alsto Co., 11052 Pearl Rd., Cleveland, OH 44136. (216)-238-7300. Illustrated catalog. BAC and MC charges. Open Mon.–Fri., 8 A.M.–5 P.M.

A variety of yard and garden

tools, such as hand cultivators, carts, storage sheds, incinerators, weather instruments, bird feeders, purple-martin houses, pruning shears, watering devices, and many more.

American Standard Co. (Ratchet-Cut), West St., Plantsville, CT 06479. (203)-628-9644. Illustrated brochure. BAC and MC charges. Open Mon.–Fri., 10 A.M.–3 P.M.

Pruning shears, loping shears, and pole pruners of various sizes, all with "ratchet" action, making cutting less effort. Available from many garden dealers or direct by mail.

Brookstone Co., Vose Farm Rd., Peterborough, NH 03458 (603)-924-7181. Illustrated catalogs, two per year, $1.00 for two year subscription. AEX, BAC, and MC charges. Open Mon.–Sat., A.M.–5 P.M.

Among the "hard-to-find tools" offered are numerous garden related items: special-purpose garden knives, water-volume regulator for lawn sprinklers, lawn aerator, plastic cold frames, soaker hoses, pruning tools, and the like.

Tune In on Your Tulips

Do your plants perk up when you talk to them? Are they lulled by soft music, jarred by loud noises? To find out, just hook them up to a "Galvanic Skin Response Monitor." A needle moving back and forth on its meter will record their reactions. You can buy a GSR Monitor (for about $160) from **American Science Center, Inc.**, 5700 Northwest Hwy., Chicago, IL 60646.

Even if you're not in the market for a monitor, you're apt to find a lot of other interesting, and less expensive, things in the company's 164-page catalog (it's 50¢ a copy). Such as a miniature still for turning flowers into perfume, a mushroom-growing kit, magnifiers, a 4½-foot working windmill, soil test kits, plant growth lights, and hundreds of other science-related gadgets. If you're in Chicago, you can visit the center Mon.–Fri., 8:30 A.M.–5 P.M.; Sat., to 3 P.M.

About Those Tulips . . .

If you're dubious about plant sensitivity, skeptical about people who talk to their plants, we suggest you read *The Secret Life of Plants,* by Peter Tompkins and Christopher Bird (an Avon paperback, $1.95 at booksellers). Chances are, after you wade through its 400-plus pages of scientific facts and theories, you'll never again feel the same about those plants on your windowsill. Right now, the authors claim, your plants are reading your mind.

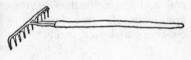

Charley's Greenhouse Supply, 12442 N.E. 124th St., Kirkland, WA 98033. (206)-827-5371. Illustrated catalog. $1.00 (credited). BAC charge. Open Tues.–Fri., 10 A.M.–6 P.M.; Sat. 10 A.M.–4 P.M.

Just about everything needed by greenhouse or indoor gardeners. Plant foods, soil test kits, plastic pots, baskets, flats, soil-heating cables, thermometers, fluorescent light fixtures and tubes, greenhouse shading materials, heaters, electrical controls, fans, shutters, sprayers, misting and watering systems, polyeth-

ylene and acrylic fiberglass sealing strips and more. As a bonus, the catalog has much information on lighting, watering, heating, and ventilating requirements in greenhouses.

Edmund Scientific Co., 555 Edscorp Bldg., Barrington, NJ 08021. (609)-547-3488. Illustrated catalog. BAC and MC charges. Open Mon.–Thurs., 8 A.M.–6 P.M.; Fri. and Sat., 8 A.M.–9 P.M.; Sun., 11 A.M.–6 P.M.

Plant growth lights, miniature greenhouses and terrariums, bonsai equipment, soil test kits, carnivorous plants, a book on construction of a solar greenhouse, magnifiers, weather instruments, and hundreds of other science-related items, many of interest to gardeners.

Garden Way Catalog, Dept. 68001, 48 Maple St., Burlington, VT 05401. Illustrated catalog. BAC and MC charges.

After you've harvested your crops, you'll find lots of tools and equipment in this catalog to help you preserve them. Such as a food dehydrator, cherry stoner and cherry pitter, apple picker, apple parer and apple peeler, fruit press for making your own cider, corn sheller, and similar items. Also garden carts in various sizes, designed to carry big loads with ease.

The Garden Way Living Center, which sells these tools and many other supplies for self-sufficient living, is open during summer months, Mon.–Fri., 8:30

A.M.–8:30 P.M.; Sat., until 5:30 P.M. It's situated at 1186 Williston Road, South Burlington, VT. (802)-863-3451.

A. M. Leonard, Inc., 6665 Spiker Rd., Box 816, Piqua, OH 45356. (513)-773-2694. Illustrated catalog. Minimum order, $10. Open Mon.–Fri., 8 A.M.–5 P.M.; Sat., 8 A.M.–noon.

Many professional-quality horticultural tools and supplies. Nursery carts, ball tongs, shovels for various purposes, pruners, hoes, weeders, spading forks, planting tools, picks, earth augers, burlap, tar wrap, weather instruments, rakes, hose and hose fittings, seed sowers, moisture meters, sprinkler heads. A number of books, primarily for nurserymen.

Lorenzen's, 421 E. Sunrise Hwy., Bellmore, NY 11710. (516)-785-7371. Illustrated brochure.

Pruning saw with a stainless-steel blade, just nine inches long, for reaching tight corners where shears or loppers can't be used. Also indestructible aluminum plant labels with special paint pen for marking (no fading after seven years' testing in the garden) and a tip-resistant miniature cement birdbath for use in miniature gardens.

Lorenzen, owner of a tool-and-die shop and specialist in miniature roses, designed these items particularly for use with his plants.

Montgomery Ward, 618 W. Chicago Ave., Chicago IL 60607

(or your nearest Ward catalog store). Illustrated *Suburban, Farm & Garden Catalog.*

Wide range of garden and related equipment such as hand and power tools, small greenhouses, indoor-light-garden units, garden hose and sprinklers, beneficial insects, pumps and waterfalls, wheelbarrows, and hundreds of other items.

Mother's General Store, 101 N. Church St., Hendersonville, NC 28739. (704)-693-4109. Illustrated catalog, 50¢ (credited). AEX, BAC, and MC charges. Open Mon.–Sat., 9 A.M.–6 P.M.; Sun., 1 P.M.–6 P.M.

Such things as grain mills, cider presses, strawberry barrels, kraut cutters, pitchforks, mole repellers, hand cultivators, scythes, and loads of other fascinating, old-timey tools and goods.

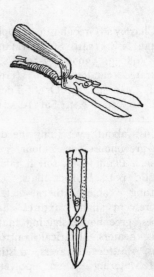

Walt Nicke, 19 Columbia Tnpk., Hudson, NY 12534. (518)-828-3415. Illustrated catalog, 25¢. Open Mon.–Fri., 10 A.M.–4 P.M.

A unique collection of garden tools and gadgets, a lot of which aren't available elsewhere. There are thatched-roof birdhouses from England, slug bait holders, plastic flowerpots that can be steam-sterilized, a pocket-size pruner just 3½ inches long, the Cape Cod Weeder, imported watering cans, cast-aluminum scoops, plant supports that grow with the plant, Scovil hoes, a transparent waterproofing tape for outdoor use on glass or plastic greenhouses —and many more.

The famous Cape Cod Weeder, with its knife-like angle and pointed tip, has served many generations of home gardeners.

Paw Paw Everlast Label Co., Box 93-V, Paw Paw, MI 49079. Illustrated brochure; send SASE.

Everlast labels with wire standards and etched-zinc nameplates. Many sizes, shapes, and types.

Jiffy Seedstarter Greenhouse

"I noticed how grass thrives in sidewalk cracks," said Arne Knutsson, specialist in new garden products. The result, after much testing, was this mini-greenhouse which grows as many as forty plants in a space just 4½ × 5 inches. Available from garden suppliers everywhere—one of the many products researchers develop to aid home gardeners.

Sears, Roebuck and Co., 925 S. Homan Ave., Chicago, IL 60607 (or from your nearest Sears catalog store). Illustrated *Suburban, Farm and Ranch Catalog.*

Necessities and extras for the home gardener or part-time farmer. Tools, beekeeping equipment, power equipment, light-garden units, saws, fences, cultivators, watering devices, etc. An item of note: a small "Mini-Composter" for hand-grinding vegetables and garden wastes.

Standard Engineering Works, Inc., 289 Roosevelt Ave., Pawtucket, RI 02860. (401)-722-0238. Illustrated brochure. Minimum order, $10. Open by appointment.

Motor-driven humidifiers and automatic controls, for greenhouses and indoor gardens; deliver from two quarts to three gallons per hour.

Tradewinds, Inc., 2339 Tacoma Ave. South, Box 1191, Tacoma, WA 98401. (206)-272-4887. Illustrated brochure. Open Mon.–Fri., 9 A.M.–5:30 P.M.

Hoeboy, a push-type rotary garden cultivator imported from Denmark. Just 8½ inches wide, with twelve revolving blades that penetrate soil surface but not so deep as to injure plant roots. Also Jarret Earth Auger, imported from Australia; in various diameters, for planting trees and vines, soil testing, and erecting fences.

Young Industries, 1033 Wright Ave., Mountain View, CA 94043.

(415)-968-8486. Illutsrated brochure.

Lawn and garden aerators, sod coring tools, tree and shrub root soakers, sod planters, mixer-proportioners for use with garden hoses or for permanent installation. Available from many garden dealers, or direct by mail.

NOTE: Several suppliers listed sell items used primarily by commercial growers or large-scale gardeners. If you don't fit into either of these categories but think they may have an item you're looking for, we suggest you inquire (enclosing SASE) instead of asking for a copy of their catalog.

Watering, Misting, and Propagating Equipment

Aquamonitor, Box 327, Huntington, NY 11743. (516)-422-5664. Illustrated brochure.

Automatic mist systems, usable with garden hoses, for plant propagation in greenhouses or outside. Valves, sensors, cables, and mist rails available separately or in kit form.

Chapin Watermatics, 368 N. Colorado Ave., Watertown, NY 13601. (315)-782-1170. Brochure.

Automatic tube watering kits for small greenhouses or home gardens. Available from many garden suppliers or directly by mail. (Note: if you write Chapin, specify that you would like their brochure on watering kits for small greenhouses.)

Hancor, Inc., Box 1047, Findlay, OH 45840. (419)-422-6521. Illustrated brochure.

Manufacturer of Turf-flow—corrugated, flexible plastic tubing, sizes from two inches in diameter and larger, for drainage in home gardens and grounds. Easily installed, with fittings, couplers, and adapters. The brochure has

information on uses of Turf-flow, but the product is available only from retail and mail-order garden suppliers.

Mist Methods Co. (Russell Kennedy), 5612 8th Court South, Birmingham, AL 35212. Illustrated brochure; send SASE.

Mistic Bubble—a mist-propagation unit, four feet in diameter, with rigid wire framework and plastic cover, plus fog nozzle, for propagation of cuttings.

Simpler Co., 487 Mathew St., Santa Clara, CA 95050. (408)-247-4535. Illustrated brochure.

Sprinkler Spikes—sprinkler spray heads easily installed in a garden hose for converting to an inexpensive sprinkling system. Available separately or in kit form with hose. From garden dealers or directly by mail.

Submatic, Inc., Box 246, Lubbock, TX, 79408. (806)-747-0902. Illustrated catalog. Open Mon.–Sat.; phone ahead.

Supplies for drip irrigation systems: emitters, hose, tubing, couplings, timers, controls, and related items. Kits available, including one for converting an old garden hose to a drip system.

"Drip irrigation may be best defined as the controlled application of water at a very low rate to a specific area of the plant. Remember the old leaky hydrant that would drip and drip and drip—and how plants nearby would grow and grow and grow? That's the way it is with drip irrigation."

Williamstown Irrigation, Inc., Box 68, Williamstown, NY 13493. (315)-964-2214. Illustrated brochure. Open Mon.–Fri., 8 A.M.–4 P.M.

Tico Tunnel—a plastic enclosure for protecting row crops, such as strawberries, tomatoes, peppers, from wind, frost, and rain damage. Minimum order is one hundred feet.

A booklet about the benefits and uses of mist, *Intermittent Mist Propagation*, Nr. 573, is 25¢ from **The Ohio State University,** Extension Office, 2120 Fyffe Rd., Columbus, OH 43210.

Plant Foods, Potting Soils, Chemicals, and Fertilizers

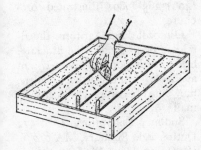

Bernard D. Greeson, Horticultural Supplies, 3548 N. Cramer St., Milwaukee, WI 53211. (414)-332-6944. Descriptive price list, 35¢. Open by appointment.

Plant foods, both organic and inorganic, specially formulated violet foods, potting soil, potting-soil additives, insecticides and fungicides, plastic pots and labels, soil test kits, plant growth lights, orchid-growing supplies, and other needs for indoor gardeners.

The Hy-Trous Corp., 3 Green St., Woburn, MA 01801. (617)-933-5772. Illustrated brochure.

Hy-Trous liquid fertilizers, Mer-Made fish-emulsion plant food, Mer-Made liquid-seaweed plant food, Solo-Gro seed-starter cubes. Available from garden dealers or directly by mail.

Mosser Lee Co., Millston, WI 54643. (715)-284-2296. Color illustrated catalog, 25¢. Open Mon.–Fri., 8 A.M.–4 P.M.

Sphagna-Mix organic growing medium, worm-bed compost, other chemicals and fertilizers, sphagnum moss, compost maker, plant markers, Dyna-Gro plant food, and other gardening supplies. Included with the catalog is a booklet, *Soilless Gardening Miracles,* and a package of Dyna-Gro plant food.

Nursery Specialty Products, 410 Greenwich Ave., Greenwich, CT 06830. (203)-661-5840. Brochure.

Manufacturers of Wilt-Pruf, an antidesiccant to protect plants from transplant shock, winter kill, and air pollution. Also Spray-Stay, a sticker-extender for prolonging spray adhesion to plants. The brochure has information on uses. The products are available from garden dealers.

Plantabbs Corp., Timonium, MD 21093. (301)-252-4620. Illustrated price list.

Houseplant and garden chemicals and fertilizers. Also Flower-Dri silica gel for preserving flowers. Available from garden suppliers or directly by mail.

Polymetrics International, Inc., 919 Third Ave., New York, NY 10022. (212)-371-2050. Illustrated brochure.

Plantgard, a polymer, applied to plants as a spray; reduces evaporation while allowing the passage of oxygen and carbon dioxide; also contains a sun-screening agent for stimulating plant growth; water-based and non-toxic; available by mail only in areas where not supplied by local dealers.

Rich Earth Products, Box 387, Charles City, IA 50616. Catalog.

Plant foods and related items, including Sea-Born (an organic soil conditioner), Start (an organic compost activator), and En-Rich (an organic additive for potting soil).

Science Products Co., Inc., 5801 N. Tripp Ave., Chicago, IL 60646. (312)-583-3171. Illustrated brochure.

Garden chemicals including Thuricide (a natural microbial insecticide), Blossom-Set, Tomato-Gro, Wonder-Brel gibberellic acid, Berry-Set, Diazinon and Sevin insecticides, animal repellents, and others. If not available from local garden dealers, they may be ordered directly by mail.

Sierra Chemical Co., 1001 Yosemite Dr., Milpitas, CA 95035. (408)-263-8080. Illustrated brochure.

Osmocote and Agriform timed-release plant foods. The brochure has information on uses. If not available from garden dealers, they may be ordered directly by mail.

Sudbury Laboratory, Inc., 572 Dutton Rd., Sudbury, MA 01776. (617)-443-8844. Illustrated catalog. Open by appointment only.

Soil test kits and refills; Sea-Power liquefied seaweed organic plant food; nitrogen, phosphorus, and potash for custom fertilizer mixes; Chaperone animal repellents; Sea-Gro seed-starter cubes, fortified with seaweed. Available from garden suppliers or order directly. Founded in 1932, the company is situated on the former Babe Ruth farm.

Windy Hills Estate, Rte. 3, Box 60, Ferguson Dr., Three Rivers, MI 49093. Descriptive price list, 25¢ (credited).

Potting mediums, developed by Von Blum Industries of Europe, blended for various types of plants—as African Violet Medium for plants requiring a 6.0–7.0 pH soil content, and Rhododendron Medium, 4.5–6.0 pH.

Aids for Organic Gardeners

EARTHWORMS

Gardeners are becoming more aware of the value of earthworms. As worms tunnel through soil, they ingest soil and waste material, pass this through their bodies, and produce "castings" far richer than the materials originally ingested. Worm casts have been found to contain five times more nitrogen, seven times more available phosphorus, and eleven times more potash than the original ingested soil.

Worms thrive in soil that has plenty of compost or organic material mixed in. A booklet on the importance of earthworms and information about making compost is available from Rotocrop, 58 Buttonwood St., New Hope, PA 18938.

Sources for Earthworms

Brazos Worm Farms, Box 4185, Waco, TX 76705. (817)-799-2034. Brochure. Visitors welcome; phone ahead.

Hybrid redworms. Detailed instructions are included in the brochure.

McMahan Farms, Rte. 3, Spring Valley, Greenwood, SC 29646. (803)-229-3287. Brochure.

Earthworms for soil improvement. Also numerous books and pamphlets on worms and their benefits in gardens.

North American Bait Farms, Inc., 1207 S. Palmetto Ave., Ontario, CA 91761. (714)-983-3677. Catalog. BAC and MC charges. Tours of farms, Tues.–Sat., at 10 A.M., 11 A.M., 2 P.M., and 3 P.M.

Hybrid redworms, worm castings, worm-raising supplies of all types, many books on worms and vermiculture.

The company, a leader in worm technology, is currently working with several U.S. cities in using worms for biodegradable waste removal. Rather than burying garbage, worms turn waste into worm-casting compost that can be used in gardening and farming.

Worms and supplies can also

be obtained from distributors in eighteen locations throughout the United States. For addresses of distributors in your area, write to North American Bait Farms, enclosing SASE.

BENEFICIAL INSECTS

Bio-Control Co., 10180 Ladybird Dr., Auburn, CA 95603. (916)-273-4006. Brochure. Open Mon.–Sat., 8 A.M.–4 P.M.

Live adult ladybugs and Chinese praying-mantis egg cases.

"Business has increased about twenty times since our first year and continues to increase as people find out the true beneficial value of ladybugs and praying mantises."

Norman Evans, 58 Cedar Grove Place, North, Grove City, OH 43123. (614)-871-0526. Send SASE for current prices.

Praying-mantis egg cases. Complete instructions are included with each order.

"While ferocious-looking, praying mantises will not sting or bite humans, even becoming tame enough to sometimes eat meat and insects from your fingers. The mantis is the only known in-

sect that can turn its head to look over its shoulder. With the forelegs bent it reminds one of the position of prayer; hence the name."

Gothard, Inc., Box 370, Canutillo, TX 79835. (915)-874-3125. Brochure.

Trichogramma wasps, which control such harmful insects as the codling moth, army worm, European corn borer, cotton bollworm, leaf rollers, the pecan casebearer, tomato fruitworm, corn-ear worm, and some cutworms. Information on use is included.

NATURAL AND NON-TOXIC INSECT CONTROLS

Animal Repellents, Inc., Box 999, Griffin, GA 30223. (404)-228-8434. Illustrated brochure.

Tack Trap, a sticky, tacky, colorless material containing no toxic ingredients, may be applied on surfaces to trap flying insects; effective against white flies. Also repellents for rabbits and other animals. Available from many garden dealers, or order directly.

Fairfax Biological Laboratory, Inc., Clinton Corners, NY 12514. (914)-266-3705. Brochure.

Doom and Japidemic—milky-disease spore powder for control

of Japanese beetles. Non-toxic to humans, beneficial insects, animals, and plants. Available from garden dealers, or order directly.

Galt Research, Inc., Rte. 1, Box 245, Trafalgar, IN 46181. Brochure.

Dipel, a naturally occurring bacterium (*Bacillus thuringiensis*) that kills leaf-eating worms and caterpillars. Non-toxic to humans, beneficial insects, bees, birds, and other wildlife. Available from garden dealers, or order directly.

Humane Traps for Nuisance Animals

Rabbits and other animal pests in your garden can be trapped alive and unharmed in Havahart traps. Animals can be moved in the traps and released in another area. Traps will not hurt children or pets. For information about using the traps, send 25¢ to **Allcock Manufacturing Co.,** Box 551, Ossining, NY 10562. Havahart traps are sold by many garden dealers, or they may be ordered directly from Allcock.

Organic Reading

The Compost Pile, E-991, 15¢. *Facts About Organic Gardening,* IB-36, 15¢. *Growing Vegetables Organically,* IB-39, 20¢. Order from **Cornell University,** Mailing Rm., Bldg. 7, Research Park, Ithaca, NY 14850.

Mulches for Weed Control, BR-1159, 15¢. From **University of Vermont,** Publications Office, Morrill Hall, Burlington, VT 05401.

Organic Soil Conditioners, A-2305, 10¢. From **University of Wisconsin,** Agricultural Bulletin Bldg., 1535 Observatory Dr., Madison, WI 53706.

Making Compost, HO-63, 20¢.

Utilizing Animal Waste as Fertilizer, ID-101, 20¢. From **Purdue University,** Mailing Rm., Agricultural Administration Bldg., West Lafayette, IN 47907.

Biological Control of Plant Pests, Handbk. 34; how to control plant pests by parasites, predators, and other natural means.

Natural Gardening, Handbk. 77; separates the wheat from the chaff of "organic" gardening; soundest methods; use of soil amendments.

The handbkooks are $1.50 each from **Brooklyn Botanic Garden,** 1000 Washington Ave., Brooklyn, NY 11225.

Beekeeping

Forbes and Johnston, Box 212, Homerville, GA 31634. (912)- 487-5881. Price list. Open Mon.–Fri., 8 A.M.–5 P.M.

Cypress beehives, various sizes, with parts and accessories. Also beekeeping equipment such as crimp-wire and cut comb foundations, gloves, hive tools, and bee veils.

Hubbard Apiaries, Onsted, MI 49625. (517)-467-2051. Also at: Belleview, FL 32620. (904)-245-2461. Illustrated catalog. Open Mon.–Fri., 7 A.M.–4 P.M.; Sat., 7–10 A.M.

Beekeeping supplies, including beeswax foundations, hives, hive parts, supers, extractors, steam-producing equipment, honey containers, miscellaneous tools and equipment, and many books on beekeeping.

The Midwestern Hive Co., 1527 E. 26th St., Minneapolis, MN 55404. (612)-724-1743. Price list. U.S. sales only. Open Mon.–Fri., 9 A.M.–5 P.M.

A full line of bee equipment: standard hives, supers, frames, covers, bottom boards, wax foundations.

"Bees are particularly useful in orchards, giving higher and better yields of fruit. We feel that most gardeners would find it interesting to raise bees and produce honey."

Sunstream Bee Supply, Box 225, Eighty Four, PA 15330. (412)-222-3330. Illustrated catalog, 50¢ (credited). Open weekdays except Tuesday, 9 A.M.–5 P.M.; Sun., 11 A.M.–4 P.M.

All types of beekeeping equipment. Bees, queen bees, plans for making equipment, honey plant seeds, many related books. Questions will be answered on request.

Wild Birds

"Birds: the best insecticide ever devised."
—Stern's Nurseries

Antiques, Inc., 2215 W. Shawnee, Muskogee, OK 74401. (918)-687-4447. Brochure. BAC and MC charges. U.S. sales only. Open every day, 10 A.M.–5 P.M.

Hand-carved birdhouses and

bird feeders. Expensive, but distinctive. For discriminating birds and bird lovers.

The shop in Muskogee also has antique garden items, gifts, and an antique-car museum with over sixty antique cars on display.

Audubon Workshop, 907 MacArthur Blvd., Northbrook, IL 60062. (312)-498-4624. Illustrated catalog, 25¢. BAC and MC charges. U.S. sales only. Open Mon.–Sat., 9 A.M.–5 P.M.

Complete selection of wild-bird products: houses, feeders, baths, food. Also books, records, and information on wild birds. Many original products not sold elsewhere.

"A company devoted to showing people how to protect and enjoy the wild birds near their home. Wild birds' survival isn't as natural as it once was. Millions of trees that once provided food and shelter have been cut down and replaced with concrete. Pollution, pesticides, technology, and a long list of other man-made problems are threatening their very existence."

Bamco, Box 700-VC, Morro Bay, CA 93442 (805)-772-8719. Illustrated brochure. Open by appointment.

Birdbath bubblers and tricklers for a constant supply of fresh water. A special adapter for a water outlet permits use of regular garden hose along with tubing for the bubbler. Also fountain heads and accessories for garden pools.

Dilley Mfg. Co., 17811 Euclid Ave., Cleveland, OH 44112. (216)-531-6764. Illustrated brochure. Open Mon.–Fri., 9 A.M.–4 P.M.

Plastic "see-through" wild-bird feeders of various types, some adjustable for small or wide openings. Also thistle seed and birdbaths.

Duncraft, Inc., 25–29 S. Main St., Penacook, NH 03301. (603)-753-6341. Color illustrated catalog, 25¢. BAC and MC charges. Open Mon.–Sat., 9 A.M.–5 P.M.

Largest selection of bird-feeding supplies on the East Coast. Specialty birdseeds, netted suet feeders and thistle feeders, books, bird records, and other accessories.

Hummingbird Heaven, 10726 Samoa Ave., Tujunga, CA 91042. (213)-352-1733. Illustrated brochure. Visitors by appointment.

Syrup-type hummingbird and oriole feeders. Original design, developed over twenty years ago.

"Once hummingbirds have become accustomed to feeding on your premises, they will return from migration year after year, looking for the feeders where they were hung before. After the young have learned to fly, the parent birds will bring them along to feed at the Hummingbird Bar."

Inco Arms, 225 N. Hull Ave., Minden, NB 68959. (308)-832-2213. Illustrated brochure. Open Mon.–Fri., 1 P.M.–5 P.M.

Electrically heated bird waterer. Withstands severe, below-zero weather; the heating element activates at 38° F.

Long Life Dial-A-Bird Home, Box 449, Westwood, NJ 07675. (201)-664-0590. Color illustrated brochure. U.S. sales only. Visitors by appointment.

Bird feeders and houses, including a combination nest home and feeder that is used all year. Various sizes, and choice of post, bracket, or swinging mounting.

"All these items are exclusive with us and are very carefully crafted. They are the outcome of years of bird feeding with inefficient, store-bought feeders.

Nature Nook, Box 362, Mineola, NY 11501. (516)-248-5579. Illustrated brochure.

Full line of best-known bird feeders, houses, accessories, and specialty seeds (thistle, sunflower, and others).

Pennyfeather Corp., 3828 Kennett Pike, Greenville, DE 19807. (302)-656-1413. Illustrated brochure. BAC and MC charges. Open Mon.–Sat., 10 A.M.–5 P.M.

Feeders, houses, baths, and seeds of all sorts for attracting birds to homes and gardens. Special feeder with separate com-

partments for unmixed seed. Also devices for keeping squirrels and other animals off feeders. Many are original designs.

Shop in Greenville has a wide selection of unusual gift items, all in a nature motif.

James R. Waite, Inc. Box 78, Manhasset, NY 11030. (516)-248-5508. Color illustrated catalog, 25¢ (credited). Open Mon.–Sat., 9 A.M.–4 P.M.

Distinctive, brightly colored lucite Satellite bird feeders, original designs of the late James Waite. Also other bird feeders and houses, bird-related items, and gifts for home gardeners and bird lovers.

Calling All Friends of Birds

An organization, formed in 1972, is dedicated to preserving America's wild birds—not only for ecological reasons but also for the beauty and enjoyment that birds add to life.

Membership in the Bird Friends Society, Essex, CT 06426, is a nominal $2.00 per year and includes, among other benefits, a semiannual publication, *Wild Bird Guide*.

Dried Flowers and Flower-arranging Supplies

Dorothy Biddle Service, VC-GT, Hawthorne, NY 10532. (914)-769-0240. Illustrated catalog, 10¢. Open weekdays 9 A.M.–5 P.M.

Just about everything needed for flower arrangers. Needlepoint holders of all sizes and shapes, flexible hairpin holders, florists' wire and tape, flower picks, pole

pins, stem cutters, clippers, floral clay, moss, pebbles, vases and flower holders, centerpiece arrangers, ceramic figurines, butterflies, pot brackets, and many books on flower arranging, preserving plants, and making corsages. Also houseplant tools and sprayers and a full line of moisture meters.

Boycan's Craft Supplies, 823–25 Spearman Ave., Farrell, PA 16121. (412)-346-5534. Illustrated catalog, $1.00 (credited).

Natural and artificial flowers and foliage, materials for making artificial flowers, baskets of many sizes and shapes, Oasis floral base, silica gel for drying flowers, styrofoam, ribbons and trims, miniatures and figurines, and a great variety of hard-to-find craft supplies.

The Cone Tree, 528 W. 4th Ave., Box 812, Albany, OR 97321. (503)-926-2984. Illus-

trated catalog. Open every day, noon–5 P.M., November 11 to December 20; other times by appointment.

About fifty varieties of cones and pods, some from Africa, Australia, and Hawaii. Sizes range from less than an inch to a foot or larger. Also wreaths, candle rings, and other decorative items made from cones.

Driftwood Co. (John Haydon), 1450 Palm Ave. S.W., Box 1021, Seattle, WA 98116. (206)-937-0537. Illustrated brochure, 50¢ (credited).

Driftwood in many sizes and shapes, for use with live or dry flower arrangements, bonsai, saikei, and other garden decorations. Sizes range from small pieces, about six inches long, to log ends, butts, and large chunks. Tools and other materials for working with driftwood. Also some finished items made of driftwood, and much information on using it.

Besides collecting and selling driftwood, Haydon is working on a book about American Samoa, of which he was governor for five years.

Junior's Plant Shop, Glen St., Rowley, MA 01969. Catalog, 40¢.

Very wide selection of natural, dried plant materials. Cones, flowers, decorative sea foliage, fruits and leaves, bearded barley, sea oats, swamp cane sprays, magnolia leaves, natural bamboo sprays, beech seeds, forsythia pods, wild-onion flowers. Also wires, picks, tape, clay, glue, and other supplies.

"In many parts of our country, we face long winter months when the outdoor picture is drab and cheerless. In our homes, gay winter bouquets can immeasurably brighten the scene. They bridge the long gap between the time we gather the last chrysanthemum of autumn and the first daffodil of spring."

Ridgehill Features, Box 744, Hillside, IL 60162. (312)-279-0160. Illustrated brochure.

Organically formulated Flourish, for prolonging the life of cut flowers, and Keepsake Flourish, an aid for drying and preserving flowers. Both are liquid concentrates.

Squirrel's Delight, 205 Mensinger Pl., Modesto, CA 95350. (209)-521-7921. Illustrated catalog. Open Tues.–Sat., 10 A.M.–5 P.M.

Dried natural items for decorative uses—cones, pods, weeds, and whatnot. Also kits of cones and other materials for wreaths, centerpieces, etc., with instructions for easy assembly.

The retail shop in Modesto also has a creative-arts center.

Some Booklets to Spark Your Imagination

Be an Artist: Make Your Own Pressed Flower Pictures, IB-34, 30¢, and *Corsages from Garden Flowers,* E-1047, 10¢. Both from **Cornell University,** Mailing Rm., Bldg. 7, Research Park, Ithaca, NY 14850.

Flower Arranging, E-410, an excellent, illustrated guide; $1.00 from **Michigan State University,** Bulletin Office, Box 231, East Lansing, MI 48824.

Dried Flower Designs, Handbk. 76, many ideas for collecting, preparing, and arranging plant parts; making wreaths and swags; designs for miniatures and others. $1.50, **Brooklyn Botanic Garden,** 1000 Washington Ave., Brooklyn, NY 11225.

The Well-Informed Gardener

Greenhouses"; "Fertilizers"; "Nut Trees"; "Balcony Gardening"; "Hollies for Your Garden"; "Propagation Guide" (two parts, $1.00); and "Fruit Gardening" (three parts, $1.50).

The Family Food Garden, Box 1014, Grass Valley, CA 95945. Tabloid style, ten issues per year, $6.00.

Covers the growing of fruits, vegetables, and meat by the homeowner; alternate energy sources; all aspects of preserving food; recipes for home-grown food; garden tools and machinery; greenhouse and hydroponic food growing; and many other aspects of food production, handling, and use.

Flower and Garden Magazine, 4251 Pennsylvania Ave., Kansas City, MO 64111. Monthly, $5.00 per year. Three regional editions.

For all home gardeners, whatever their interests. Indoor and outdoor gardening, in wide variety, with emphasis on practical, how-to information that gardeners can use. A regular column each month for children. Well illustrated.

Horticulture, 300 Massachusetts Ave., Boston, MA 02115. Monthly, $9.00 per year. Published by the Massachusetts Horticultural Society.

Articles, written by experts in their fields, cover the broad spectrum of gardening throughout the country. Outstanding color

Reading one or more of these regularly is about the best way to keep up with the gardening world. Some of these publications are general; others focus on a limited area. And most plant societies, as well as many botanical gardens, have periodicals with in-depth coverage of their specialties.

The Avant Gardener, Box 489, New York, NY 10028. An eight-page newsletter, published twice a month, $10 per year. (Three sample copies are available for $1.00.)

Reports the latest developments in all areas of horticulture—plants, products, techniques, research. Frequent special issues, including the following, which are 50¢ unless otherwise noted: "Gardening for the Busy, Tired, and Retired"; "Soilless Indoor and Terrace Gardening"; "Groundcovers"; "Dwarf Conifers"; "Wildflowers"; "Dream photos. Received the National Magazine Award for Visual Excellence in 1976.

House Plants & Porch Gardens Magazine, Box 428, New Canaan, CT 06840. Bimonthly, $6.00 per year.

Deals with houseplants and their culture and small-scale outdoor gardening. Regular features include artificial-light gardening, plant remedies, basics, organic gardening, and the greenhouse. Has eighty-eight pages, with thirty-two pages in full color.

Organic Gardening and Farming, 33 E. Minor St., Emmaus, PA 18049. Monthly, $6.85 per year.

A wealth of information each month on natural gardening, living on the land, and related subjects. Much material on food preparation, energy conservation, and ecological problems, as well as gardening.

Ozark Gardens, Box 68, Glenn Dale, MD 20769. Mimeographed bimonthly, $3.00 per year. (Sample copy, 40¢.)

A friendly, down-to-earth publication on outdoor and indoor gardening, with interesting personal accounts from readers who share their growing joys and sorrows.

Photosynthesis, Box 4121, Grand Central Station, New York, NY 10017. Monthly newsletter, $6.00 per year. (Send SASE for sample copy.)

Features how-to articles on plant care, diagnosing plant problems, propagation, specifics on different types of plants, and reviews of plant products. Will answer plant questions of subscribers who enclose a SASE with their queries.

Plants Alive Magazine, 5509 1st Ave. South, Seattle, WA 98108. Monthly, $9.00 per year. (Send subscription orders to *Plants Alive,* 1255 Portland Pl., Boulder, CO 80302. Sample copies available by writing the Circulation Department, at the Seattle address.)

Focuses on indoor, greenhouse, and outdoor container gardening. Well-illustrated, authoritative articles cover all phases of growing bulbs, and flowering and foliage plants, as well as fruits, vegetables, trees, and shrubs indoors or in containers.

Popular Gardening Indoors, 383 Madison Ave., New York, NY 10017. Bimonthly, $5.97 for six issues. (Sample copy, $1.25.)

For all indoor gardeners, from beginners to the more advanced growers who would like to specialize or get involved in more advanced techniques. Emphasizes living with plants and all that this implies, such as decorating with plants and plant-related crafts.

Under Glass, Box 114, Irvington, NY 10533. Bimonthly, $2.50 per year.

Written exclusively for greenhouse gardeners. Regular features include a column on window greenhouses, information on a particular plant species, planting notes, a question-and-answer column, and reports on new and timely products and innovations

New books and classic—on every phase of gardening—many of which are not stocked by most booksellers.

Aurora Book Companions, Box 5852 Denver, CO 80217. (303)-778-8383. Illustrated catalog. BAC and MC charges.

Many garden-related subjects, such as organic gardening, food preservation, natural foods, herbs, ecology, survival, wild foods, and homesteading.

H. Lawrence Ferguson Books, Box 5129-V, Ocean Park Sta., Santa Monica, CA 90705. (213)-670-4246. Catalog. Open by appointment.

Rare and out-of-print books on gardening, botany, horticulture, natural history. Free search service for hard-to-find books.

Garden Way Publishing Co., Charlotte, VT 05445. (802)-425-2171. Illustrated catalog, $1.00 (credited).

Books on gardening and self-

in the greenhouse-gardening world.

Books by Mail

sufficient living. Many are published by Garden Way from ideas generated by its staff, such as *The Complete Homesteading Book, Heating with Wood,* and *How to Make a Living in the Country (Without Farming)*. Wide range of titles on indoor and outdoor gardening, preserving foods, using mulches, keeping bees, and dozens of other topics.

HHH Horticultural, 68 Brooktree Rd., Hightstown, NJ 08520. (609)-448-9345. Catalog plus periodic flyers, $1.00 (credited). MC charge. Visitors by appointment.

Almost every gardening book in print in English. Most of these are in stock. The company also publishes *Plant Finders* (hardy and tender plant-source reference lists) and *House Plant Finder,* which includes as a bonus "House Plant Latin," a cross-referenced listing of common names to botanical names.

"We are a small business with Service as our principal premise. We are ardent gardeners ourselves with memberships in many of the Plant Societies and Professional Associations and have been and are Accredited Judges in some of these."

Hilltop House, 1 The Loch, Roslyn, NY 11576. Catalog, $1.00.

A great many out-of-print

books on botany, horticulture, orchids, and natural history.

Horticultural Books, Inc. (Dr. Edwin A. Menninger), Box 107, Stuart, FL 33494. (305)-287-1091. Price list.

Specialist in horticultural books for gardens in warm climates, including many books from foreign publishers. The titles cover all phases of gardening. A number of the books were written by Dr. Menninger.

Mother's Bookshelf, Box 70, Hendersonville, NC 28739. Illustrated catalog. BAC and MC charges.

Very wide selection of books on topics such as gardening, homesteading, wild foods, stocking up, herbs, nature, environment, solar energy, do-it-yourself, spinning and weaving, building fences, organic growing, etc. Many books not readily available elsewhere.

Pomona Book Exchange (The H. F. Jansons), Rockton, Ont. LoR 1Xo. Catalog, 50¢. Visitors by appointment.

Books on horticulture and related subjects, such as agriculture, food science, nature, birds, and insects; many out-of-print, antiquarian, and rare. All horticultural books in print, including foreign books, may be ordered (although not all are stocked).

"We are a husband and wife team who, after many years in food science and horticulture, operate our book business from our Rockton fruit farm (a hobby). Our specialty is fruit science, expressed by our name 'Pomona,'

for the ancient Italian goddess of fruit."

Richards' Flowerbooks, Box 507, Fort Collins, CO 80522. Catalog, $1.00.

New, old, and rare horticultural books and prints. Good selection of orchid literature, and rare prints and reproductions from classic antiquarian orchid books.

S. J. Singer Co., 1133 Broadway, New York, NY 10010. Catalog, $1.00.

Botanical and gardening books —rare, antiquarian, out-of-print, and collectors' books—some ranging back to the sixteenth century.

Spring Church Book Co., Box 127, Spring Church, PA 15686. (412)-354-2359. Brochure.

Current books of interest to gardeners, homesteaders, and do-it-yourselfers, sold at a discount. Stocks books of all publishers and emphasizes personalized and efficient service.

Wildcrafters (J. Kelly), Box 7, Looneyville, WV 25259. Circulars and price list; send stamp.

Variety of new and used books on herbs, gardening, and crafts.

Elisabeth Woodburn, Booknoll Farm, Hopewell, NJ 08525. (609)-466-0522. Catalog, $1.00. Open by appointment only.

Many one-of-a-kind old books, as well as some new books, on horticulture, landscaping and gardens, herbs, and beverages. Catalogs are issued on specific subjects in these fields; state your particular interest when ordering a catalog.

Plant Societies

Among the benefits of joining a plant society are up-to-the-minute information written by experts in their specialties, loan libraries, exchanges of rare plants and seeds, round robins, conventions, tours, and, most of all, a chance to meet other gardeners who share your interests.

Howard A. McCready, secretary of the American Penstemon Society, states this very well:

"Annual get-togethers which include field trips in scenic country are, to people interested in wild plants and the society of those with mutual interests, almost beyond price."

Even though you're not a member, you can order plant-society publications marked * in the following lists.

And a word about dues: With increasing costs, many societies find it necessary to raise their dues almost every year. If you're sending a check for a membership, we suggest you include a self-addressed postcard and ask the society to let you know if dues have increased.

African Violet Society of America, Inc., Box 1326, Knoxville, TN 37901. Annual dues, $6.00. *African Violet Magazine,* five issues per year.

*A brochure, *How to Grow African Violets,* will be sent without charge.

American Begonia Society,

Inc. Membership Secretary: Mrs. Jacqueline Garinger, 5950 Canterbury Dr., Apt. C-201, Culver City, CA 90230. Annual dues, $5.00. Monthly magazine, *The Begonian.* Founded in 1932.

American Bonsai Society, 228 Rosemont Ave., Erie, PA 16505. Annual dues, $10. *Bonsai Journal,* four issues per year plus six newsletters annually. Founded in 1967.

*Information pamphlet with reading list of pertinent books will be sent without charge.

The American Boxwood Society, Box 85, Boyce, VA 22620.

Annual dues, $5.00. *The Boxwood Bulletin,* quarterly. Founded in 1961.

*Back issues of *The Boxwood Bulletin* are available at $1.50 per copy.

American Camellia Society, Box 212, Massee Ln., Fort Valley, GA 31030. Annual dues, $7.50. *The Camellia Journal,* quarterly, and *The American Camellia Yearbook,* annually. Founded in 1945.

The Camellia: Its Culture for Beginners, $1.25. *Camellia Nomenclature,* $3.00.

American Daffodil Society, Inc. Executive Director: Geo. S. Lee, Jr., 89 Chichester Rd., New Canaan, CT 06840. Annual dues, $7.50. *Daffodil Journal,* quarterly, plus occasional special publications.

The Daffodil Handbook, $3.40. Single copies of *Daffodil Journal,* $1.00. *A Brief Guide to Showing and Growing Daffodils,* $1.00.

The American Dahlia Society, Inc. Secretary: Mrs. Irene B. Owen, 345 Merritt Ave., Bergenfield, NJ 07621. Annual dues, $7.00. *Quarterly Bulletin* and *Annual Classification List.* Founded in 1927.

American Fern Society. Records Treasurer: Terry W. Lucansky, Department of Botany, University of Florida, Gainesville, FL 32601. Annual dues, $5.00. *American Fern Journal,* quarterly. *Fiddlehead Forum,* a newsletter, five or six times yearly. Organized in 1893.

Americn Fuchsia Society, Hall of Flowers, Golden Gate Park, San Francisco, CA 94122. Annual dues, $5.00. *American Fuchsia Society Bulletin,* monthly. Founded in 1929.

Third Fuchsia Book covers culture and other topics; $2.00.

American Gesneria Society, Box 549, Knoxville, TN 37901. Annual dues, $6.00. Bimonthly on *Gesneriad Saintpaulia News* (also official publication of Saintpaulia International); joint membership in both societies is $5.75 annually. Founded in 1951.

*A brochure, *Gesneriad Growing Suggestions;* send SASE.

American Gloxinia & Gesneriad Society, Inc. Membership Secretary: Mrs. Charlotte M. Rowe, Box 174, New Milford, CT 06776. Annual dues, $7.00. *The Gloxinian,* six issues per year. Founded in 1951.

How to Know and Grow Gesneriads, $1.00. Culture sheet with membership information included: send SASE.

American Gourd Society, Box 274, Mount Gilead, OH 43338. Annual dues, $2.50. *The Gourd,* three issues per year. Organized in 1970.

*Send SASE for a list of books and bulletins on gourd culture and crafts.

American Hemerocallis Society. Secretary: Mrs. Arthur W. Parry, Signal Mountain, TN 37377. Annual dues, $7.50. Quarterly publication *The Hemerocallis Journal.* Founded in 1946.

American Hibiscus Society.

Executive Secretary: Mrs. Gordon A. Fore, Rte. 1, Box 491F, Fort Myers, FL 33905. Annual dues, $5.00. Quarterly publication *The Seed Pod*. Founded in 1950.

Official Nomenclature List describes over six hundred hibiscus; $3.00. *Supplement No. 1 to Nomenclature* describes over 175 newer varieties; $3.00.

The American Hosta Society. Secretary: Mrs. Nancy Minks, 114 The Fairway, Albert Lea, MN 56007. Annual dues, $3.00. *Annual Bulletin* plus newsletters.

American Iris Society, 2315 Tower Grove Ave., St. Louis, MO 63110. Annual dues, $7.50. *AIS Bulletin* quarterly. Founded in 1920.

Sections of the American Iris Society (dues sent to the St. Louis address):

Japanese, $2.00 annually;
Median, $2.00 annually;
Rebloom, $3.00 annually;
Siberian, $2.00 annually;
Spuria, $2.00 annually;

What Every Iris Grower Should Know, $1.10.

American Magnolia Society. Secretary: Mrs. W. B. Melnick, Rte. 6, Box 347A, Jackson, TN 38301. Annual dues, $5.00. Newsletter twice a year.

*A seventy-two-page book, *Check List of the Cultivated Magnolias*, compiled by society members, is available for $5.00 from **Plant Sciences Data Center, American Horticultural Society,** Mount Vernon, VA 22121.

American Orchid Society, Inc., Botanical Museum of Harvard University, Cambridge, MA 02138. Annual dues, $15. *AOS Bulletin* monthly.

*A seventy-six-page book on orchid culture is available for $1.50.

American Penstemon Society. Secretary: Howard McCready, 1547 Monroe St., Red Bluff, CA 96080. Annual dues, $3.00. Annual *Bulletin*.

American Peony Society, 250 Interlachen Rd., Hopkins, MN 55343. Annual dues, $7.50. *American Peony Society Bulletin* quarterly. Founded in 1904.

*Issues of quarterly bulletins available for $2.00 each.

The American Plant Life Society and The American Amaryllis Society Group, Box 150, La Jolla, CA 92038. Annual dues, $7.00. Annual publication *Plant Life and Amaryllis Year Book*. Founded in 1934.

American Pomological Society. Business Manager: Dr. Loren D. Tukey, 103 Tyson Bldg., University Park, PA 16802. Annual dues, $10. *Fruit Varieties Journal* quarterly. Founded in 1848.

*A 450-page book with sixty-four illustrations, *History of Fruit Growing and Handling in the United States of America and Canada*, is $15.45. (Canadian orders should be sent to: Regatta City Press Ltd., 3030 Pandosy St., Kelowna, B.C. V1Y 1W2.)

American Primrose Society. Treasurer: Mrs. Vickey Sauer, 16864 124th S.E., Renton, WA 98055. Annual dues, $5.00. Publication *American Primrose Society Quarterly*.

*Back issues of the quarterlies are $3.65 for ten copies.

American Rhododendron Society. Executive Secretary: Mrs. Bernice Lamb, 2232 N.E. 78th Ave., Portland, OR 97213. Annual dues, $12. Quarterly bulletin. Founded in 1945.

*A booklet, *Fundamentals of Rhododendron and Azalea Culture,* is 50¢.

American Rock Garden Society. Secretary: William T. Hirsch, 3 Salisbury Ln., Malvern, PA 19355. Annual dues, $7.00. Quarterly *Bulletin.* Established in 1934.

American Rose Society, Box 30,000, Shreveport, LA 71130. Annual dues, $15.50. *The American Rose* monthly, and a yearly, *American Rose Annual.*

*Handbook for Selecting Roses, 25¢ plus SASE.

The Aril Society, International. Membership Chairman: Mrs. Richard A. Wilson, 11500 Versailles Ave., N.E., Albuquerque, NM 87111. Newsletters several times yearly. *The Aril Society International Yearbook* annually.

*Yearbooks available for $2.50 each. Newsletters are two for 25¢.

Bonsai Clubs International, Box 2098, Sunnyvale, CA 94087. Annual dues, $7.50. *Bonsai,* ten issues per year. Founded in 1962.

The Bromeliad Society, Inc., Box 3279, Santa Monica, CA 90493. Annual dues, $7.50. *Bromeliad Society Journal* bimonthly. Founded in 1950.

Cactus and Succulent Society of America, Box 3010, Santa Barbara, CA 93105. Annual dues, $10 (send to Abbey Garden Press, Box 3010, Santa Barbara, CA 93105). *The Cactus and Succulent Journal* bimonthly.

Cymbidium Society of America, Inc., Box 208, Whittier, CA 90608. Annual dues, $10. Bimonthly magazine.

The Delphinium Society. U.S. Vice-President: Phillip H. Smith, 1630 Midwest Plaza Bldg., Minneapolis, MN 55402. Annual dues, $3.00. (Send dues to H. R. Lucas, Treasurer, 25 Sladbury's Lane, Holland-on-Sea, Essex, England CO154BE.) U.S. members receive the annual *Delphinium Yearbook* plus a packet of choice English delphinium seed.

*Booklets available from the treasurer: *Delphiniums from Seed,* 50¢; *Delphinium Culture Simplified,* $1.00; *Delphiniums Are Versatile* (flower arranging), 50¢.

Dwarf Fruit Tree Association, Box 143, Hartford, MI 49057. Annual dues, $5.00. Bimonthly publication *Compact Fruit Tree.* Annual *Compact Composite.*

Epiphyllum Society of America, 218 E. Greystone Ave., Monrovia, CA 91016. Annual dues, $3.00 (send to Velma Featherstone, 23500 The Old Road, Newhall, CA 91321). *Epiphyllum Bulletin,* six or more times a year. Founded in 1940.

Epiphyllum Handbook available for $4.00 plus postage.

Herb Society of America, 300

Massachusetts Ave., Boston, MA 02115. Annual dues $14. (New members must be elected, and require two sponsors.) Annual publication *The Herbarist*.

A Primer for Herb Growing, available for 50¢ plus 13¢ postage. Annual *The Herbarist*, $2.00 plus 45¢ postage.

Hobby Greenhouse Association, 45 Shady Dr., Box 695, Wallingford, CT 06492. Annual dues, $5.00. Bimonthly publication *The Planter*.

Holly Society of America, Inc. Secretary-Treasurer: Mr. Bluett C. Green, Jr., 407 Fountain Green Rd., Bel Air, MD 21014. Annual dues, $5.00. *Holly Letter* three issues per year. *Proceedings*, report of the annual meeting.

Handbook of Hollies, $5.50. *Holly Letter*, $1.00 per issue. Send SASE for list of available bulletins.

Hydroponic Society of America. Executive Officer: Paul W. Droll, Box 516, Brentwood, CA 94513. Annual dues, $24. Monthly newsletter plus quarterly journal. Founded in 1974.

Indoor Light Gardening Society of America, Inc., 128 W. 58th St., New York, NY 10019. Annual dues, $5.00 (send to Mrs. James Martin, 423 Powell Dr., Bay Village, OH 44140). Bimonthly publication *Light Garden*. Founded in 1966.

Learn to Grow Under Fluorescent Lights, $1.50. *Ferns Under Fluorescents*, 50¢. *Seed Propagation*, 50¢. *Orchid Culture Under Lights*, 50¢ *Flowering Plants for Light Gardens*, 75¢. *Light Garden Primer*, $1.00. *Begonias for Light Gardens*, 50¢.

International Cactus and Succulent Society, Box 691, Breckenridge, TX 76024. Annual dues, $5.00. *ICSS Newsletter* three or more times yearly. Founded in 1973.

International Geranium Society. Secretary: Arthur Thiede, 22551 Thrush, Colton, CA 92324. Annual dues, $5.00. *Geraniums Around the World* quarterly. Founded in 1953.

International Lilac Society, Inc. Secretary: Walter W. Oakes, Box 315, Rumford, ME 04276. Annual dues, $5.00. *Pipeline* monthly newsletter. *Lilacs* annually.

*Copy of *Pipeline* sent without charge. *Lilacs*, $1.00 per copy.

Los Angeles International Fern Society, 2423 Burritt Ave., Redondo Beach, CA 90278. Annual dues, $4.50. *LAIFS*, a twenty-four-page monthly bulletin. *Fern Lessons* monthly. Founded in 1959.

*Send SASE for list of available publications.

National Chrysanthemum Society, Inc., USA. Secretary: Mrs. Walter A. Christoffers, 394 Central Ave., Mountainside, NJ 07092. Annual dues, $7.50. Quarterly publication *Chrysanthemum* plus a show issue in January. Founded in 1944.

*Available books (include 25¢

postage for each): *Beginners Handbook*, $2.00; *Breeders Handbook*, $1.50; *Advanced Growers Handbook*, $3.00; *Show and Judges Handbook*, $3.50; *Chrysanthemum Classification Register*, 75¢. A pamphlet, *Care of Stock Plants—Rooting Cuttings*, 50¢ plus 15¢ postage.

National Fuchsia Society. Membership Secretary: Mrs. Martha Rader, 10934 E. Flory St., Whittier, CA 90606. Annual dues, $5.00. *The Fuchsia Fan* monthly.

*A brochure, *The Culture of Fuchsias;* send SASE.

National Oleander Society, 5127 Avenue 0-½, Galveston Island, TX 77550. Annual dues, $3.00 (send to Mrs. R. Wayne Gaido, Treasurer, 2819 Beluche, Galveston Island, TX 77550). Book and slide loans to members. Founded in 1968.

New England Wild Flower Society, Inc. Executive Director: Ann Spence Dinsmore, Hemenway Rd., Framingham, MA 01701. Annual dues, $7.50. Quarterly newsletter. Founded at the turn of the century.

*Send SASE for a list of publications on wildflowers.

North American Fruit Explorers. Secretary: Robert Kurle, 10 S. 55 Madison St., Hinsdale, IL 60521. Annual dues, $5.00. Quarterly magazine *Pomona.*

North American Gladiolus Council. Secretary: R. E. Dorsam, 30 Highland Place, Peru, IN 46970. Annual dues, $6.00. *NAGC Bulletin* quarterly. Annual classification list. Founded in 1945.

The North American Lily Society, Inc. Executive Secretary Earl A. Holl, 8812 Nora Lane, Indianapolis, IN 46240. Annual dues, $7.50. Quarterly bulletin and annual yearbook. Founded in 1947.

*A forty-eight-page handbook, *Let's Grow Lilies*, $2.00. *Growing Lilies from Seed*, 25¢ plus postage. Send orders and payments to the society, Box 40134, Indianapolis, IN 46240.

Northern Nut Growers Association, 4518 Holston Hills Rd. Knoxville, TN 37914. Annual dues $8.00. A newsletter, *The Nutshell,* four times per year, and *Annual Report,* proceedings of the annual meeting. Founded in 1910.

*A 421-page book, *Handbook of North American Nut Trees* $9.50. Copies of each *Annual Report* from 1910 available; for prices, write R. A. Jaynes, Conn. Agr. Exp. Sta., Box 1106, New Haven, CT 06502.

The Palm Society, 1320 S. Venetian Way, Miami, FL 33139 Annual dues, $12.50. *Principes.* quarterly journal. Founded in 1956.

Principes, $1.50 per copy or $6.00 for yearly subscription *Hardy Palms*, 75¢.

Saintpaulia International, Box 549, Knoxville, TN 37901. Annual dues, $6.00. Bimonthly publication *Gesneriad Saintpaulia News* (joint publication with American Gesneria Society; membership in both societies is $5.75 annually).

*A brochure, *Helpful Hints for Success with African Violets;* send SASE.

The Sempervivum Society, 11 Wingle Tye Rd., Burgess Hill, Sussex, England, RH15 9HR. Annual dues, $6.00. Three journals plus three international newsletters per year. The yearbook is also available to members.

**The Sempervivum Handbook* describes species and natural hybrids; many color plates, $10.

Society for Louisiana Irises, University of Southwestern Louisiana, Lafayette, LA 70504. Annual dues, $5.00 (send to Mrs. Ira S. Nelson, Box 4-0175, University of Southwestern Louisiana, Lafayette, LA 70504). Quarterly newsletter. Occasional special publications. Founded in 1941.

*Copies of newsletter available for $1.00 each. Special publications, $2.00 each.

Southern Fruit Council, Rte. 3, Box 40, Summit, MS 39666. Annual dues, $1.00. *The Southern Fruit Garden,* three issues per year.

*Sample copy of *The Southern Fruit Garden* will be sent without charge.

The Terrarium Association, 57 Wolfpit Ave., Norwalk, CT 06851. Annual dues, $7.00. Illustrated newsletter, *Terrarium Topics,* six times per year.

*Back copies of *Terrarium Topics,* 50¢ each.

Not-for-Profit Gardening

From planting flowers in village squares to using horticulture as therapy for the mentally retarded, hundreds of thousands of gardeners—sponsored by the following organizations—freely donate their time, talents, and money.

The Garden Club of America, 598 Madison Ave., New York, NY 10022.

Among the "Objects" of this organization, founded in 1913, are "to stimulate the knowledge and love of gardening" and "to restore, improve and protect the quality of the environment." Activities of the club and its more than twelve thousand members include establishing The Redwood Grove in California to save these endangered trees, developing "vest-pocket" parks in many cities, providing educational material for teachers and schoolchildren, and awarding scholarships and fellowships to qualified students of horticulture.

Men's Garden Clubs of America, 5560 Merle Hay Rd., Des Moines, IA 50323. Members of more than two hundred affiliated clubs work for civic beautification and do much to promote and teach gardening. Special emphasis is placed on youth programs of all types.

National Council of State Garden Clubs, Inc., 4401 Magnolia Ave., St. Louis, MO 63310. Representing almost a million members in the United States, the council recently inaugurated a youth-and-aging program to bring together young people and the elderly with the common denominator of a love of gardening. Other current projects include ACE—Action Committee for the Environment—and compiling information about a comprehensive network of historic trails throughout the country.

National Council for Therapy and Rehabilitation through Horticulture, Mount Vernon, VA 22121. Members in the United States, Canada, and England promote the development of horticulture and related activities as a therapeutic and rehabilitation medium. Two of its many outstanding accomplishments: a young woman who was mentally handicapped is now responsible for mounting, labeling, and storing rare plant

specimens at the National Arboretum; a nurseryman who became blind over ten years ago ha adapted to working in a green house and teaches other blind persons the pleasure and satisfaction of working with plants.

Fifteen dollars well spent Yearly membership in The American Horticultural Society, Mount Vernon, VA 22121, at $15, has many benefits. Among them are an attractive bimonthly magazine The American Horticulturist, and a bimonthly newsletter, both filled with gardening advice, an annual seed distribution of well over one hundred rare and uncommon varieties, special tours, and conferences. The society also prepares many publications, provides an information service, and sponsors awards and incentive programs.

A membership is an excellent way to become part of a nonprofit organization dedicated to promoting the interests of all segments of American horticulture.

The USDA and Cooperative Extension Services

The U. S. Department of Agriculture and the Cooperative Extension Services (a joint venture of the USDA and state land-grant universities) provide a huge source of information for gardeners. Three ways to tap this source follow:

1. Read USDA publications. Aids for gardeners range from ad-

vice on growing pansies to advice on storing potatoes. The *List of Available Publications of the USDA*, Nr. 11, is 45¢ from the **Supt. of Documents**, Washington DC 20402.

2. Read CES publications. Each state CES also publishes a great deal of material on gardening, usually geared to its own

area. However, some state publications are useful to gardeners throughout the country. Lists may be obtained by writing to state CES publications offices. In this book we have mentioned some USDA and CES publications of general interest, but there are many more.

3. Consult your county exten- sion agent. Almost every U.S. county has a local CES office where personnel are ready to help you with gardening problems. Check county-government headings in your phone book for location of your office—or get the address from your state extension service.

Addresses of State CES Publications Offices

Alabama Cooperative Extension Service, Auburn University, Auburn, AL 38630

Alaska Cooperative Extension Service, University of Alaska, Box 95151, Fairbanks, AK 99701

Arizona Cooperative Extension Service, University of Arizona, Tucson, AZ 85721

Arkansas Cooperative Extension Service, University of Arkansas, Box 391, Little Rock, AR 72203

California Public Service, University Hall, University of California, Berkeley, CA 94720

Colorado Bulletin Room, Colorado State University, Fort Collins, CO 80521

Connecticut Agricultural Publications, University of Connecticut, Storrs, CT 06268

Delaware Mailing Room, Agricultural Hall, University of Delaware, Newark, DE 19711

Florida Bulletin Room, Building 440, University of Florida, Gainesville, FL 32601

Georgia Cooperative Extension Services, University of Georgia, Athens, GA 30601

Hawaii Publications Distribution Office, Krauss Hall, University of Hawaii, 2500 Dole Street, Honolulu, HI 96822

Idaho Mailing Room, Agricultural Science Building, University of Idaho, Moscow, ID 83843

Illinois Agricultural Publications Office, 123 Mumford Hall, University of Illinois, Urbana, IL 61801

Indiana Mailing Room, Agricultural Administration Building, Purdue University, West Lafayette, IN 47907

Iowa Publications Distribution Center, Printing and Publications Building, Iowa State University, Ames, IA 50010

Kansas Distribution Center, Umberger Hall, Kansas State University, Manhattan, KS 66506

Kentucky Bulletin Room, Experiment Station Building, University of Kentucky, Lexington, KY 40506

Louisiana Publications Librarian, Room 192, Knapp Hall, Louisiana State University, Baton Rouge, LA 70803

Maine Department of Public Information, PICS Building, University of Maine, Orono, ME 04473

Maryland Agricultural Duplicating Services, University of Maryland, College Park, MD 20742

Massachusetts Cooperative Extension Service, Stockbridge Hall, University of Massachusetts, Amherst, MA 01002

Michigan MSU Bulletin Office, Box 231, Michigan State University, East Lansing, MI 48823

Minnesota Bulletin Room, Coffey Hall, University of Minnesota, St. Paul, MN 55101

Mississippi Cooperative Extension Service, Mississippi State University, State College, MS 39762

Missouri Publications, B-9, Whitten Hall, University of Missouri, Columbia, MO 65201.

Montana Extension Mailing Room, Montana State University, Bozeman, MT 59715

Nebraska Department of Information, College of Agriculture, University of Nebraska, Lincoln, NB 68503

Nevada Agricultural Communications, University of Nevada, Reno, NV 89507

New Hampshire Mail Service, Hewitt Hall, University of New Hampshire, Durham, NH 03824

New Jersey Bulletin Clerk, College of Agriculture, Rutgers University, New Brunswick, NJ 08903

New Mexico Bulletin Office, Department of Agricultural In-

formation, Drawer 3A1, New Mexico State University, Las Cruces, NM 88001

New York Mailing Room, Building 7, Research Park, Cornell University, Ithaca, NY 14850

North Carolina Publications Office, Department of Agricultural Information, Box 5037, North Carolina State University, State College Station, Raleigh, NC 27607

North Dakota Department of Agricultural Information, North Dakota State University, Fargo, ND 58102

Ohio Extension Office, Ohio State University, 2120 Fyffe Road, Columbus, OH 43210

Oklahoma Central Mailing Services, Oklahoma State University, Stillwater, OK 74074

Oregon Extension Hall 118, Oregon State University, Corvallis, OR 97331

Pennsylvania Sales Supervisor, 230 Agricultural Administration Building, Pennsylvania State University, University Park, PA 16802

Rhode Island Resource Information Office, 16 Woodward

Hall, University of Rhode Island, Kingston, RI 02881

South Carolina Publications, Department of Public Relations, Trustee House, Clemson University, Clemson, SC 29631

South Dakota Bulletin Room, Extension Building, South Dakota State University, Brookings, SD 57006

Tennessee Agricultural Extension Service, University of Tennessee, Box 1071, Knoxville, TN 37901

Texas Department of Agricultural Communications, Texas A&M University, College Station, TX 77843

Utah Publications Room, Agricultural Science Building, Utah State University, Logan, UT 84321

Vermont Publications Office, Morrill Hall, University of Vermont, Burlington, VT 05401

Virginia Extension Division, Virginia Polytechnic Institute, Blacksburg, VA 24061

Washington Cooperative Extension Service, Bulletin Room, Publications Building, Washington State University, Pullman, WA 99163.

West Virginia Mailing Room, Communications Building, Patterson Drive, West Virginia University, Morgantown, WV 26506

Wisconsin Agricultural Bulletin Building, 1535 Observatory Dr., University of Wisconsin, Madison, WI 53706

Wyoming Bulletin Room, College of Agriculture, University of Wyoming, Box 3354, University Station, Laramie, WY 82071.

Canada Department of Agriculture

Both the Canada Department of Agriculture and provincial departments have lists of publications for gardeners.

The Canada Department of Agriculture *List of Publications* is available without charge from Information Division, Canada Department of Agriculture, Ottawa, Ont. K1A 0S9.

For copies of provincial lists, write to the communications offices at the following addresses.

Provincial Cooperative Agricultural Communications Offices

Alberta Communications Branch, Alberta Agriculture, 1B Agriculture Building, 9718 107th St., Edmonton, Alta. T5K 2C8

British Columbia Information Branch, Department of Agriculture, Parliament Buildings, Victoria, B.C. V8W 2Z7

Manitoba Communications Division, Department of Agriculture, 307-200 Vaughan St., Winnipeg, Man. R3B 2N6

New Brunswick Communications, Department of Agriculture, Fredericton, N.B. E3B 5H1

Newfoundland Extension Division, Department of Forestry and Agriculture, Building 812, Pleasantville, St. John's, Nfld. A1A 1R1

Nova Scotia Coordinator of Publications, Department of Agriculture, Hollis Building, Halifax, N.S. B8J 2M4

Ontario Publications Information Branch, Ministry of Agriculture and Food, Parliament Buildings, Toronto, Ont. M7A 1A5

Prince Edward Island Information Officer, Extension Services Branch, Department of Agriculture, P.O. Box 2000, Charlottetown, P.E.I. C1A 7N8

Quebec Director, Information Branch, Department of Agriculture, Quebec, Que. G1A 1E4

Saskatchewan Extension Division, University of Saskatchewan, Saskatoon, Sask. S7N 0W0

Appendix

On the following pages you will find the companies, plantsmen, and suppliers, included in this book, listed geographically, first the Americans (listed by state), then the Canadians (by province).

When you're traveling, take this guide along. Many of these sources have retail greenhouses, nurseries, or shops where you can buy the items offered by mail and, frequently, many other things. A number have outstanding display gardens or greenhouses that are well worth a special trip. Others welcome visitors who share their interests in plants.

It's a good idea to phone ahead, even when days and hours are listed; these may have changed. Normal "open" hours usually do not apply to holidays, although some companies are, as they say, open every day. And when "visitors by appointment" is specified, it means just that. Don't just drop in.

Some companies are not open to visitors. But this guide may be useful in ordering by mail—it might be more convenient to buy from a source in your area rather than from one half a continent away—if both offer similar things.

Alabama
BESSEMER
Arant's Exotic Greenhouses
BIRMINGHAM
Mist Methods
GREENVILLE
Fern Hill Farm
MOBILE
Gothic Arch Greenhouses
Orchard Nursery
G. C. Robinson Nursery

Arkansas
AUGUSTA
Conner Co.
CAMDEN
House of Violets
LITTLE ROCK
Fox Orchids
WEST MEMPHIS
Mary Walton

California
ALTADENA
Nuccio's Nursery
APTOS
Dome Greenhouses
John Ewing Orchids
AROMAS
Cactus Gem Nursery
ATHERTON
Tonia
AUBURN
Bio-Control Co.
BAKERSFIELD
Cactus by Mueller
BARSTOW
Kirkpatrick's
BELLFLOWER
The Green House
BEVERLY HILLS
Casaplanta
BREA
Golden Earth Enterprises
CAPITOLA
Shaffer's Tropical Gardens
CARMEL
Hollow Hills Succulent Farm

CARPINTERIA
  Abbey Garden
  Armacost & Royston
CASTRO VALLEY
  King's Chrysanthemums
  Clyde Robin Seed Co.
CERRITOS
  Clark Day, Jr.
CHICO
  Vallombrosa Gardens
COLTON
  Environmental Dynamics
DALY CITY
  San Francisco Plant Co.
EL CERRITO
  Water Works Gardenhouses
EL MONTE
  Tinytrees Nursery
ENCINITAS
  Cox's Epiphyllum Nursery
ESCONDIDO
  Seaborn Del Dios
FALLBROOK
  Dick Wright
FELTON
  Green Valley Seeds
FOUNTAIN VALLEY
  Modular Hydroponic Gardens
FREMONT
  California Nursery
FRESNO
  Henrietta's Nursery
GALT
  K&L Cactus
LEMON GROVE
  McDaniel's
LOS ANGELES
  Collector's Succulents
  Exotica Seed Co.
  Fuchsia Land
  Kent's Bromeliads
  Rheinfrank & Assoc.

MALIBU
  Arthur Freed Orchids
MARINA DEL REY
  Velco's Bromeliads
MIDPINES
  The Shop in the Sierra
MILPITAS
  Sierra Chemical Co.
MODESTO
  Squirrel's Delight
MOORPARK
  Marz Bromeliads
MORRO BAY
  Bamco
MOUNTAIN VIEW
  Young Industries
NORTH HOLLYWOOD
  Orchid Imports
ONTARIO
  Armstrong Nurseries
  North American Bait Farms
PALO ALTO
  ECOREF
  Ecology Action
PARAMOUNT
  Loehman's Cactus Patch
PASADENA
  Western Arboretum
PERRIS
  Hamner's Iris Garden
PLACERVILLE
  Hortica Gardens
RANCHO SANTA FE
  Burwell Geoponics
REDWOOD CITY
  J. L. Hudson
  Pacific Coast Greenhouses
RESCUE
  Discovery Trails Gardens
RESEDA
  Singers' Growing Things
RIDGECREST
  Aril Iris Farm

ROSEMEAD
  Taylor's Garden
ST. HELENA
  Bolduc's Greenhill Nursery
SAN CARLOS
  Tsang and Ma
SAN GABRIEL
  Fred A. Stewart
  Sunnyslope Gardens
SAN JOSE
  Kitazawa Seed Co.
SAN JUAN CAPISTRANO
  De Sylva Seeds
SAN MARCOS
  Cordon Bleu Farms
SAN PEDRO
  Exotiks
SANTA BARBARA
  Abbey Garden Press
  Santa Barbara Orchid Estate
SANTA CLARA
  Simpler Co.
SANTA CRUZ
  Antonelli Bros.
  Bay View Gardens
  Beach Garden Nursery
  Capitola Violet Gardens
  Herb Hager Orchids
  McGregor Greenhouses
  Peter Reimuller
SANTA MONICA
  H. Lawrence Ferguson
SANTA ROSA
  Country Garden Nursery
SCOTTS VALLEY
  Redfern Greenhouses
SEBASTOPOL
  Miniature Plant Kingdom
  Redwood Empire Camellias
SOUTH SAN FRANCISCO
  Rod McLellan Co.
STOCKTON
  Melrose Gardens

TOPANGA
  Fernwood Plants
TUJUNGA
  Hummingbird Heaven
UPLAND
  Van Ness Water Gardens
VAN NUYS
  California Epi Center
VISALIA
  Sequoia Nursery
VISTA
  Foster Iris
  Grigsby Cactus Gardens
  Hawks Nursery
  Kent's Bromeliads
  Modlins Cactus Gardens
  Taylor's Garden
WATSONVILLE
  John Ewing Orchids
  Rod McLellan
  Tillotson's Roses
  Vetterle's Begonia Gardens
WEST COVINA
  Jack's Cactus Garden
WILLITS
  Little Lake Nursery

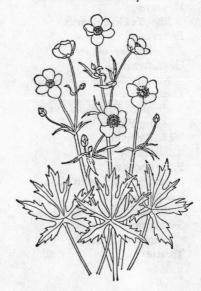

WILLOWS
World Gardens
YORBA LINDA
Pixie Treasures
YUCAIPA
Valley's End Iris Garden
YUCCA VALLEY
A. Hugh Dial
Colorado
COLORADO SPRINGS
Hydro-Gardens
DENVER
Aurora Book Companions
Rocky Mountain Seed Co.
The Violet House
FORT COLLINS
Richards' Flowerbooks
GUNNISON
Hansen Weatherport
LOVELAND
Kroh Nurseries
ROCKY FORD
D. V. Burrell
Connecticut
BRIDGEPORT
John Caschetto
DANIELSON
Logee's Greenhouses
EASTFORD
Buell's Greenhouses
GREENWICH
Nursery Specialty Products
LITCHFIELD
Hemlock Hill Herb Farm
White Flower Farm
NEW FAIRFIELD
Baums Nursery
PLANTSVILLE
American Standard Co.
ROCKY HILL
Brimfield Gardens
SALISBURY
Lauray of Salisbury
TRUMBULL

Heavenly Violets
WATERBURY
Piedmont Gardens
WETHERSFIELD
Comstock, Ferre & Co.
Chas. C. Hart Seed Co.
Delaware
BRIDGEVILLE
Orinda Nursery
GREENVILLE
Pennyfeather Corp.
SELBYVILLE
Buntings' Nurseries
Florida
BELLE GLADE
Everglades Orchids
BELLEVIEW
Hubbard Apiaries
BOYNTON BEACH
Alberts & Merkel
COCOA BEACH
John Brudy's
ELLENTON
Bates Orchids
FORT MYERS
Greenbrier Orchids
GAINESVILLE
Violet House
HOMESTEAD
Fennell Orchid
Kerry's Nursery
HOMOSASSA SPRINGS
Homosassa Springs Orchids
JACKSONVILLE
Paul F. Duke
LAKE PLACID
Joyner's Caladiums
MIAMI
Jerry Horne
Jones and Scully
Joseph Redlinger
NORTH FORT MYERS
Cornelison's Bromeliads

ORANGE LAKE
  Florida's Vineyard
ORLANDO
  Ann Mann's Orchids
PLANTATION
  Shadow Lawn Nursery
RIVERVIEW
  Southern Gardens
SARASOTA
  Sarasota Bonsai Gardens
SEBRING
  Spaulding Bulb Farm
STUART
  Horticultural Books
TALLAHASSEE
  The Yarb Patch
TAMPA
  Topiary
WINTER HAVEN
  Slocum Water Gardens

Georgia
ALBANY
  Piedmont Plant Co.
ALMA
  Sweet Gum Farms
ATLANTA
  H. G. Hastings
BALL GROUND
  Lawson's Nursery
BLAIRSVILLE
  William Bradley Co.
BROOKS
  Ison's Nursery
DECATUR
  Davidson Gardens
GRIFFIN
  Animal Repellents
  Greenlife Gardens
HOMERVILLE
  Forbes and Johnston
MADISON
  Pennington
MORELAND

  Enclosures, Inc.
ROCKMART
  Hidden Springs Nursery
SAVANNAH
  Bloom 'N Vine
THOMASVILLE
  Thomasville Nurseries
TY TY
  Evans Plant Co.

Hawaii
HILO
  Kuaola Farms
  Lehua Anthurium Nursery
HONOLULU
  Hurov's Tropical Seeds
WAIMANALO
  Maile's Anthurium Nursery

Idaho
BOISE
  Winston Roberts
JEROME
  Oscar W. Johnson
MOSCOW
  Northplan Seed Producers

Illinois
CENTRALIA
  Southern Meadows Gardens
CHICAGO
  American Science Center
  Germania Seed Co.
  Science Products Co.
CORNELL
  Imperial Flower Garden
CRYSTAL LAKE
  Thon's Garden Mums
ELMHURST
  Orchids by Hausermann
HILLSIDE
  Ridgehill Features
MONTICELLO
  Illini Iris
NORTHBROOK
  Audubon Workshop

OAKFORD
  Lounsberry Gardens
O'FALLON
  Geraldi Nursery
PANA
  National Greenhouse Co.
ROCKFORD
  Interior Products
  H. Shumway, Seedsman
ROCKTON
  Midwest Wildflowers
SOUTH ELGIN
  Ed-Lor Glads
WYOMING
  Sunshine Seed Co.

Indiana
BLOOMINGTON
  Dr. Raymond Smith
CARMEL
  Baumer, Inc.
GREENSBURG
  Henderson's Botanical Gardens
HUNTINGBURG
  Ahrens & Son
INDIANAPOLIS
  Bash's Seed Store
  Species Specialties
MIDDLEBURY
  Krider Nurseries
ROACHDALE
  Wilson Bros. Floral Co.
SOUTH BEND
  Council Oaks
TRAFALGAR
  Galt Research
WASHINGTON
  Gardening Without Cultivation

Iowa
AMES
  Ames Greenhouses
CHARLES CITY
  Rich Earth Products

COUNCIL BLUFFS
  DeGiorgi Co.
DAVENPORT
  Gruber's Gladiolus
DECORAH
  Decorah Nursery
FARMINGTON
  Rider Nurseries
HAMBURG
  Inter-State Nurseries
HAMPTON
  Earl Ferris Nursery
SHENANDOAH
  Henry Field Seed Co.
  Earl May Seed Co.
STANHOPE
  Wilder Iris Garden

Kansas
ABILENE
  Mrs. Rosetta White
BURLINGTON
  Huff's Gardens
HUMBOLDT
  Schoonover Gardens
LYONS
  Cook's Geranium Nursery
MORAN
  Harper's Orchard Gardens
TOPEKA
  J. A. Demonchaux
  Ben Haines Co.

Kentucky
FINCHVILLE
  Uncle Charlie's Rose Products
LEXINGTON
  Mohr Gardens

Louisiana
BATON ROUGE
  Amaryllis, Inc.
BOSSIER CITY
  Barnett Cactus Garden
CHENEYVILLE
  Tanner's Garden

Duson
  Vincent Greenhouses
Lafayette
  Charjoy Gardens
  C. G. Simon Nursery
New Orleans
  Reuter Seed Co.
Opelousas
  Louisiana Nursery
Prairieville
  Crochet Daylily Garden
Slidell
  Tammia Nursery

Maine
Albion
  Johnny's Selected Seeds
Boothbay Harbor
  Conley's Garden Center
Brunswick
  Carobil Farms
Camden
  Howe Hill Herbs
  Merry Gardens
Falmouth
  Allen, Sterling & Lothrop
Fryeburg
  Western Maine Forest Nursery
Greenfield
  Thoreau Wildgarden
Hancock
  Riverside Studio
Kennebunk
  Armstrong Associates
Litchfield
  The Rock Garden
South Harpswell
  Dr. Currier McEwan
Winthrop
  Thomas Seeds
Maryland
Baltimore
  Meyer Seed Co.

Beltsville
  J. A. Nearing Co.
Cambridge
  The House Plant Corner
Frederick
  Gene & Gerry's Gardens
Gaithersburg
  Starmont Daylily Farm
Kensington
  Kensington Orchids
Lilypons
  Three Springs Fisheries
Pittsville
  Tingle Nursery
Princess Anne
  Bountiful Ridge
Ruxton
  Village Greenhouse
Salisbury
  W. F. Allen Co.
  Brittingham Plant Farms
  Rayner Bros.
  Otis S. Twilley Seed Co.
Timonium
  Plantabbs Corp.
Westminster
  Carroll Gardens
Massachusetts
Agawam
  Pleasant Valley Glads
Allston
  Sun Dew Environments
Beverly
  S&G Exotic Plant Co.
Boston
  Sun Dew Environments
Bridgewater
  Hall Nursery
Haverhill
  Gray & Cole
Holbrook
  Blackthorne Gardens
Ipswich
  Common Fields Nursery

John Messelaar Bulb Co.

LOWELL
Indoor Garden Sales

MIDDLEBORO
Alexander's Blueberry Nursery

NORTHFIELD
Gladside Gardens

NORWELL
Reliable Greenhouses

PITTSFIELD
Knowlton's African Violets

REHOBOTH
Tranquil Lake

ROWLEY
Junior's Plant Shop
Nor'East Miniature Roses

SANDWICH
F. W. Schumacher Co.

SOUTH DEERFIELD
Nourse Farms

SOUTH HAMILTON
P. DeJager & Sons

SUDBURY
Sudbury Laboratory

VINEYARD HAVEN
Nelson Coon

WESTPORT
Exoticus Tropical Plants

WHITMAN
Paradise Gardens

WILMINGTON
A. E. Allgrove Nursery
Kartuz Greenhouses

WOBURN
Hy-Trous Corp.

WORCESTER
Verandel Co.

Michigan
AUGUSTA
Dutch Mountain Nursery

BARODA
Zilke Bros. Nursery

BIRMINGHAM
Lake Angelus Gardens
Southmeadow Fruit Gardens

BURTON
Rakestraw's Gardens

DETROIT
Indoor Gardening Supplies
Lienau Peony Gardens

FARMINGTON
International Growers Exchange

GALESBURG
Burgess Seed & Plant Co.

GROSSE ILE
Island Gardens

HARTFORD
Dean Foster Nurseries
Hilltop Orchards

HOPKINS
Englerth Gardens

JACKSON
Al's Violets

KALAMAZOO
A. H. Hazzard

KALEVA
Fruit Haven Nursery

LIVONIA
Far North Gardens

MILLINGTON
Theo Jensen

MONROE
Ilgenfritz Orchids

NORWAY
Woodlot Seed Co.

ONSTED
Hubbard Apiaries

PARMA
Fox Hill Farm

PAW PAW
Paw Paw Everlast Label Co.

PLYMOUTH
Ackman's Dahlia Gardens

PONTIAC
  Lake Angelus Gardens
SOUTH HAVEN
  Black River Orchids
STEVENSVILLE
  Emlong Nurseries
THREE RIVERS
  Windy Hills Estate
VICKSBURG
  Louise Barnaby
VULCAN
  David Reath
WEST OLIVE
  Vans Pines
YPSILANTI
  Makielski Berry Farm
ZEELAND
  H. L. Hubbell, Inc.

Minnesota
  ALBERT LEA
    Minks' Fairway Gardens
  ASKOV
    Ferndale Nursery
  BATTLE LAKE
    Swedberg Nurseries
  EDINA
    Savory's Greenhouses
  FARIBAULT
    Brand Peony Farm
    Farmer Seed
    The Lehman Gardens
  GRAND RAPIDS
    Orchid Gardens
  HUTCHINSON
    Dooley Gardens
  MINNEAPOLIS
    Flor-L-Pot
    Gable Iris Gardens
    Riverdale Iris Gardens
    The Midwestern Hive Co.
  ROGERS
    Julius Wadekamper

ST. CHARLES
  Noweta Gardens
ST. PAUL
  Park Nursery

Mississippi
  DUCK HILL
    Archway Green Houses
  MENDENHALL
    Early Garden Greenhouses

Missouri
  BUNKER
    Bee Fork Water Gardens
  CAPE GIRARDEAU
    Mueller's Garden
  INDEPENDENCE
    David Buttram
  KANSAS CITY
    Lenington Gardens
  LECOMA
    ABC Herb
  LOUISBURG
    Routh's Greenhouses
  LOUISIANA
    Stark Bro's
  OZARK
    Wilson's Greenhouse
  ROLLA
    Ponzer Nursery
  RUSSELLVILLE
    L. Volkart's
  ST. LOUIS
    Finck Floral
  SARCOXIE
    Gilbert H. Wild
  SEDALIA
    Archias Seed Store

Montana
  HELENA
    Valley Nursery

Nebraska
  ASHTON
    Tom's Garden Mums

LEXINGTON
  Hildenbrandt's Iris Gardens
LINCOLN
  Fleming's Flower Fields
MINDEN
  Inco Arms
MURDOCK
  Schliefert Iris Gardens
NORFOLK
  N. Freudenburg
New Hampshire
EXETER
  Francis M. Sinclair
NEW IPSWICH
  Sundials & More
PENACOOK
  Duncraft, Inc.
PETERBOROUGH
  Brookstone Co.
New Jersey
ALPINE
  North Jersey Bromeliads
BARRINGTON
  Edmund Scientific
BRICKTOWN
  Beaver Dam Creek Nursery
COLTS NECK
  Cummins Garden
EGG HARBOR CITY
  Helen & John Braniff
HACKETTSTOWN
  Grace's Gardens
HAMMONTON
  Galletta Bros.
HIGHTSTOWN
  HHH Horticultural
HOPEWELL
  Elisabeth Woodburn
JACKSON
  Mincemoyer Nursery
  Woodstream Nursery
LINWOOD
  Fischer Greenhouses

MINOTOLA
  Desert Dan's Cactus
NUTLEY
  Shoplite Co.
OAKLAND
  House of Orchids
PORT MURRAY
  Well-Sweep Herb Farm
ROBBINSVILLE
  Edelweiss Gardens
SADDLE RIVER
  William Tricker
SEWELL
  Orol Ledden
SOMERDALE
  Thompson & Morgan
SUMMIT
  Lager & Hurrell
SUSSEX
  Rocky Hollow Herb Farm
WARREN
  E. B. Nauman
WESTWOOD
  Long Life
New Mexico
BELEN
  New Mexico Cactus Research
ROSWELL
  Roswell Seed
New York
BABYLON
  Van Bourgondien Bros.
BALDWIN
  Joel Spingarn
BAYSIDE
  Annalee Violetry
BELLMORE
  Lorenzen's
BELLVALE
  Baldsiefen Nursery
BOHEMIA
  Louis A. Hindla

BRONX
  N. Y. Botanical Garden
BROOKVILLE
  Louis Smirnow
BUFFALO
  Stokes Seeds
CANANDAIGUA
  J. E. Miller Nurseries
  Peter Pauls Nurseries
CANASTOTA
  Hermitage Gardens
CATSKILL
  Walther's Exotic House
    Plants
CLINTON CORNERS
  Fairfax Biological Laboratory
DANSVILLE
  Kelly Bros.
DOLGEVILLE
  Lyndon Lyon
EAST AURORA
  Mardon Gardens
EAST MORICHES
  Leuthardt Nurseries
FAIRPORT
  D. S. George Nurseries
GENEVA
  Legg Dahlia Gardens
  N. Y. State Fruit Testing
    Coop. Assoc.
  Stern's Nurseries
HALL
  Seedway
HAWTHORNE
  Dorothy Biddle
HEUVELTON
  St. Lawrence Nursery
HUDSON
  Walt Nicke
HUNTINGTON
  Aquamonitor
  Panfield Nurseries

HUNTINGTON STATION
  Garden of Eden Greenhouse
    Center
IRVINGTON
  Lord & Burnham
JAMESVILLE
  Schmelling's African Violets
LIVINGSTON MANOR
  Heirob Bonsai
LYONS
  Mayo Nurseries
MANHASSET
  James R. Waite
MARION
  Rich Glads
MINEOLA
  Nature Nook
NEW YORK CITY
  Burnett Bros.
  Home Plant Displayers
  Polymetrics, Inc.
  John Scheepers
  S. J. Singer Co.
  Vegetable Factory Green-
    houses
NIAGARA FALLS
  Ordev Mfg. Co.
NORTH BELLMORE
  Green Planter System
OSSINING
  Allcock Mfg. Co.
PAVILION
  Gratwick Tree Peonies
ROCHESTER
  Joseph Harris
ROCKVILLE CENTRE
  Ruschmohr Dahlia Gardens
ROSLYN
  Hilltop House
  Alex J. Summers
  Tara Eden
SARATOGA SPRINGS
  Saxton Gardens

SCHENECTADY
  Alprax Enterprises
SHRUB OAK
  Peekskill Nurseries
SOUTH SALEM
  Carlson's Gardens
  Practical Products
WATERTOWN
  Chapin Watermatics
WILLIAMSTOWN
  Williamstown Irrigation

North Carolina
DUNN
  Jernigan Gardens
GOLDSBORO
  Turner Greenhouses
HENDERSONVILLE
  Mother's Bookshelf
  Mother's General Store
KINGS MOUNTAIN
  Iron Gate Gardens
MARSHALL
  Griffey's Nursery
MT. VERNON SPRINGS
  Paul P. Lowe
PINEOLA
  Gardens of the Blue Ridge
PRINCETON
  Powell's Gardens
RALEIGH
  Wyatt-Quarles

Ohio
BAINBRIDGE
  Boatman Nursery & Seed Co.
BUTLER
  L. Easterbrook
CANTON
  R. L. Holmes Seed
  Letherman's
CHARDON
  Wildwood Gardens
CHESTERLAND

  Sunnybrook Farms Nursery
CLEVELAND
  Alsto Co.
  Aluminum Greenhouses
  Dilley Mfg. Co.
  Tube Craft
FINDLAY
  Hancor, Inc.
GENEVA
  Girard Nurseries
GROVE CITY
  Norman Evans
INDEPENDENCE
  William Tricker
LONDON
  F&R Farrell
MENTOR
  Bluestone Perennials
  Garden Place
  Joseph J. Kern
  Melvin E. Wyant
METAMORA
  Glecklers Seedmen
NEW STRAITSVILLE
  McComb Greenhouses
NORTH LIMA
  Mellinger's
PERRYSVILLE
  Summerlong Iris Gardens
PIQUA
  A. M. Leonard
SALEM
  Bakers' Tree Nursery
SANDUSKY
  Doris Drennen
SEAMAN
  Millstone, Inc.
SOUTH EUCLID
  A. Shammarello & Son
TIPP CITY
  Spring Hill Nurseries

WARREN
  Taroko Co.
Oklahoma
MUSKOGEE
  Antiques, Inc.
Oregon
ALBANY
  The Cone Tree
  Nichols Garden Nursery
ASHLAND
  Open Season
BROOKS
  Thomas Henny Nursery
CANBY
  McCormick Lilies
  Grant E. Mitsch
  Swan Island Dahlias
DALLAS
  Oakhill Gardens
DAYS CREEK
  Casa Yerba
ELMIRA
  Wilson's Dahlias
EUGENE
  Greer Gardens
  Island Gardens
GRANTS PASS
  Harrold's
GRESHAM
  Oregon Bulb Farms
HILLSBORO
  E. Ray Miller's Dahlia Gar-
    dens
LAKE GROVE
  Edgar L. Kline
MEDFORD
  Jackson & Perkins
  Siskiyou Rare Plant Nursery
MILWAUKIE
  White Dahlia Gardens
MONMOUTH
  Herbs 'N Honey Nursery

NEWBERG
  Rex Bulb Farms
OREGON CITY
  Fleur de Lis Gardens
PORTLAND
  Bateman's Dahlias
  The Bovees Nursery
  Sturdi-Built Mfg.
RIDDLE
  LaVonne's Greenhouse
SALEM
  Infer Landscape
  Schreiner's Gardens
SCIO
  Maco Home Greenhouses
SILVERTON
  Cooley's Gardens
  Silver Falls Nursery
SPRINGFIELD
  Gossler Farms Nursery
  Laurie's Garden
WILDERVILLE
  Pilley's Gardens
WILSONVILLE
  Roses by Fred Edmunds
Pennsylvania
ASPERS
  Adams County Nursery
BAINBRIDGE
  Natural Development
BUTLER
  Orlando S. Pride
CHELTENHAM
  Pennypack
COLLEGEVILLE
  Sven Van Zonneveld
EIGHTY FOUR
  Sunstream Bee Supply
FARRELL
  Boycan's Craft Supplies
FEASTERVILLE
  Raraflora

GLADWYNE
  Vick's Wildgardens
HUNTINGDON VALLEY
  Tinari Greenhouses
INDIANA
  Carino Nurseries
  Musser Forests
NORTHAMPTON
  Metro Myster Farms
PENN RUN
  Pikes Peak Nurseries
PHILADELPHIA
  Rainbow Sand
POINT PLEASANT
  Ference's Nursery
PORT MATILDA
  Greenland Flower Shop
QUAKERTOWN
  Palette Gardens
REEDSVILLE
  Appalachian Wildflower
    Nursery
RIMERSBURG
  Eccles Nurseries
SAGAMORE
  Flickingers' Nursery
SNOW SHOE
  Edward Owen Engineering
SPRING CHURCH
  Spring Church Book Co.
TANNERSVILLE
  Dutch Bulb Import Co.
WARMINSTER
  W. Atlee Burpee
WEST GROVE
  Conard-Pyle
WYNNEWOOD
  Penn Valley Orchids
Rhode Island
PAWTUCKET
  Standard Engineering Works

South Carolina
CLEMSON
  Double Daylilies
COLUMBIA
  The Garden Spot
GREENWOOD
  McMahan Farms
  Geo. W. Park
HODGES
  Wayside Gardens
NEWBERRY
  Carter & Holmes
South Dakota
YANKTON
  Gurney Seed
Tennessee
CLEVELAND
  Boatman Nursery & Seed Co.
DRESDEN
  Fred's Plant Farm
GLEASON
  Margrave Plant Co.
  Steele Plant Co.
MCMINNVILLE
  Terry Barnes Nursery
  Cumberland Valley
    Nurseries
MEMPHIS
  Brussel's Bonsai
NASHVILLE
  Aladdin Industries
SMYRNA
  Clover Garden Products
Texas
BRENHAM
  Yankee Peddler Herb Farm
BROWNSVILLE
  Helen's Cactus
CANUTILLO
  Gothard, Inc.
CORPUS CHRISTI
  Coastal Gardens

DALLAS
  Horticultural Enterprises
  Mini-Roses
  Nicholson-Hardie
EDINBURG
  Cactusland
FARMERSVILLE
  Texas Onion Plant Co.
FORT WORTH
  Moores Reblooming Iris
  Ed Storms
  Texas Greenhouse Co.
  Peggy Williams Garden
GRANBURY
  Loyce's Flowers
HOUSTON
  Wheeler's Daylily Farm
KERRVILLE
  Green Horizons
LUBBOCK
  Submatic, Inc.
MANSFIELD
  Hughes Garden
MARFA
  Desert Plant Co.
OMAHA
  Brown's Omaha Plant Farm
REKLAW
  Mason's Plant Farms
SOUR LAKE
  Louise's Greenhouse
TYLER
  Arp Roses
  P. O. Tate Nursery
WACO
  Brazos Worm Farms
WILLS POINT
  Kimbrew-Walter
Utah
  OGDEN
    Squires Bulb Farm
  OREM
    Tell's Garden

ROY
  Mission Bell Gardens
Vermont
  CENTER RUTLAND
    French's Bulb Importer
  CHARLOTTE
    Garden Way Publishing
  JOHNSON
    Shyhook Farm
  MANCHESTER CENTER
    Vermont Bean Seed Co.
  PUTNEY
    Putney Nursery
  SOUTH BURLINGTON
    Garden Way Living Center
  WEST DANVILLE
    Le Jardin du Gourmet
Virginia
  ANNANDALE
    Mailex
  BLAND
    William P. Newberry
      Gardens
  NORTH
    The Daffodil Mart
  RADFORD
    Avonbank Iris Gardens
  RICHMOND
    Semispheres
  WAYNESBORO
    Waynesboro Nurseries
Washington
  BELLEVUE
    JD-21 Lighting Systems
  BOTHELL
    Wileywood Nurseries
  CASHMERE
    J&J Iris Garden
  CASTLE ROCK
    S&K Gardens
  COLLEGE PLACE
    Iris Test Gardens

EDMONDS
  Jack C. Williams Co.
ENUMCLAW
  Klinkel's African Violets
KIRKLAND
  Charley's Greenhouse Supply
LONG BEACH
  Clarke Nursery
LYNNWOOD
  Wileywood Nurseries
MOUNT VERNON
  Darst Bulb Farms
SEATTLE
  Abundant Life Seeds
  Driftwood Co.
  Hewston Green
  Laura's Collectors' Garden
  Northwest Hybridizers
  Rainier Mt. Alpine Gardens
SEQUIM
  Cedarbrook Herb Farm
SPOKANE
  Alpines West Nursery
  Jamieson Valley Gardens
  Lamb Nurseries
  Stanek's Garden Center
TACOMA
  Aqua-Pots
  Connell's Dahlias
  H. L. Larson
  Tradewinds, Inc.
VASHON ISLAND
  Beall Co.
WALLA WALLA
  Baldwin's Iris
WENATCHEE
  C&O Nursery
  Eden Road Iris Garden

YAKIMA
  May Nursery
West Virginia
  LOONEYVILLE
    Wildcrafters
  PETERSTOWN
    Hickory Hollow
  RAINELLE
    Appalachian Root & Herb
  RAMSEY
    Green Thumb Home
      Nursery
Wisconsin
  CRIVITZ
    Woodland Acres Nursery
  GLIDDEN
    North Central Comfrey Pro-
      ducers
  MADISON
    Flad's Glads
    Olds Seed Co.
  MILLSTON
    Mosser Lee
  MILWAUKEE
    Bernard Greeson
  OAK CREEK
    Floralite Co.
  OMRO
    Game Food Nurseries
  PLAINFIELD
    George Melk
  RACINE
    Flowerland
  RANDOLPH
    J. W. Jung Seed
  WAUKESHA
    Hydro-Growth Greenhouses
  ZENDA
    Feather Hill Industries

CANADA

Alberta
  BOWDEN
    Alberta Nurseries
  EDMONTON
    Devon Nurseries
  STONY PLAIN
    Miniature Gardens
British Columbia
  SURREY
    Alpenglow Gardens
  VICTORIA
    Bailey Orchids
    The Butchart Gardens
    Harborcrest Nurseries
Manitoba
  BRANDON
    Lindenberg Seeds
  ROBLIN
    Skinner's Nursery
  WAWANESA
    Gaybird
Ontario
  AGINCOURT
    Chrysler's Gesneriad House
  ANCASTER
    Edward Lowden
  BROOKLYN
    Dynarose
  ETOBICOKE
    Sheridan Nurseries
  GOODWOOD
    Otto Richter
  HORNBY
    The Plant Room

  MISSISSAUGA
    Sheridan Nurseries
  OTTAWA
    Ritchie Feed
  PROTON STATION
    Wood's African Violets
  ROCKTON
    Pomona Book Exchange
  TORONTO
    C. A. Cruickshank
    Sheridan Nurseries
  UNIONVILLE
    Sheridan Nurseries
  VIRGIL
    Carl Pallek
  WEST FLAMBORO
    William Dam Seeds
Prince Edward Island
  YORK
    Vesey's Seeds
Quebec
  BEACONSFIELD
    Sheridan Nurseries
  LAVAL
    Perron
  MONTREAL
    Sheridan Nurseries
Saskatchewan
  PARKSIDE
    Honeywood Lilies
  SASKATOON
    Early Seed
    Riverside Gardens

Under "additional sources," page numbers are followed by the letter "a" or "b" to indicate the first or second column of that page.